Cultural Encyclopedia of LSD

Cultural Encyclopedia of LSD

Wayne Glausser

McFarland & Company, Inc., Publishers

Jefferson, North Carolina, and London

LIBRARY OF CONGRESS CATALOGUING-IN-PUBLICATION DATA

Glausser, Wayne.
Cultural encyclopedia of LSD / Wayne Glausser.
p.   cm.
Includes bibliographical references and index.

ISBN 978-0-7864-4785-5
illustrated case binding : 50# alkaline paper ∞

1. LSD (Drug)—social aspects.
2. LSD (Drug)—History.
I. Title.
HV5822.L9G53   2011   362.29'403—dc22   2011005801

BRITISH LIBRARY CATALOGUING DATA ARE AVAILABLE

On the cover: Timothy Leary, 1965 (Strand Releasing/Photofest);
background art by Desiree Walstra

Manufactured in the United States of America

*McFarland & Company, Inc., Publishers
Box 611, Jefferson, North Carolina 28640
www.mcfarlandpub.com*

For Meg and Annie

Acknowledgments

DePauw University supported my work with research grants and a sabbatical. In addition to all the scholarly, journalistic, and biographical sources acknowledged in the bibliography, I have benefited greatly from conversations with colleagues, friends, and family. I especially want to thank Michael Sinowitz for his help with music and popular culture, Istvan Csicsery-Ronay and Tom Chiarella for our chats about sundry matters psychedelic, and Keith Nightenhelser for the many useful suggestions that flowed from his truly encyclopedic mind. My DePauw students in two seminars about drugs, literature, and culture provided an abundance of ideas and provocative questions. I am grateful to all of them, and especially to Shelby Sleight and Michael Schmidt, who spent a summer with me researching several of these topics.

I am sorry that my brother Grant, who had a lively curiosity about this subject, did not live quite long enough to see the finished book. I hope that Marnie McInnes will decide that it was worth the trouble, and that Meg and Annie Glausser—sisters and scientists, to whom I dedicate this encyclopedia—will take some pleasure in browsing through it.

Table of Contents

Preface

As Swiss chemist Albert Hofmann was synthesizing compounds from lysergic acid in 1938, he had no idea that his work would have such a dramatic influence on history: he was simply looking for a drug to aid circulation. The compound he labeled LSD-25 surprised him with unprecedented mind-altering effects. Fortunately, the Prometheus of LSD was a well-read, intellectually curious man, and he began to probe psychiatric, religious, and artistic implications of the drug he had brought into the world. Three decades later, his discovery made headlines and changed lives in ways he could never have imagined.

LSD holds a special place among drugs. Because it is not addictive and its effects are as unpredictable as they are powerful, it affects humans live very differently from drugs like heroin, cocaine, and methamphetamine, which deliver predictable pleasure and damage. Even among its cousin drugs, the psychedelic family that includes mescaline and psilocybin, LSD stands out for its exceptional psychotropic potency. At the height of its popularity, LSD influenced all areas of culture, as people tried to harness its power for a broad range of purposes: to heal neuroses, to fight Communists, to inspire art, to subvert the political establishment, to catalyze human evolution, to put humans in touch with God. The study of LSD opens up a rich vein of historical and phenomenological ironies. From Hofmann's very first trip, the drug induced a spectrum of emotions ranging from panic to euphoria. LSD could make someone crazy, or restore someone's mental health. It was a tool for therapy and a weapon to deploy against an enemy; a threat to social order, and a sacrament; an inspiration to artists, and their nemesis. The government that ended up denouncing and criminalizing LSD had earlier encouraged its production and introduced it to budding countercultural prophets.

This encyclopedia attempts to record the cultural impact of LSD in all its complexity—especially in America and England, the two countries that dominated psychedelic culture, and their respective psychedelic capitals, San Francisco and London. Although a substantial number of entries relate to the prime psychedelic years of the mid to late 1960s, other entries treat earlier and later periods as well as the lingering contemporary influence of LSD. The selection of topics and the entries themselves reflect no position of advocacy regarding LSD. This encyclopedia necessarily presents many entries about psychedelic enthusiasts and their reasons for taking the drug, but LSD's critics and risks are also given due attention. A curious but cautious approach seems fitting for a drug so full of contradictions that Albert Hofmann referred to it as "my problem child" (*Sorgenkind*): something he loved but worried about.

Introduction

My interest in this subject derives both from personal experience—as a college student in California during the later years of the psychedelic era—and from scholarly inquiry—as an English professor who has addressed various questions surrounding drugs, literature, and culture. Writing a cultural encyclopedia of LSD has turned out to be a surprisingly tall order. Although the peak of the psychedelic era lasted only a short time, LSD had an enormous and lasting influence. The drug became famous for its association with countercultural lifestyles and values, but these hippie elements quickly infiltrated mainstream culture; moreover, it was the mainstream (if secretive) cultures of psychiatry and Cold War military intelligence that first explored LSD and paved the way for the psychedelic half-decade of the mid to late 1960s.

The roughly 400 entries in this encyclopedia can be sorted into several topical categories. A small number of people who devoted themselves to promoting LSD all figure prominently—from cautious intellectuals like Albert Hofmann and Aldous Huxley, to acid evangelists Timothy Leary and Ken Kesey, psychedelic wizards of the East and West, respectively. More surprising advocates of LSD also appear, such as nutritionist Adelle Davis and conservative stateswoman Clare Boothe Luce. Equally surprising are a few countercultural heroes

who deplored the use of the drug, including Jack Kerouac and Frank Zappa. Prominent manufacturers and brands of LSD are covered, from the official "Delysid" brand that Sandoz distributed to psychiatric researchers, to Owsley's color-coded batches of pills, to more recent sheets of blotter acid adorned with images sacred and secular.

Because LSD first entered the world in the context of psychiatry, many entries address psychiatrists who ran clinical trials and tested the effectiveness of the drug in therapy for various conditions; other psychiatric entries summarize the results of such therapy in treatment for alcoholism, depression, schizophrenia, autism, sexual problems, and anxiety in dying patients. Animal testing also enters, as in the sad story of Tusko, the elephant who died in an LSD experiment gone wrong. (Happier results came in tests with spiders and dolphins.) Several Hollywood celebrities took LSD for therapeutic reasons. The first to acknowledge this public was Cary Grant, who told magazines that psychedelic therapy had made him a saner, happier man. Other movie stars had mixed reactions and kept their LSD use more private: Sean Connery, for one, who took a tumultuous trip right after *Goldfinger,* and Groucho Marx, who dropped acid to prepare for a movie role as God. Other entries record LSD's influence on celebrities from a variety of fields, including Nobel

Prize–winning scientists, captains of industry (among them Steve Jobs and Bill Gates), and sports stars (notably Phil Jackson from basketball, and baseball's Dock Ellis, who threw a no-hitter while high on LSD).

During the 1950s, at the same time psychiatrists were evaluating LSD's potential as a therapeutic drug, the CIA and the military were testing it for use as a weapon in the Cold War. Several entries address the people who conducted these experiments and their results. The CIA program known as MK-ULTRA funded careful clinical trials as well as wilder operations such as "Midnight Climax," in which a martini-drinking narcotics cop watched prostitutes interact with clients who had been dosed with acid. One of the most controversial episodes in LSD history involved CIA scientist Frank Olson, who was given a surprise acid trip by his boss and apparently committed suicide in the aftermath. CIA and military tests introduced LSD to a number of people who became psychedelic enthusiasts and countercultural leaders—among them Ken Kesey, Allen Ginsberg, and Grateful Dead lyricist Robert Hunter (who passed the secret to his friend Jerry Garcia). The encyclopedia records LSD connections for several political activists and utopians who participated in 1960s counterculture. Their opinions about the political value of the drug varied considerably: within the Haight-Ashbury group known as the Diggers, for example, some saw LSD as a crucial tool for subverting complacency about the social status quo, while others criticized tripping as a self-indulgent distraction from the real work of social change. A number of entries focus on people, places, and events associated with the political utopians of the era. Also included is the demented utopian vision of Charles Manson, who used LSD within his "family," and ended up in Folsom prison talking about acid trips with his cell neighbor, Timothy Leary.

Many entries explore LSD's associations with religion and spirituality. Some scholars contend that the sacramental core of the Eleusinian Mysteries of ancient Greece was an organic hallucinogen similar to LSD. LSD's influence on religion in the 1960s was profound. Psychedelic alliances with Zen Buddhism and other Eastern religious traditions were very common, but the drug also had an impact on mainstream religions: professors at divinity schools speculated about its sacramental value, and even Catholic priests—most notably the Jesuits—took acid trips as spiritual voyages. There was silliness as well as sublimity in psychedelic religion, as some acid enthusiasts fabricated churches in an attempt to circumvent drug laws (see, for example, Chief Boo-Hoo). The encyclopedia includes entries about the legal status of LSD, including the only relevant Supreme Court cases, and explains recent attempts to revive legal psychiatric and medical experiments. Legislators in the United States and elsewhere made LSD illegal because of what they judged to be serious risks to health. One general entry summarizes what is known about health risks, both physical and psychological. A separate entry addresses the controversial theory that LSD damages chromosomes, a scare that was much more effectively publicized than the scientific paper that retracted the claim a few years later. Another entry explains what is known about the death of Diane Linkletter, whose father linked her suicide to an acid trip and led the movement for anti–LSD legislation.

Quite a few entries address topics related to LSD's influence on the arts. Nowhere was this influence greater than in popular music. One entry describes typical features of psychedelic rock as a subgenre, and many others treat bands that produced popular music during the psychedelic era. For the most part, information about music comes under headings for band names, with cross listings for notable songs and artists; a few of the most prominent individuals, such as Jerry Garcia and all four Beatles, receive more than just a cross-listing. A handful of entries record LSD-related music from pre-psychedelic years (e.g., "LSD-25" by the Gamblers) and post-psychedelic years (including The Clash and Talking Heads). Several entries are devoted to psychedelic visual art. There is a general entry on the subject, separate entries for the major poster artists and a few psychedelic mainstream artists, Zap Comix, light shows, and tie-dye designs. Literature is also covered extensively. Topics include works of fiction that feature LSD, ranging from highbrow *The Crying of Lot 49* to pulpy *Sexual Paradise of LSD*. Other literary entries address poets who used LSD as a muse, a handful of journalists who wrote insider or outsider accounts, and assorted nonfiction books (including both Leary's guidebook for acid trippers, *The Psychedelic Experience*, and its cultural antithesis, the pseudo-nonfictional *Go Ask Alice*). A number of entries describe films in which the drug plays a role, from the very earliest cinematic depiction of an LSD trip—taken by Vincent Price in *The Tingler* (1962)—to Ang Lee's acid scene from his 2009 film about Woodstock. Most of the films included come from the psychedelic era proper, and range in quality from *The Acid Eaters* to *2001: A Space Odyssey*. Television shows are also well represented. The most famous single episode is Jack Webb's "Blue Boy" from *Dragnet*, but other entries treat hippie-themed episodes from *Star Trek* as well as satirical perspectives from *Saturday Night Live* and *The Simpsons*. Psychedelic themes influenced commerce as well as art. In fashion, hippie styles became quite popular for a time, and retro-psychedelic looks still appear from time to time in designer collections. There was a hippie Barbie for one year, and more recently, Ben and Jerry's has featured flavors of ice cream that allude to the world of psychedelic rock. Advertisers for mainstream companies like Disney, McDonald's, and Campbell's Soup deployed psychedelic images during the late 1960s to make their wares more attractive to Boomers.

Because this is a cultural and not a technical encyclopedia, I have not addressed the chemistry of LSD or its interaction with neurotransmitters (still an open question in neuroscience). In composing these entries, I have tried as much as possible to focus on LSD-specific information about a given person, event, place, organization, or text. The entry about Aldous Huxley, for example, addresses his connections with LSD and leaves a full account of his interests and accomplishments to other reference sources. When information about a particular subject is ambiguous or incomplete, I have done my best to present an accurate, impartial account of what is known. We may never find out definitively what happened in the Frank Olson case, for instance, and the Olson entry presents competing theories of his death without choosing one as most likely. My hope is that readers with a great variety of perspectives on LSD will find this encyclopedia informative, engaging, and amusing. It is not necessary, in other words, to declare oneself "on the bus" or "off the bus" to enter these pages in the right frame of mind.

For those who decades ago participated in the enthusiasm surrounding LSD, and recall nostalgically the nobler aspirations of the psychedelic era—socio-political reformation, musical sublimity, renovation of consciousness, spiritual enlightenment—the appearance of a retrospective encyclopedia may be unsettling. It signals that the period has withdrawn into history, preserved and neatly packaged for inspection. The same might be said of a museum exhibit about the psychedelic era, such as the recent show mounted by the Denver Museum of Art. I can only offer my own experience at the Denver exhibit as comfort. After the initial shock of seeing docents with laser pointers decoding Rick Griffin posters (not to mention a full-scale simulation of a Haight-Ashbury apartment), I found the experience thought-provoking, even refreshing. I hope something similar might happen for readers of this encyclopedia.

The Encyclopedia

Abraham, Ralph. A prominent mathematician and one of the pioneers of Chaos Theory, Abraham used LSD frequently as he developed his ideas. For Abraham, LSD was not simply a way of freeing up his mind and sparking creativity: what he saw on his psychedelic trips contributed substantive elements of the theory he developed. In a profile of Abraham's work on Chaos Theory, John David Ebert wrote, "Abraham had been experimenting with LSD since his first ingestion of it in 1967, whereupon it had catalyzed a series of visions of radiant mathematical topologies which he later termed 'dynamatons.'" He took LSD many times and gradually worked toward a new field of study based on what he saw during his trips. Abraham told Ebert, "The sacred geometry of our time is fractal geometry and the space-time patterns of Chaos Theory.... And some of these patterns we see just by closing our eyes in psychedelic trips and meditations." Abraham taught at Berkeley, Columbia, and Princeton before moving in 1968 to the University of California, Santa Cruz (see *Santa Cruz*).

Abramson, Harold. Abramson was an American psychiatrist who in 1953 received one of the earliest grants for LSD research from the CIA. He published several papers on his experiments and organized a series of international conferences on the psychiatric implications of LSD. Among those Abramson introduced to LSD was anthropologist Gregory Bateson (see *Bateson, Gregory*).

Acid. The most common nickname for LSD comes from the English translation of *Säure*, the German word that puts the "S" in LSD. A strictly English initialization would be LAD, for Lysergic Acid Diethylamide. The *Oxford English Dictionary* cites a Neal Cassady letter from 1965 as the earliest use of "acid" in this sense: "Got up late that night, got loaded on acid and went bar-hopping to hear some great Rock and Roll" (see *Cassady, Neal*). The year 1966 saw the first use of "acid head," a frequent user of LSD, as well as "acid test" (see *Acid Test*).

Acid Eaters. This 1968 B-movie follows a group of secretaries and bikers on a weekend of tripping and sex. They make their way to a sugar-cube pyramid that appears to be the gateway to Hell. One of the bikers transforms into the devil and offers LSD to all; their psychedelic experiences focus almost exclusively on the fulfillment of sexual fantasies. *Acid Eaters* is also the title of a 1993 album by The Ramones, which includes covers of songs by Jefferson Airplane, Rolling Stones, and other bands of the psychedelic era (see *Jefferson Airplane; Rolling Stones*).

Acid House. In the mid 1980s, club DJs in

America and England began playing a pulsing, repetitive style of music that became known as "acid house." The first acid house artists used a synthesizer that produced sounds resembling certain features of psychedelic music. Acid house earned its name not only for its sound, but for its association with raves, where many partiers took psychedelic drugs—most commonly MDMA (see *Ecstasy*), but also LSD.

Acid Queen. In Peter Townshend's rock opera *Tommy* (1969), Tommy's parents take him to a character called "The Acid Queen" in an attempt to cure his traumatized psyche. As her name suggests, she favors psychedelic therapy (combined with sexual advances); her efforts do not work, and the song "The Acid Queen" portrays her drug world as menacing. The Who follow up this song with "Underture," an instrumental in high psychedelic style.

Acid Rock. Although this term and "psychedelic rock" are often used synonymously, some critics prefer to reserve "acid rock" for the intense, beat-driven music that led to heavy metal. The acid rock band Iron Butterfly is commonly cited as a forerunner of heavy metal music (see *Iron Butterfly*), and the phrase "heavy metal" itself comes from "Born to Be Wild," a song by acid rock band Steppenwolf (see *Steppenwolf*). See *Psychedelic Rock*.

Acid Test. In 1965, Ken Kesey and the Merry Pranksters began hosting large public parties that they called "Acid Tests" (see *Kesey, Ken; Merry Pranksters*). Kesey borrowed the name from a chemical test used by gold miners, but the phrase also brought to mind the CIA-sponsored clinical tests that introduced Kesey to LSD. The Pranksters held approximately a dozen Acid Tests over the next year, culminating in an "Acid Test Graduation" that marked the end of the Prankster saga.

The Acid Tests were held at an assortment of venues on the West Coast, including both outdoor and indoor locations. The basic idea was to extend to a larger audience the psychedelic adventures that the Pranksters had been experiencing during their bus trip across the country. Organizers advertised the events with colorful posters built around the slogan, "Can YOU pass the Acid Test?" At the Tests, most attendees took LSD—sometimes without knowing they were doing so. They were surrounded by an array of sights and sounds intended to stimulate an interesting trip and help forge a sense of community among the trippers. Rooms (or trees) were painted in day-glo colors, with strobe lights enhancing the visual effects. Psychedelic light shows were projected all around, as well as excerpts from films taken by the Pranksters during their road trip. Music was usually provided by the Grateful Dead, who served as house band for the Acid Tests. In playing at the Tests, the Dead developed their free-flowing improvisational style that established them as the quintessential psychedelic band. Jerry Garcia has said that these events let them experiment and evolve without the pressures of a traditional concert performance (see *Grateful Dead*). The sound system for Acid Tests included amplifiers, speakers, and microphones scattered throughout the venue; attendees were free to contribute sounds of their own whenever they felt inspired to do so. Acid Test attendees talked, sang, danced, or sat alone in psychedelic rumination.

Timothy Leary and his friends from the Eastern wing of American psychedelia criticized the Acid Tests as reckless. Leary emphasized the importance of careful preparation and stress-free settings for acid trips, and he saw great risks for people like whose trips came suddenly and chaotically. Even among the Pranksters, there were disagreements about how Acid Tests should be organized and whether they should continue at all. The police had begun to take notice of the Tests and sometimes intervened. Kesey returned from exile in Mexico with the idea that psychedelic enthusiasts should no longer need the drug. He organized one last Test, the "Acid Test Graduation," to convey his message; this Test produced disappointing results, however, and no sequels were planned. Literary journalist Tom Wolfe met up with Kesey and the Pranksters near the end of their run, just before the Acid Test Graduation. The resulting book became a bestseller and gave the American public its most detailed description of the psychedelic perspective (see *Electric Kool-Aid Acid Test*).

The Acid Tests from the 1960s have often been cited as the ancestors of the dance parties known as "raves" that flourished in later decades. Like Acid Tests, raves feature light shows, a distinctive musical style, and the widespread use of hallucinogens (including LSD, but more commonly MDMA or "Ecstacy": see *Ecstasy*). And like Acid Tests, raves have faced pressure from public authorities who raised health concerns.

Acid Western. Critic Jonathan Rosenbaum coined the term "Acid Western" in a review of Jim Jarmusch's 1995 film *Dead Man*. Rosenbaum considered *Dead Man* the most impressive example of this subgenre, which he dated back to the 1960s and 1970s. He labeled as Acid Westerns a number of films from those years, including three that featured principals from *Easy Rider,* itself a kind of Acid Western (see *Easy Rider*): *Ride in the Whirlwind* (written by and starring Jack Nicholson), *The Hired Hand* (directed by and starring Peter Fonda), and *Kid Blue* (starring Dennis Hopper). As Rosenbaum defines them, Acid Westerns differ from traditional Westerns in their associations with countercultural values and their reversals of mythic archetypes. For example, *Dead Man* links a westward journey "with death rather than rebirth, and with pessimism rather than hope." *Dead Man* also has certain cinematic qualities that resonate with the psychedelic experience: a defamiliarized landscape, languid pacing, a few hallucinatory images, and Neil Young's spacey electric soundtrack. Jarmusch welcomed Rosenbaum's idea of the Acid Western. He explained that he filmed in black and white "to keep the atmosphere eerie and a little trippy." Jarmusch improvised his own casual definition of the subgenre—"Westerns made by people who have taken acid, I guess"—and when asked whether he had taken acid, he replied, "Not recently."

Advertising. The psychedelic style that defined 1960s counterculture spread quickly to mainstream corporate advertising. Although this marriage of Haight-Ashbury and Madison Avenue might seem ironic, it was certainly predictable, given the importance of the Baby Boom generation to marketers. Ads with hippie imagery became commonplace in magazines, but it was in television commercials—the quintessential vehicle for reaching Boomers—that psychedelic style found its best expression.

Some well known brands simply adopted psychedelic styling without making any attempt to link their products with countercultural values. Campbell's Soup, for example, created a commercial that used their traditional themes and icons, but added psychedelic decorations. The background song delivered a familiar message—"When you have a sandwich, Campbell up"—while the guitar in the background played a few psychedelic licks. The iconic Campbell kids appeared with rosy cheeks, but they were surrounded by psychedelic images of suns, butterflies, and abstract swirls that resemble liquid light shows. McDonald's ran a similar commercial that embedded their usual cast in a psychedelic landscape. The McDonald's ad was trippier than the Campbell's: in part because of the inherent surrealism of smiling cheeseburgers and such, but also because McDonald's took more trouble with the effects and made a reference to tripping. They reworked their theme song as psychedelic soft-rock: "Get yourself ready for a trip through McDonald's Land." Other brands made a more direct attempt to link their products with the counterculture. Seven Up started to call itself the Un-cola and made commercials in high psychedelic animation. The best example, from 1968, borrowed images from *Yellow Submarine*. However authentic the psychedelic style, the underlying message was far from countercultural: Seven Up offered an array of grand prizes to consumers, such as cars, clothing, boats, and skiing vacations. They did their best to disguise these ordinary prizes with psychedelic animation, and they pitched the offer in hippie-friendly terms—"Now you can do your own thing and win your un-thing."The company that most successfully linked its product with psychedelic style was Levi-Strauss, whose jeans already had strong associations with the counterculture. Levi-Strauss reinforced this connection in commercials with highly wrought psychedelic animation. One notable example was "The Stranger" from the early 1970s. A pink and orange man walks into a town populated by sketchy black and white figures: "There was a stranger who came to our town. He was tall and had eyes that could look right to the bottom of you." When the man finally turns so that his face becomes visible, the imagery resembles something from a Carlos Castaneda hallucination: at first it's not a face but a bug-like alien, which starts glowing and transforms into a Janus-faced figure, until finally resolving into more ordinary human form. As this is going on, the narrator is saying, "Then in his strange way he transformed us to a world of Levi slacks and jeans. Life will never be dull again in our town." The ad both applauded hippie consumers for their style and encouraged them to trade in the old blue jeans for fancier models.

Psychedelic commercials were also created for non-profit causes. The American Cancer Society hired Peter Max to produce a psychedelic anti-smoking commercial (see *Max, Peter*). Max animated a young man in profile, with checkerboard hair, with a flower floating in front of him. As the flower gradually transforms into the face of a young

woman, who kisses him, the narrator says, "Nice things start when you stop smoking." The American Cancer Society implicitly deployed LSD against tobacco, with flower power trumping the Marlboro Man.

In the twenty first century, psychedelic gestures have appeared mainly in nostalgic ads aimed at Boomers facing retirement. An ad for financial services shows a graying executive thinking fondly of his adventures in a VW bus. One company that maintains a non-nostalgic link with psychedelic culture is Apple, whose iPod commercials show young people grooving to their music as psychedelic colors splash the background (see *Jobs, Steve*).

Agora Scientific Trust. In 1962, John Beresford founded this trust in New York City, the first organization devoted to the study of LSD. See *Beresford, John*.

Alcoholism. In the early years of LSD-assisted psychotherapy, some psychiatrists saw great promise in the drug as a tool for curing alcoholism. The first psychiatrist to try LSD therapy on alcoholics was Humphry Osmond, the man who coined the term "psychedelic" (see *Osmond, Humphry; Psychedelic; Psychiatry*). Osmond and colleague Abram Hoffer, working in a Saskatchewan mental hospital, carried out a series of trials with surprisingly good results. Overall, approximately half of the alcoholics who underwent psychedelic therapy successfully gave up drinking. This was a significantly better rate than had been achieved by other methods of treatment, including pharmaceutical interventions and traditional psychotherapy.

Osmond and Hoffer originally conceived of the LSD experience as a psychotomimetic event, perhaps similar to what an alcoholic would face with *delirium tremens*. In their first theory of how LSD might assist alcoholics, they speculated that patients subjected to the negative effects of *delirium tremens*—but without the physical risks of that condition—might receive a therapeutic scare. However, as they examined the results of their trials, Osmond and Hoffer generated a more positive theory of what was happening: instead of patients frightened into sobriety by a simulation of psychosis, they saw patients who had developed greater self-awareness. The LSD helped alcoholics to recognize and distance themselves from previous behavioral patterns. As their studies continued, Osmond and Hoffer observed patients gaining not only self-awareness but a deeper sense of spiritual purpose. Bill Wilson, founder of Alcoholics Anonymous, also believed that a spiritual foundation greatly improved chances for permanent sobriety; when Wilson tried LSD himself, he was impressed by its entheogenic potential and welcomed psychedelic therapy as an adjunct to his own methods (see *Wilson, Bill*).

Osmond and Hoffer would give patients a single dose of 200–400 micrograms. Patients had been screened for psychological conditions that might lead to bad experiences, and those who qualified as good risks were carefully supervised during their trips. As medical historian Erika Dyck notes in her study of Osmond and Hoffer's work, "In the early trials, no concerted efforts were made to create a stimulating environment, but as the trials progressed, stimuli such as music, fresh cut flowers, paintings and other visual aids were added to intentionally create an environment with perceptual distractions. Staff encouraged patients to enjoy the experience and either talk to, or withdraw from, others in the room.... The following day, subjects were encouraged to compose a written description of their experience, without interference from hospital staff." It was precisely these relaxed conditions for the trials, Dyck explains, that made other scientists skeptical. A rival group in Toronto complained that Osmond and Hoffer had imposed insufficient controls for factors besides LSD that might be influencing the results. The Toronto researchers proposed a new procedure that would control environmental variables and thereby ensure a strict focus on the drug itself. In the Toronto design, patients would wear blindfolds and in some cases physical restraints, and remain in isolation from other people. Their goal was "to ascertain whether the drug offered genuine benefits, or whether the perceived advantages merely inspired clinical enthusiasm that corrupted the real outcome" (Dyck). The Toronto trials did not reproduce the striking results from Saskatchewan. Advocates of traditional methods believed they had exposed LSD therapy as nothing special, but Osmond and his supporters blamed the unimpressive results on the blindfolds, restraints, and isolation. Psychedelic therapy would only work, they maintained, if the trips were taken in more stimulating, congenial surroundings.

Although some psychiatrists continued to use psychedelic psychotherapy for alcoholism through the early 1960s, the work ended when LSD became illegal. Advocates including the Multidisciplinary Association for Psychedelic Research have been pressing for the resumption of such research (see *MAPS*).

Alexander, Marsha. Alexander wrote *The Sexual Paradise of LSD*. See *Sexual Paradise of LSD*.

Alice in Acidland. This 1968 B-movie tried to capitalize on the psychedelic vogue. Its loose plot involves the adventures of a recent high school graduate named Alice, who takes various drugs and joins in unconventional sexual activities. Cinematically, *Alice in Acidland* offers little in the way of psychedelic effects; when Alice takes LSD about 45 minutes into the film, however, it does shift from black and white to color. See *Alice in Wonderland*.

Alice in Wonderland. In 1960s counterculture, Lewis Carroll's books about Alice were strongly associated with the use of LSD and other hallucinogenic drugs (see *Carroll, Lewis*). Various elements of plot and imagery in Carroll's books contributed to this connection, including sudden shifts of visual perception and subversions of logic, language, and conventional behavior. The Disney company noted an opportunity to re-market their animated film of *Alice in Wonderland* for the psychedelic era: according to David Koenig, "The studio prepared ads with copy such as 'Down the rabbit hole and through the talking door lies a world where vibrant colors merge into shapes of fantasy, and music radiates from flowers,' 'Nine out of ten Dormice recommend Walt Disney's *Alice in Wonderland* for visual euphoria and good, clean nonsense,' and 'Should you go see it? Go ask Alice'" (see *Disney, Walt*). This last promotional nugget was quoting the chorus of Grace Slick's "White Rabbit," a popular song from 1967, which had been particularly influential in forging the connection between Alice and psychedelic culture (see *"White Rabbit"; Slick, Grace*). A bestselling anti-drug narrative, *Go Ask Alice* (1971), drew its title from the chorus of "White Rabbit" (see *Go Ask Alice*). Other connections included the B-movie *Alice in Acidland* (1968), in which a college girl takes LSD and the film turns from black and white to color; many examples of Alice-themed blotter art (see *Blotter Art*); and various dramatic adaptations of the Alice books that emphasized the psychedelic implications of her adventures. A recent example of such an adaptation was performed at UCLA in 2008 by "Bruin Live" theater: Lewis Carroll appeared as a character and gave Alice LSD as her ticket to Wonderland.

Alpert, Richard. Alpert met Timothy Leary when both were working in the Harvard psychology department (see *Leary, Timothy; Harvard*). Trained as a therapist, he shared Leary's enthusiasm for LSD and other psychedelic drugs; Alpert believed that LSD could help individuals improve self-awareness, and help humanity as a whole make spiritual progress. Alpert was later dismissed from Harvard for his involvement in drug experiments that school officials con-

sidered irresponsible. He joined Leary at Millbrook to continue their psychedelic and social experimentation. Along with Leary and Ralph Metzner, Alpert wrote *The Psychedelic Experience*, a manual for trippers based on The Tibetan Book of the Dead (see *Psychedelic Experience*).

In the later 1960s, Alpert traveled to India to study with guru Neem Karoli Baba. Alpert took the name "Ram Dass" and has devoted himself to spiritual counseling ever since. He credited LSD with weaning him from what he regarded as the superficial "games" of academia and directing him to a richer focus on spiritual growth. In a televised interview from 1967, he emphasized how LSD had nurtured his sense of oneness with all humanity. On an acid trip, one realizes, "There is no 'other': it is all one." Ironically, the creators of the television show *Lost* gave the name "Richard Alpert" to the belligerent leader of a group known as "The Others."

Altamont. On December 6, 1969, the Rolling Stones headlined a huge free concert at the Altamont Speedway, east of San Francisco. The event was envisioned as a one-day, West Coast version of Woodstock (see *Woodstock*). The major San Francisco psychedelic bands were all booked for the concert, including Grateful Dead, Jefferson Airplane, and Santana. Altamont proved to be no Woodstock, however: instead of a hippie festival of peace and love, it turned into an unruly, violent scene. One concertgoer was killed, three others died accidentally, and two performers were seriously injured.

Several factors contributed to the tragic outcome. Many attendees took LSD, which contributed somewhat to the chaos; but a similar level of LSD use at Woodstock had not caused much disruption. The man killed at Altamont had started behaving erratically from the influence of methamphetamine, not LSD. Because the concert had been moved to Altamont at the last minute, preparations for crowd control and security were hasty and inadequate. The crowd of 300,000 jostled for position nearer the small stage as the headline acts began playing. Members of the Hell's Angels had been paid with beer to protect the bands, but they reacted to the chaotic scene with excessive force (see *Hell's Angels*). One Angel punched Marty Balin of Jefferson Airplane and knocked him unconscious; when the Grateful Dead heard the news, they cancelled their performance and left Altamont. The Rolling Stones stayed to perform, but as they played "Under My Thumb," a man ran toward the stage with a gun, and a Hell's Angel stabbed him to death.

The tragic events of Altamont were seen by many as the inevitable flipside of Woodstock, with LSD and other drugs implicated in the uncivilized behavior. Robert Hunter wrote "New Speedway Boogie" for the Grateful Dead as a bleak commentary on the concert. The Altamont story is recorded in the 1970 documentary film *Gimme Shelter*.

Altered States. This 1980 film was based on the psychedelic experiments of John C. Lilly (see *Lilly, John*). Paddy Chayefsky wrote *Altered States* first as a novel and then as a screenplay. William Hurt stars as a psychology professor who, like Lilly, uses psychedelic drugs in conjunction with a sensory deprivation tank. The professor finds himself undergoing evolutionary regression: he transforms temporarily into a more primitive primate, and later into much more elemental protozoic material. His wife ultimately intervenes to bring him back to normal identity. Lilly liked the film and said that the regression theme came from the real psychedelic experience of one of his colleagues. In a 1983 interview with Judith Hooper, Lilly recalled how his friend "suddenly 'became' a chimp, jumping up and down and hollering for twenty five minutes." The "chimp" later explained to Lilly, "I was in a tree. A leopard was trying to get me. So I was trying to scare him away."

"And She Was" This hit song by Talking Heads from 1985 offers a subtle lyric about LSD written two decades after the psychedelic golden age. David Byrne explained that it was "a song I wrote about a girl I knew in high school in Baltimore, Maryland, who used to take LSD and lie out in a field behind the Yoo-hoo chocolate drink factory" (spoken in performance, from "Live at Union Chapel"). Byrne attended high school in the later 1960s, which places the tripping girl squarely within the hippie era. Unlike psychedelic rock songs from the 1960s, "And She Was" looks at a psychedelic moment from an outsider's point of view. Byrne views the tripping girl both skeptically and sympathetically: he positions himself as a detached and somewhat amused observer, but to some degree he appreciates her psychedelic elevation. Although the song has a hint of satire, the title lyric suggests a certain respect for that most fundamental of hippie goals, simply to be—as in the Human Be-In (see *Human Be-In*).

Apocalypse Now. In Coppola's Vietnam epic, LSD appears in two adjacent scenes that are among the most memorable in the film. An officer who served in the Army Security Agency testified to the accuracy of the film's depiction: "*Apocalypse Now*—that's how it really was. After a while, Vietnam *was* an acid trip. Vietnam was psychedelic, even when you weren't tripping" (Lee and Shlain).

In the first scene, a boat with American soldiers has arrived at the Do Lung Bridge, the last outpost where they can receive supplies. One of the soldiers (Lance the surfer) has taken LSD for the occasion. Asked what he thinks about the ominous scene they are approaching, Lance says, "It's beautiful." Lance has painted his face green and holds a puppy inside his jacket. With images of violence and desperation all around him, he appears mellow and fascinated. Coppola arranged the Do Lung Bridge scene so that both aural and visual elements suggest a psychedelic experience. He alternates between frames of complete darkness and sudden illumination of confused soldiers, producing a slow-paced stroboscopic effect. Bright flares periodically arc across the darkness; their purpose is violent (for aiming artillery), but from Lance's psychedelic point-of-view, they look beautiful. The bridge itself is framed by strings of lights suggestive of a carnival. As Lance sits happily with his puppy, Captain Willard has to keep reminding him to take cover. The soundtrack reinforces the hallucinatory chaos of the scene. Coppola uses a synthesizer to create an eerie calliope-like sound, with distorted pitch and rhythm. Later a Hendrix guitar riff is heard amidst the sounds of battle. As Willard anxiously searches for someone in charge to sort things out, Lance tags along but revels in the spectacle. In the next scene, with the boat crew past the bridge and back in daytime, Lance remains high. He lights a canister of purple smoke and improvises a little "Purple Haze" routine. As he is doing this, Viet Cong soldiers open fire and kill the boat's captain. The soldiers panic over the loss, and Lance's psychedelic playfulness seems somehow to blame.

The two scenes suggest an ambiguous message about the confluence of the psychedelic era and the Vietnam era. On the one hand, LSD allowed Lance to retain a noble innocence in the middle of a hellish scene, as he transcended (and ultimately survived) his role as a soldier. On the other hand, the acid trip distracted Lance and endangered his friends. The aesthetic pleasure he took from the scene contrasts grotesquely with the flesh-and-blood tragedy playing itself out in front of him. See *Vietnam.*

Artichoke. The CIA program for testing LSD that began as "Bluebird" was renamed "Artichoke" before ending up as "MK-Ultra." See *MK-Ultra; Bluebird.*

Asher, Harry. Physiologist Asher volunteered to take LSD and be observed by psychiatric researchers in Birmingham, England. Asher's account of his trip was published as a *Saturday Review* cover story in 1963: "Experiment with LSD: They Split My Personality." Except for earlier stories about Cary Grant's success with psychedelic therapy (see *Grant, Cary*), this was the first prominent piece about LSD to appear in a mainstream American magazine. (For a similar article in a Canadian magazine that ran a decade earlier, see *Katz, Sidney; Macleans*). Asher's trip journal detailed both positive and negative effects, but the overall impression slanted toward the negative, with Asher revealing very disturbing impulses set loose by the drug.

At first he enjoyed the altered state: "The early experiences were wholly delightful. There was a feeling of exhilaration and self-confidence, such as is rarely experienced, and an exaggerated tendency to laugh at anything at all." Later, with his eyes closed, he has a euphoric vision of a beachscape with three women. "It was not just that I liked or loved these women very, very much," he recalled. "Rather I felt a wonder that was really there, really there in the illusion, if you follow me; it just cannot be described in words." More often, though, Asher recorded unpleasant effects. Mid-trip he divided into two selves: a shadowy entity off to the left, "the naughty one," and the main person, who was "really me, but in an improved form. He was a very strong character." The naughty self suggested that he jump out a window. Later, back home but still under the drug's influence, Asher recognized "a compulsive urge to do violence to my children"; he urged his wife to keep them away until he returned to normal consciousness. His return to normality took much longer than he expected. For a few days he cried and talked emotionally about events from his past. In a sidebar giving background on LSD, *Saturday Review* dismissed early hopes that the drug would serve as an aid to therapy: "Unfortunately, LSD is not dependable in therapy.... LSD is not used as a medicine but as a research tool to uncover secrets of the mind."

Austin Powers. Mike Myers' 1997 spoof of 1960s spy movies briefly renewed interest in old school psychedelic culture. Near the beginning of *Austin Powers: International Man of Mystery,* Austin enters the "Electric Psychedelic Pussycat Swinger's Club," as "Incense and Peppermints" plays on the soundtrack (see *Strawberry Alarm Clock).* In the sequel, Myers invents the portmanteau word "shagedelic"—"psychedelic" combined with "shag"—to express his appreciation for a female spy's mind-blowing sexual attractiveness.

Autism. In the middle of the twentieth century, autism was thought by many experts to be a childhood manifestation of schizophrenia. Because established methods of treating autism showed minimal success, and because psychiatrists had experimented with LSD as a means of treating adult schizophrenics (see *Schizophrenia*), they began testing LSD in therapy for autistic children. The first results were reported at a Princeton conference in 1959, and several studies followed over the next few years. A recent article summarizes the results of LSD therapy for autism from 1959–1974: "Several positive outcomes were reported with the use of LSD, but most of these studies lacked proper experimental controls and presented largely narrative/descriptive data" (Sigafoos). Among the psychiatrists who reported promising results in the early 1960s was Gary Fisher (see *Fisher, Gary*). Less successful was a 1962 study of twelve mute children diagnosed with autism: doctors observed "rapid mood swings from elation to depression," "decreased alertness in most but increased alertness in a few," and no evidence of "the hoped-for change from muteness to speech" (Freedman).

Avalon Ballroom. This smallish San Francisco venue was the site of psychedelic concerts produced by Chet Helms and the Family Dog from 1966 to 1968 (see *Helms, Chet; Family Dog*). The Avalon could accommodate approximately 500 people, many of whom tripped on acid and danced as the bands performed. Liquid light shows accompanied the music (see *Light Shows*). At a typical concert, two bands would play two sets each; all of the major San Francisco bands played there, as did many lesser known local acts. Helms employed psychedelic poster artists to advertise Avalon concerts, including Stanley Mouse and Alton Kelley, Rick Griffin, and Victor Moscoso (see *Psychedelic Posters*). Concerts at the Avalon are considered by many hippie veterans to have been the epitome of the psychedelic scene in San Francisco.

Babbs, Ken. Babbs was a member of the Merry Pranksters and one of Ken Kesey's closest friends (see *Merry Pranksters; Kesey, Ken*). They first met in the late 1950s in a creative writing class at Stanford. Babbs graduated with an ROTC commission as a Marine officer; he went to Vietnam, where he flew helicopter missions. When Babbs returned, he got back together with Kesey, and the two men began to form a loose community of LSD enthusiasts that became the Merry Pranksters. During their famous trip across the country, Babbs's engineering knowledge helped them hold the old bus together. Later, he devised improvements for concert sound equipment that would enable psychedelic bands to play at maximum volume without undue distortion. When Kesey went to Mexico as a fugitive in 1966, Babbs and fellow Prankster Wavy Gravy emerged as unofficial leaders of the group (see *Wavy Gravy*). In later years, he and Kesey remained close friends and collaborated on various writing projects.

Bananas. One of the more intriguing legends that developed in the psychedelic era had to do with the supposed hallucinogenic properties of bananas. According to the widely disseminated story, if banana peels were dried out, scraped, and smoked, they would induce an LSD-like high. Smoking banana peels actually produces no such effect. However, the idea of psychedelic bananas was taken so seriously that FDA scientists tested the fruit for over three weeks to see if a new drug threat might be lurking in the middle of the supermarket.

The myth of the psychedelic banana originated early in 1967 during a concert tour by Country Joe and the Fish (see *Country Joe and the Fish*). One of the Fish, drummer Gary "Chicken" Hirsh, suggested that bananas could deliver a high. The band decided to give it a try that night at their Vancouver concert. They scraped and baked banana peels, rolled them into joints, and smoked them before their last set of the night. This set turned into an extended improvisation, more like The Grateful Dead than typical Country Joe. Members of the band attributed their psychedelic sublimity to the bananas. In their enthusiasm, they had forgotten the actual cause of their high: before the concert started, they had drunk water that roadies had spiked with LSD.

The next day, though, Country Joe went back home to Berkeley and spread the story about psychedelic bananas. The news got around so quickly that bananas sold out at local supermarkets. Newspapers in San Francisco picked up the story, and wire services distributed it nationally: "Banana Turn On, New Hippy Craze" (*San Francisco Chronicle*, February, 1967). At about the same time, writers at the *Berkeley Barb* published a detailed recipe for making hallucinogenic bananas; the recipe was a hoax concocted by skeptical *Barb* satirists, but many readers took it seriously. One gullible reader was William Powell, who reprinted the recipe in his *Anarchist Cookbook:* after scraping 15 pounds of bananas, make a paste, and "spread this paste on cookie sheets and dry it in an oven for about 20–30 minutes. This will result in a fine black powder (bananadine). Usually one will feel the effects of bananadine after smoking three or four cigarettes." The FDA assigned a lab team to cook up some "bananadine" and test for hallucinogenic properties. After three weeks of testing on a smoking machine, the scientists found nothing psychedelic: "The Bureau of

Science has made an analysis of the smoke obtained from several recipes for dried banana peel and concentrated banana juice. There were no detectable quantities of known hallucinogens in these materials" (FDA press release, May, 1967).

One accidental beneficiary of the banana myth was Donovan (see *Donovan*), who had recorded the song "Mellow Yellow" in 1966, before Country Joe's revelation. "Mellow Yellow" nevertheless blended with psychedelic bananas in a way that helped to strengthen both of them as memes. Listeners assumed that Donovan's "electrical banana" referred to the LSD-like banana high. Donovan welcomed the association, although years later he admitted that he heard about psychedelic bananas only after "Mellow Yellow" had been written and recorded. "Electrical banana" actually referred to a vibrating sex toy.

Barbie. The Barbie doll briefly joined the world of psychedelic fashion and music. "Arriving fairly concurrently in the Age of Aquarius was Barbie in all her psychedelic glory," notes Sharon Verbeten. A "Live Action Barbie" model from 1970 wore pink and orange hippie pants, a brown headband, and fringe that dangled from her wrists. Once activated, she could jerk her limbs around in an approximation of hippie dancing. "I dance to your favorite music," Barbie said on the box, but she also had her own music: a faux psychedelic song about being free. This incarnation of Barbie lasted about a year.

Barrett, Syd. Barrett led the English rock band Pink Floyd during its early period of innovative psychedelic music. His heavy use of LSD sparked his creativity but may have triggered the mental illness that ended his career prematurely. See *Pink Floyd*.

Barron, Frank. A classmate of Timothy Leary's in graduate school at Berkeley, Barron worked in the 1950s on CIA-funded psychological research. He became interested in psychedelic drugs, and in 1960 he started the Harvard Psychedelic Drug

Research Center. Barron invited Leary to join him at Harvard for experiments with LSD and other psychedelics (see *Harvard; Leary, Timothy*). In 1969 Barron took a position at the University of California, Santa Cruz, where he worked on research related to creativity (see *Santa Cruz*). He served as a member of the Albert Hofmann Foundation until his death in 2002.

Bateson, Gregory. An English anthropologist who developed the theory of "double bind" and the field of "psychocybernetics," Bateson ran clinical trials of LSD at Stanford starting in the late 1950s. Among the volunteer trippers at these trials was Ken Kesey (see *Kesey, Ken*). Bateson became a regular at the Esalen Institute (see *Esalen*) and late in his career took a position at the University of California, Santa Cruz (see *Santa Cruz*).

Beach Boys. Brian Wilson, creative leader of The Beach Boys, has said that both his life and his music were significantly influenced by LSD experiences in the mid 1960s. Wilson started using LSD in 1965, and the drug had both positive and negative effects on his life. He told writer Tom Nolan in 1966, "I took LSD ... and I learned a lot of things, like patience, understanding. I can't teach you or tell you what I learned from taking it, but I consider it a very religious experience" (Cateforis). In interviews many years later, he gave more mixed reviews of his acid experiences. "It got me deeper into the music, but it scared me, too" (Chapman). He "mostly got over" his fears, Wilson said, "but when you take a drug like LSD, you're never going to be the same again" (Lester). Indeed, Wilson's struggles with paranoia and depression damaged his life and work for many years following the heyday of The Beach Boys.

Wilson's first acid trip provides a good illustration of these mixed results. He told reporter Geoff Boucher that his first impulse was to bury his head under a pillow: "He was stricken. He had images of his mother and father in his mind and, most of all, fear." It was on that night that he "first heard another voice in his head, one that was threatening and stayed with him for years." After a while, though, Wilson felt better, went to his piano, and ended up composing "California Girls." "I was thinking about the music from cowboy movies," he recalled. "And I sat down and started playing it, bum-buhdeeda, bum-buhdeeda. I did that for about an hour. I got these chords going. Then I got this melody, it came pretty fast after that." He "kept working at the keyboard and, turning his thoughts to fashion magazines, he came up with one of the most famous opening lines in pop music"—a lyric about fashionable Eastern girls (Boucher). If "California Girls" seems an unlikely candidate for a psychedelic song, it was LSD that triggered the unexpected combination of cowboy music and fashion models. Wilson's "Good Vibrations" from the following year has more obvious psychedelic qualities. He worked on the song for six months and incorporated technical innovations—including complex overdubbing—that influenced The Beatles' *Sergeant Pepper's Lonely Hearts Club Band* (see *Beatles*). The lyrics to "Good Vibrations" contain no explicit references to drugs, but some of them suggest an early hippie landscape of colors, flowers, and sunshine.

Beat Generation. Novelist Jack Kerouac gave this polysemous name to a group of bohemian writers of the 1950s: "Beat" suggested tired or dejected, but also cool, even beatific. Prominent Beat figures played significant roles in the transition from Beat to hippie counterculture. Poet Allen Ginsberg, who participated in government tests of LSD, became close friends with Timothy Leary and other psychedelic enthusiasts in the early 1960s. Ginsberg more than any other Beat celebrity embraced the new generation of hipsters. He helped shape psychedelic history in New York, San Francisco, and London (see *Ginsberg, Allen*). Another prominent Beat, Neal Cassady, joined with the Merry Pranksters as an Acid Test regular and the driver of their colorful bus (see *Cassady, Neal; Merry Pranksters*). An important if less famous transitional figure was jazz critic and magazine editor David Solomon: drawing inspiration from Aldous Huxley, Solomon edited writings about LSD, promoted its use, and eventually served a jail sentence for helping to manufacture LSD microdots (see *Solomon, David; Operation Julie*). Among the best known Beats, only Kerouac clearly rejected the newer generation of countercultural rebels. Kerouac had no appetite for psychedelic drugs: he memorably commented, "Walking on water wasn't built in a day." When Cassady drove the Pranksters to visit his old friend, Kerouac reacted angrily to their anti-patriotic gestures and sulked in a corner until they left.

Beatles. The Beatles' use of LSD strongly influenced their music, and their music influenced psychedelic culture all over the world. John Lennon and George Harrison were the first Beatles to take the drug. In April of 1965, Lennon, Harrison, and their wives attended a dinner party hosted by Harrison's dentist. After dinner, the dentist slipped some LSD into their coffee, and the two Beatles found themselves unexpectedly tripping in a small London apartment. According to Steve Turner, Harrison said that night that he felt as if he were "falling in love with everyone." Harrison and Lennon became enthusiastic acidheads, taking hundreds of trips; McCartney and Starr tripped less frequently, but enough to understand the drug's mind-altering appeal. Beatles' music soon took a psychedelic turn.

Revolver (1966) was the first Beatles' album to show the influence of LSD. The one obviously psychedelic song is Lennon's "Tomorrow Never Knows," which begins with words borrowed from Timothy Leary's manual for tripping, *The Psychedelic Experience* (see *Psychedelic Experience*); the end of the song engages Leary's themes of detach-ment and transcendence, with life seen as a series of games. Lennon, the other Beatles, and producer George Martin worked hard in studio to produce sound effects appropriate for the song's psychedelic content. Lennon wanted his vocals to have an eerie vibrato quality. He suggested that they suspend him by a rope and spin him around as he sang, but Martin came up with a more practical idea: he recorded Lennon's voice through a special kind of speaker that produced the desired effect. Instrumentally, they created an Eastern sound with the use of sitar and tambur. Other innovations included drum and guitar riffs played backwards, and a complicated system of tape looping that created strange seagull-like sounds in the background. All of these innovations helped make the song a pioneer in psychedelic music. In other *Revolver* songs, the psychedelic influence is less apparent, except for a few clues that could be understood only in retrospect. "She Said She Said" includes a line about death that Lennon later explained he had heard from Peter Fonda during a California acid trip. "Yellow Submarine" became a psychedelic song mainly after the fact, by association with the movie of the same name (see *Yellow Submarine*). But "Yellow Submarine" and various other *Revolver* songs show the Beatles experimenting with new recording techniques to create unfamiliar sounds.

These new techniques and sounds reached their pinnacle in the next album, *Sergeant Pepper's Lonely Hearts Club Band* (1967), probably the single most influential album from the psychedelic era in rock music. The first song they recorded in full-blown psychedelic style, "Strawberry Fields Forever," was intended for the new album, but ended up being released only as a single. "Strawberry Field" was a park where young Lennon enjoyed himself with his friends. McCartney said in an interview, "We transformed it into the sort of psychedelic dream, so it was everybody's childhood place instead of just ours." Lennon originally recorded a simple version of "Strawberry Fields Forever" with just his voice and guitar; gradually, the Beatles and producer George Martin transformed it into a musical collage that sounded like nothing else before it. The weird alterations of tones and tempos were so suggestive of hallucinogenic perception that "one is almost tempted to doubt [George Martin's] assurances that he never tried LSD" (Hertsgaard).

In many songs on *Sergeant Pepper,* the Beatles altered vocal and instrumental textures to produce otherworldly effects. The two songs most closely associated with LSD were both banned from BBC radio play for that very reason: "Lucy in the Sky with Diamonds" and "A Day in the Life." Although John Lennon denied the significance of the first song's title—he said he took it from a drawing by his son—people were skeptical that "L.S.D." was a mere coincidence of initials. Whether or not the title encoded a reference to LSD, "Lucy in the Sky with Diamonds" has undeniable psychedelic resonance. Certainly Lennon was taking plenty of LSD at the time. The lyrics to "Lucy" sketch a dreamy landscape that sounds like a children's version of paradise. Natural features are not only colorful but edible. However, like many Lennon songs, "Lucy" has a core of sadness. The flowers are plastic and the people artificial. Indeed, the landscape brings to mind Timothy Leary's warnings to trippers about the world appearing plastic, and people turning into puppets. The girl at the center of the song, Lucy, is very different from her predecessors in early Beatles songs: there is no holding hands or kissing or falling in love. Lucy calls you but always eludes you. The only part of her body that materializes is her eyes, and all she does is look at you looking at her. "Lucy in the Sky with Diamonds" presents a psychedelic world that is simultaneously attractive for its visionary freshness and unsettling for its hints of alienation and detachment.

"A Day in the Life" is the final and most critically admired song on the album. It in-cludes a climactic lyric about turning on (which triggered the BBC ban), followed by a famous orchestral improvisation that quickly became associated with psychedelic sublimity. Although Lennon and McCartney denied the drug allusion, the BBC had good reason to link "A Day in the Life" with psychedelic counterculture. The lyrics contrast the tedium and emptiness of even the most successful ordinary lives with the excitement of "turning on." In the last verse, this contrast comes through most sharply: with bureaucrats busy counting the holes in their streets, the song invites us to turn on and discover new ways to fill our senses. As Lennon sings the last words, his voice begins to undulate, leading into a famous orchestral passage that sound like nothing else ever recorded. McCartney and producer George Martin led a 40-person orchestra that had been hired for this unusual psychedelic gig. Martin asked all of them to start with the lowest note possible on their instruments, then to move gradually higher so that they ended exactly 24 bars later on the highest possible note. As Martin later recounted, "Of course, they all looked at me as though I were completely mad." The Beatles went even further to initiate the orchestra as psychedelic conspirators: they had them add little joke-shop novelties to the standard formal dress— fright wigs, rubber noses, stick-on nipples. The unique 24-bar product stands as one of the most recognizable musical indices of psychedelic perception.

The cover of *Sergeant Pepper* completed its psychedelic credentials: the four Beatles appear in colorful satin uniforms, surrounded by a collage of lifesize cutouts of famous people, including psychedelic pioneer Aldous Huxley (see *Huxley, Aldous*). Rock critics praised *Sergeant Pepper* extravagantly. Even the academic world took notice, with prominent literary scholar Richard Poirier writing an extended interpretive analysis of the album. Timothy Leary weighed in with characteristic hyperbole, referring to the Beatles as "evolutionary agents sent by God, endowed with a mysterious power to create a new human species." The Rolling Stones flattered the Beatles with an album that imitated both the psychedelic style and the cover art of *Sergeant Pepper: Their Satanic Majesties Request* (see *Rolling Stones*). Only Frank Zappa reacted scornfully, with a parody of *Sergeant Pepper* called "We're Only in It for the Money" (see *Zappa, Frank*).

The third album from the Beatles' peak psychedelic period fell flat. They had conceived of *Magical Mystery Tour* (1967) as a multimedia experience, with an album to be released simultaneously with a film of their adventures in a Prankster-like bus. The music received lukewarm reviews, and the film simply flopped. The "tour" itself ended prematurely. The idea seemed passé to begin with, and the bus trip caused mainly traffic jams instead of adventures.

The Beatles' enthusiasm for LSD waned about this time, although they continued to make interesting music for a while longer. McCartney in later years acknowledged the influence of LSD on their work but warned against overemphasizing its importance: "'Lucy in the Sky,' that's pretty obvious. There's others that make subtle hints about drugs, but you know, it's easy to overestimate the influence of drugs on the Beatles' music. Just about everyone was doing drugs in one form or another and we were no different, but the writing was too important for us to mess it up by getting off our heads all the time." See *Psychedelic Rock; Harrison, George; Lennon, John; McCartney, Paul; Starr, Ringo; Martin, George.*

Beckley Foundation. Like MAPS in America (see *MAPS*), England's Beckley Foundation supports research involving potential benefits of LSD and other mind-altering drugs. See *Feilding, Amanda.*

Ben and Jerry's. The co-founders of the famous ice cream company, Ben Cohen and Jerry Greenfield, graduated from a New York high school in the year of Woodstock. The hippie atmosphere of the time influenced their business partnership to come. Ben and Jerry's consistently supported non-profit organizations with hippie-friendly causes. In 2003, they attempted to stage a music festival called "One Heart, One World" at the site of Woodstock, but the event was cancelled due to poor ticket sales. Several of their flavors reflected their ties to the psychedelic era. The first such product honored Jerry Garcia of the Grateful Dead (see *Garcia, Jerry*): "Cherry Garcia" was a vanilla-based flavor with chunks of chocolate and cherries, and a carton designed in the psychedelic style of Grateful Dead posters. Garcia threatened legal action until Ben and Jerry signed a licensing agreement. "Cherry Garcia" remained in the lineup, along with "Wavy Gravy" (named for Prankster and Grateful Dead clown: see *Wavy Gravy*), "Phish Food" (after the jam band that succeeded the Grateful Dead: see *Phish*), and "Imagine Whirled Peace" (in honor of John Lennon: see *Lennon, John*). A Ben and Jerry's store is now located at the iconic intersection of Haight and Ashbury in San Francisco.

Bercel, Nicholas. Los Angeles psychiatrist Bercel was one of the first Americans to try LSD. He heard about LSD in 1950 from Swiss psychiatrist Werner Stoll, the first scientist to publish a study of the new drug (see *Stoll, Werner*). Bercel took some back home and began experimenting with it in his psychiatric practice. In the early 1950s, the CIA asked Bercel to assess the plausibility of the Soviets using LSD to poison the water supply of a major American city; Bercel tested a sample in a glass of tap water and found that the chlorine neutralized the drug (see *Water Supply*).

Beresford, John. While working in New York City in 1961, English pediatrician Beresford applied to Sandoz for LSD to conduct research (see *Sandoz*). The package he received was the most important supply of LSD ever shipped: he gave a good portion of it to Michael Hollingshead, who turned on Timothy Leary and a host of others who became psychedelic enthusiasts (see *Hollingshead, Michael; Leary, Timothy*). Beresford founded the Agora Scientific Trust in 1962 to carry out LSD experiments. His results from the early 1960s are described in Masters and Houston's *The Varieties of Psychedelic Experience.* In 1991, Beresford founded the Committee on Unjust Sentencing, which advocated for revision of laws governing prison sentences for those convicted of crimes related to psychedelic drugs (see *Laws*).

Berg, Peter. Berg was a civil rights activist and member of the San Francisco Mime Troupe who became a founder of the Diggers (see *Diggers*). In a 1982 interview (Lee and Noble), Berg defined two Digger catch phrases related to LSD: "social acid" and "hard kicks." "Social acid" meant that the drug should properly be used within a social context to catalyze useful change, not just "to find out the inner truth and mystery of life." "Hard kicks" meant a freedom to experiment with drugs that blew away inhibitions and opened up creative resources; but for Berg and the Diggers, such creativity needed to be directed toward the transformation of social realities.

Bicycle Day. April 19th is celebrated as "Bicycle Day" by LSD enthusiasts. This was the day in 1943 when Albert Hofmann first took a full dose of the drug he discovered. Hofmann, who had no idea how strong LSD would turn out to be, bicycled home from the Sandoz labs in Basel shortly after ingesting the acid. He described the odd sensation of pedaling his bicycle vigorously but feeling as though he were going nowhere. In 1993, 25 Swiss cyclists (in honor of LSD-25) commemorated the 50th anniversary of Bicycle Day by riding the same route that Hofmann took in 1943 at the start of the world's first acid trip. See *Hofmann, Albert; Sandoz.*

Big Brother and the Holding Company. This San Francisco psychedelic band formed in late 1965 under the guidance of promoter Chet Helms (see *Helms, Chet*). Helms knew the guitarists from jam sessions at his house in Haight-Ashbury; he found them a drummer and arranged their first major gig, at the Trips Festival in January 1966 (see *Trips Festival*). A few months later, Helms brought in Janis Joplin, a friend from his native Texas, to sing in a bluesy style for the band. Big Brother began playing regularly at the Avalon Ballroom. After their impressive performance at the Monterey Pop Festival, Columbia signed them to a recording contract. Their first work for Columbia, *Cheap Thrills,* was their most successful album and remains a classic of the San Francisco musical scene during the late 1960s. Zap Comix artist R. Crumb designed the cover in his distinctive style (see *Crumb, Robert; Zap Comix):* he drew little cartoons for each song and band member, including one that depicted guitarist James Gurley as a psychedelic guru with one eye in the middle of his forehead. On the back of the album cover, Columbia simply put a photo of Joplin, whom they had decided to promote as the star of the band. Reviews of their performances increasingly praised Joplin for her soulful singing but raised questions about the skills of the rest of the band. The guitarists liked to play at maximum amplification with a "raw" sound, and in general their style did not go over as well in New York as it did in San Francisco. In late 1968 Joplin split from Big Brother. She continued to perform with other musicians until her death from a heroin overdose in 1970.

Blewett, Duncan. Blewett was one of the doctors invited to Saskatchewan by Humphry Osmond in the early 1950s to experiment with psychiatric uses of LSD (see *Osmond, Humphry; Psychiatry*). Blewett was particularly interested in two aspects of psychedelic therapy: LSD as a catalyst for human evolution, and parapsychological effects associated with the drug. He wrote in *The Frontiers of Being* that use of LSD was "accelerating exponentially" the evolution of humans toward a "more loving and joyful" appreciation of life. He also gave papers analyzing people who experienced precognition, clairvoyance, and other forms of extrasensory perception while on LSD.

Bloom, Hyman. Bloom was a noted American painter who became one of the earliest volunteers to try LSD. According to supervising psychiatrist Max Rinkel (see *Rinkel, Max*), Bloom first jotted down the phrase "Hindu religion," then "drew monsters" and a picture of "a butchered beef or ox"; sometimes he simply made "dots and dashes" (quoted in Stevens).

Blotter Art. Beginning in the late 1960s, LSD began to appear in "blotter" form. The earliest blotters were rudimentary: a small square of paper dosed with a blotch of LSD in the middle. As production became more organized, blotters were printed on letter-size sheets and divided into little squares; each square contained a small dose of LSD, usually between 30 and 100 micrograms. Blotter producers began adorning each square with a design. Over the years, blotter designs became increasingly sophisticated, with images culled from a variety of cultural sources. Blotter acid became a kind of folk art. The artists were (necessarily) anonymous, and their work survived through collectors who thought highly enough of the design to forego the drug.

Early blotters displayed well established icons of psychedelia, including Tenniell's Alice in Wonderland illustrations and Mouse and Kelley's skeleton and roses. Later images came from popular culture, including Disney characters (a famous blotter shows Mickey Mouse as Sorcerer's Apprentice), superheroes from comic books, and characters from television shows (e.g., Bart Simpson, Beavis and Butthead). Other blotter designs took on a more spiritual tone: Masonic pyramids, Buddhas, sphinxes, yin/yang, even images of saints and the crucifixion.

The most famous collector of blotter art is Mark McCloud, an artist from San Francisco with an M.F.A. from UC Davis. McCloud amassed an impressive collection of blotters from the earliest to very recent examples. He put on an exhibit in 1987 at the San Francisco Art Institute, and later took the show to New York and Houston. His work caught the attention of the FBI, however, and McCloud was twice arrested and put on trial for possession and distribution of LSD. Both times he was acquitted. His lawyer argued successfully that the blotters were essentially works of folk art, and in any case, they were no longer functional as doses of LSD. McCloud told Jack Shafer in *San Francisco Weekly* (August 30, 1995) that "exposure to sunlight and heat had destroyed the illegal drug in every one of the blotters ... reducing the LSD to an inert and legal compound."

Art critic Carlo McCormick, in notes for McCloud's exhibit, reflected on the curious interplay between blotter-as-art and blotter-as-drug: "The knowledge that the paper is dosed cannot but affect how one looks at the picture. Even odder, however, is that the picture has a way of influencing one's notion of the acid. So mighty is the power of suggestion here that it seems to signify some secret knowledge or expectation of the trip, as if the ink could predict, direct, or code one's experience" (quoted in Shafer). Blotter artwork could alter expectations for a trip: anything from deep mystical experience to giggly recreation, depending on whether you swallowed Buddha or Butthead.

Blue Boy. A famous episode of *Dragnet* entitled "The LSD Story" goes more commonly by "Blue Boy," the nickname of the memorable main character. Jack Webb wrote "The LSD Story" as the first episode of his revived *Dragnet*, which returned to television on January 12, 1967. (See *Dragnet* for a later episode based on Timothy Leary.) Because Sergeant Friday met his first acidhead in the summer of 1966, before LSD became illegal, he had to improvise; but in the middle of the show, his boss brings him the October law that changed all that. "The LSD Story" thereby dramatizes new legal problems facing users as well as the risks to mental and physical health. Thirty years later, *TV Guide* named it the 85th greatest episode in television history.

"The LSD Story" narrates a struggle between mainstream culture and dissolute psychedelic behavior. Carrying the banner for the losing side is Blue Boy, an eighteen-year-old freelance seeker who has painted his face blue and yellow. Opposing him are Sergeant Joe Friday and Officer Bill Gannon. Joe and Bill dress relentlessly in gray, whereas Blue Boy flaunts his psychedelic access to colors: "Brown, blue, yellow, green," he announces, "orange, red, red, red: I can hear them all!" During his arrest, he rips out the shoulder seam of Bill's gray coat. In this version of civil war, the union is gray and the rebels are blue. At first, because there is no law against LSD, the officers book Blue Boy on "section 601 of the Welfare and Institution Code: in danger of leading an idle, dissolute, or immoral life." The danger seems to reside in Blue Boy's unconventional religious gestures. His acid experience prompted a version of pagan animism. Blue Boy has "painted himself up like an Indian," chewed on tree bark, and buried his face in the ground to gaze at the "purple pilot light of all creation." He taunts the police with evidence of his mental vitality. As different as they are, Blue Boy and Sergeant Friday do share one prosaic drug: tobacco. In one scene, Joe is standing outside Juvenile Hall, about to light a cigarette; Blue Boy intercepts Joe's match and uses it to light his own cigarette. Blue Boy momentarily joins the gray world of suits and cigarettes, and thereby alerts us to Joe's use of a dangerous drug.

Blue Boy doesn't stay with gray drugs for long: he becomes a "pusher" and sneaks around schools trying to "hook" kids on acid. Webb, in his eagerness to condemn LSD, muddles it with very different drugs. He borrows terms and plots that do not make sense for LSD, which is neither addictive nor expensive. Near the end, when Joe and Bill raid an acid party, the tripping teens are harmlessly painting and listening to music. But Joe and Bill roust them as if they were armed robbers: "All of you! Stay where you are! Freeze! You're all under arrest!" Bill grabs one boy and pulls him roughly to his feet. The bullying tactics seem incongruous, because these trippers are mellow and civil. Webb's conflation of LSD with other drugs becomes most obvious at the end of the episode, when Joe and Bill discover Blue Boy dead in a motel room. After Blue Boy's friend tells them, "He kept saying he wanted to get further out," Joe offers a climactic irony, "Well, he made it: he's dead." It turns out, though, that Blue Boy had taken an array of barbiturates along with his LSD, as the coroner's jury notes in its verdict of accidental overdose. In the end, it was not the acid, but the reds, that killed Blue Boy.

Blue Cheer. This San Francisco band took their name from a popular issue of Owsley acid, which Owsley named after a laundry detergent (see *Owsley*). Blue Cheer had a reputation for playing very loudly, and their musical style fit the profile of Acid Rock, the forerunner of Heavy Metal (see *Acid Rock*).

Blue Star Acid. A flyer warning about "Blue Star Acid" has appeared from time to time in American cities over the last four decades, copied and distributed by well-meaning parents and school officials. The flyer warns that drug dealers have been making LSD-soaked tattoos in the shape of blue stars and giving them to children. When a child puts on the tattoo, the flyer explains, LSD (and possibly some strychnine) enters the bloodstream through the skin. The story is an urban legend. Investigators have found no such tattoos or evidence of children accidentally tripping by such means. Nevertheless, the Blue Star Acid scare continues to pop up now and then.

Bluebird. "Bluebird" was the first code name given to the covert CIA testing program involving LSD and other mind-altering drugs.

Bluebird became Artichoke in 1951 and MK-Ultra in 1953. See *MK-Ultra; Artichoke*.

Bosstown Sound. In late 1967, producer Alan Lorber of MGM records promoted "The Boston Sound" or "Bosstown Sound" as a rival to the San Francisco Sound that was dominating the psychedelic rock scene (see *San Francisco Sound*). Reviews of the bands and the surrounding marketing campaign were not kind, and the Bosstown Sound faded quickly. The best known of the Bosstown bands was Ultimate Spinach (see *Ultimate Spinach*).

Bott, Christine. Bott and boyfriend Richard Kemp were hippie idealists who produced millions of doses of microdot LSD at their lab in rural Wales, until their 1977 arrest in "Operation Julie." See *Kemp, Richard; Operation Julie*.

Brand, Stewart. The man who became famous as creator of the *Whole Earth Catalog* started his countercultural career as one of the Merry Pranksters (see *Merry Pranksters*). Brand first took LSD as a volunteer subject in the Menlo Park experiments sponsored by the CIA and the American military. In the waning days of the Acid Tests, he organized the Trips Festival in January 1966, which amounted to an Acid Test on a much larger scale (see *Trips Festival*). As Fred Turner has explained, Brand later played a very important role as liaison between the old psychedelic community and the technological entrepreneurs who were developing personal computers and the internet (see *Internet*). In 1985 he gathered members of both groups to found WELL (Whole Earth Lectronic Link) and later *Wired*.

Brotherhood of Eternal Love. This southern California group supplied much of the country's LSD in the late 1960s and early 1970s. Its origins go back to 1966, when biker-surfer John Griggs and some of his friends stole Sandoz acid from a Hollywood producer, had a psychedelic epiphany in the desert, and visited Timothy Leary to find out

more. At Leary's suggestion, they chose a spiritual name for their organization, reminiscent of Leary's own League for Spiritual Discovery (see *Leary, Timothy; League for Spiritual Discovery*). The group settled in Orange County and established connections for the distribution of LSD and other drugs. The Brotherhood had many trappings of a hippie lifestyle, but they were serious about their business: they sold marijuana, hashish, and plenty of Orange Sunshine acid (see *Orange Sunshine*). At one point around 1970, law enforcement agents estimated that they were responsible for half of the American LSD supply. After Griggs's death in 1969 and the departure of chief chemist Tim Scully (see *Scully, Tim*), production and banking were headed by the mysterious Ronald Stark, who allegedly had connections with international finance, organized crime, and the intelligence community. As Stewart Tendler and David May explain in their book about the Brotherhood, Nixon-era drug officials went to considerable lengths to arrest members of the Brotherhood and disrupt their operations. The group was effectively shut down with arrests in 1972 (although Stark remained free in Europe for a few more years). *Rolling Stone* dubbed the Brotherhood a "hippie mafia," entangled in corruption and more interested in money than psychedelia.

Bummer. The most common nickname for a bad LSD trip, "bummer" entered American usage in the mid 1960s. According to Tom Wolfe, the term originated with the Hell's Angels: "'Bummer' was the Angels' term for a bad trip on a motorcycle, and very quickly it became the hip world's term for a bad trip on LSD." The *OED* cites Timothy Leary to convey the word's broad range of reference: "The Western world has been on a bad trip, a 400-year bummer" (*Politics of Ecstasy*). See *Health Risks*.

Burning Man. This annual gathering has been described by both enthusiasts and detractors as a neo-hippie carnival. Held during Labor Day week in the desert north of Reno,

Burning Man is dedicated to communal improvisation and unconventional self-expression. It is also one of the last places in the world where LSD remains in fairly heavy use. In 1998, Nevada law enforcement agents seized 100,000 doses of LSD at Burning Man. Informal data gathered from participants suggests that LSD has a conspicuous presence at the festival, although it is not as widely used as marijuana and ecstasy.

Burroughs, William S. Novelist Burroughs experimented with hallucinogens but did not respond to them as enthusiastically as did his friends Allen Ginsberg and Timothy Leary (see *Ginsbery, Allen; Leary, Timothy*). In a 1965 interview (Knickerbocker), Burroughs began by offering a strong warning about LSD and other psychedelics: "I think they're extremely dangerous, much more dangerous than heroin. They can produce overwhelming anxiety states. I've seen people try to throw themselves out of windows." But he added that his own experiences had not been so dire: "I've tried most of the hallucinogens without an anxiety reaction, fortunately. LSD-25 produced results for me similar to mescaline. Like all hallucinogens, LSD gave me an increased awareness, more a hallucinated viewpoint than any actual hallucination. You might look at a doorknob and it will appear to revolve, although you are conscious that this is the result of the drug. Also, van Goghish colors, with all those swirls, and the crackle of the universe."

Busby, John. *Life* magazine's influential cover story on LSD (see *Life*) included a note about Busby, the retired Navy captain who "used LSD just once and solved an elusive problem in pattern recognition while developing intelligence equipment for a Navy research project." Captain Busby said that LSD helped him circumvent "the normal limiting mechanisms of the brain."

Busch, Anthony K. Along with fellow psychiatrist Warren C. Johnson, Busch received LSD from Sandoz for use in clinical trials on hospitalized psychotic patients in St. Louis. They published the results in a 1950 paper that was the first of its kind. Busch and Johnson concluded, "LSD-25 may offer a means for more readily gaining access to the chronically withdrawn patients. It may also serve as a new tool for shortening psychotherapy." See *Psychiatry*.

Byrds. The Byrds were one of the first bands to produce rock music that showed a psychedelic influence. They first came to prominence when their electric version of Bob Dylan's "Mr. Tambourine Man" (see *Dylan, Bob*) rose to #1 on both American and British charts in the middle of 1965. Roger McGuinn sang Dylan's trippy lyrics and played a 12-string Rickenbacker guitar that produced a distinctive chiming sound. At the end of 1965, they recorded "Eight Miles High," one of the earliest examples of psychedelic rock. The title refers literally to the cruising altitude of an airplane, and the song on one level records impressions of a trip to London. However, the lyrics also seem to describe the disorienting effects of an LSD trip. Roger McGuinn's spacy guitar work at the beginning of the song contributes to the psychedelic effect: McGuinn used his electric 12-string Rickenbacker to play a solo loosely based on jazz riffs by John Coltrane. Because of what they assumed were drug references, the BBC and several American radio stations banned "Eight Miles High" from radio play.

David Crosby of the Byrds later made his feelings about LSD quite plain. At the Monterey Pop Festival in 1967, Crosby lectured the audience about the beneficial effects of acid trips, and he urged everyone in the country to turn on. The other Byrds, not happy about Crosby's acid evangelism and other assertive stances, eventually pushed him away from the band. Before he left, however, the Byrds produced *The Notorious Byrd Brothers*(1968), an album that mixed psychedelic elements with many other musical styles, including country.

"California Girls." This song was the unlikely product of Brian Wilson's first LSD trip. See *Beach Boys.*

Cargill, Melissa. Cargill, a chemistry graduate student at Berkeley in the mid 1960s, became Owsley's girlfriend and collaborator in LSD production. She helped produce the famously pure tablets called "White Lightning." See *Owsley; White Lightning.*

Carroll, Lewis. Oxford professor Charles Dodgson wrote *Alice's Adventures in Wonderland* and *Through the Looking-Glass* under this pseudonym. Because the Alice books became associated with psychedelic culture in the 1960s (see *Alice in Wonderland*), speculation abounded concerning Dodgson's own use of hallucinogenic drugs. There is no evidence to indicate that Dodgson used an ergot derivative or any drug strong enough to merit comparison with LSD. However, as a man who suffered chronically from headaches and insomnia, he took an interest in a variety of medicinal drugs. Dodgson owned books on homeopathic herbal remedies, stimulants, and narcotics, as well as *Mental Physiology,* W.H. Carpenter's authoritative Victorian treatment of drugs and their effects. Scholar Michael Carmichael has suggested that Dodgson read about Siberian shamans' use of hallucinogenic mushrooms.

Cassady, Neal. Cassady became famous as friend and inspiration to Beat writers Jack Kerouac and Allen Ginsberg, but he had a second phase of celebrity in the psychedelic era. Cassady met Ken Kesey in the early 1960s and joined the Merry Pranksters (see *Kesey, Ken; Merry Pranksters*). Cassady did much of the driving in the Pranksters' colorful bus; his driving skills were legendary, even in altered states. Tom Wolfe describes one day on the bus when Cassady, high on LSD, decided to negotiate a winding, downhill road without ever using the brakes. By all accounts, Cassady rarely used the brakes

in conversation: he carried on rambling monologues that touched on matters philosophical, political, poetic, and personal. He was adept at talking the Pranksters out of jams with police and other authorities. Cassady's son heard one such story from Jerry Garcia about a favorite memory. At one of the Acid Tests (see *Acid Test*), they ran into trouble parking the "Furthur" bus. A tripping Cassady, guided by a tripping Garcia, had backed the bus into a stop sign and sheared it off near ground level. At just that moment, a police car pulled into view. Cassady calmly lifted the sign back into place and held it there, with "the other hand in his pocket and his legs crossed like Buster Keaton." He chatted briefly with the police, who only wondered why Garcia had collapsed to the ground in laughter.

Cassady died not long after his Prankster adventures, apparently from complications related to the use of alcohol and barbiturates. Although he never wrote a book of his own, his life is chronicled in several books by others, including Kerouac's *On the Road* and Wolfe's *The Electric Kool-Aid Acid Test.* The Grateful Dead paid tribute to him in the song "That's It for the Other One."

Castaneda, Carlos. Author of some of the most famous and controversial psychedelic books, Castaneda met Timothy Leary a few years before the publication of his first book, *The Teachings of Don Juan* (1969). Leary had been fired from Harvard and was living in Mexico, conducting further experiments with LSD (see *Leary, Timothy*). As Leary tells the story in his memoir *Flashbacks,* Castaneda came to Leary's hotel—"La Catalina"— in an attempt to join the group of LSD adventurers. Leary was suspicious of Castaneda's motives and sent him away. Castaneda then visited a local woman known for her shamanistic powers and asked for her help. He presented himself as a professor and fledgling shaman doing battle with an American, Leary, who had stolen substances of great power from the local people. The woman knew Leary and told Castaneda that she trusted him.

In *The Teachings of Don Juan*, Castaneda presented an evil character with the same name as Leary's hotel: "La Catalina" was a witch determined to harm Castaneda and his mentor, don Juan. That book ended with Castaneda abandoning his training in sorcery due to fear of La Catalina and doubts about his own powers. He resumed his training, however, and wrote a series of sequels about the wisdom passed along by don Juan. Although the books sold well and made Castaneda a countercultural celebrity, many psychedelic experts—including Leary, and mushroom specialist Gordon Wasson (see *Wasson, R. Gordon*)—raised doubts about their authenticity. They suspected that Castaneda had borrowed or invented many of his supposed experiences with don Juan.

Chandler, Arthur. Chandler was a Beverly Hills psychiatrist who, with partner Mortimer A. Hartman, used LSD as a tool for psychotherapy and published a study of their results. See *Hartman, Mortimer A.; Grant, Cary.*

Charlatans. Pioneers of the musical scene that developed into psychedelic rock (see *Psychedelic Rock*), the Charlatans are remembered less for their music than for their lifestyle and performance personae. They dressed in Western garb (vests, string ties, hats), and their use of LSD inspired a Prankster-like playfulness and carefree atmosphere at their concerts.

The Charlatans were founded by San Franciscan George Hunter in 1964. In June of 1965, they began a series of concerts at the Red Dog Saloon in Virginia City, Nevada. The renovated saloon fit their image perfectly, and the concerts attracted the psychedelic avant garde then gathering in San Francisco. The Charlatans took LSD before their first performance at the Red Dog Saloon. According to bass player Richard Olsen, they were so high they "weren't really playing together," but they laughed and improvised. By all accounts, many members of the audience joined in the tripping. The concerts had been advertised around San Francisco with a poster designed by Hunter and fellow Charlatan Mike Ferguson; the poster has become famous as a collectible nicknamed "The Seed," the earliest example of a psychedelic poster (see *Psychedelic Posters*). The poster announces "The Amazing Charlatans.... Direct from San Francisco, The Limit of the Marvelous." The lettering is more easily legible than in posters from the mature psychedelic style, but key elements of the genre are in place: wavy lines and a gentle subversion of linear organization; hippie-themed images of flowers, vines, and stars; and a few letters with the "melting" look that would become a staple of psychedelic design.

The Charlatans' musical style was influenced mainly by traditional American folk materials. As rock historian Richie Unterberger summarizes, "While they occasionally delved into guitar distortion and fractured, stoned songwriting, The Charlatans' music was rooted in good-time jug-band blues, not psychedelic freakouts." The Charlatans signed a recording contract with Kama Sutra Records in 1966, but Kama Sutra refused to release the album after a dispute over which song would become the single. The band insisted on "Codine," Buffy Sainte-Marie's lament about drug addiction, which the record company thought too dark for popular consumption. The Charlatans' version of "Codine" eventually came out in Europe, but by that time they had faded from American attention. The Charlatans' signature song, Leadbelly's "Alabama Bound," was occasionally covered by more successful San Francisco bands as a tribute to their precursors in psychedelic performance.

Chicago. This band's song entitled "25 or 6 to 4" (1970) has often been mistakenly interpreted as referring to LSD. See *"25 or 6 to 4."*

Chief Boo-Hoo. This was the pseudonym

adopted by Arthur Kleps, self-anointed "Patriarch of the East" in the Neo-American Church. Boo-Hoo's church called for the sacramental use of LSD but was known more for satire than theology. See *Kleps, Arthur; Neo-American Church; Religion.*

Chromosomes. Just when interest in LSD was at its apex, shortly before the Summer of Love, researchers discovered a frightening risk for those who took the drug: LSD appeared to damage human chromosomes. *Science* published the first study connecting LSD with genetic abnormalities in March of 1967 (Cohen and Marmillo). From there the story spread sensationally, transmitted by newspapers, television news, popular magazines, documentaries, and government agencies. Dozens of follow-up studies were funded in the months following those first published results.

As things turned out, it was the science that was defective, not the offspring of acidheads. In 1971 *Science* published a lengthy, painstaking correction of the first chromosome study. The 1971 authors (Dishotsky *et al.*) reviewed all the studies, compared their own lab results, and concluded there was nothing to worry about: "In the past 4.0 years, 68 studies and case reports directly related to this issue have been published.... From our own work and from a review of the literature, we believe that pure LSD ingested in moderate doses does not damage chromosomes in vivo, does not cause detectable genetic damage, and is not a teratogen [a substance that can cause birth defects] or a carcinogen in man."

Andrew Weil has summarized a number of problems with the methods and conclusions of the original studies. To begin with, their conclusions were based on retrospective analysis, not prospective studies with strict controls. Retrospective studies are much more vulnerable to errors related to *post hoc ergo propter hoc* reasoning. More careful research has shown that similar chromosomal breakage can be caused by other very

common drugs and conditions, including aspirin and viral infections. Furthermore, results based on test tube experiments can be unreliable: cells behave differently in test tubes than they do inside a living body. Finally, as Weil explains, "chromosomal breaks are seen in cells of all people," which weakens the case for something special and dangerous in the case of LSD. "In fact, through the whole controversy no one showed *why* it was bad to have broken chromosomes in your lymphocytes. It sounds bad, certainly, but one cannot say that it is bad without making a number of shaky assumptions."

Shaky science was necessary but not sufficient to cause the chromosome uproar. After all, the original paper in *Science* was tucked away in the middle of the issue, not even one of the headliners. The real story was not so much the faulty science as the sensational publicity that quickly surrounded it. By contrast, the 1971 correction received very little attention.

The major news magazines presented the story with rhetorical flair. They wanted not only to warn hippies but to punish them for being foolish. *Time* began, "LSD, the substance that was supposed to open the doors to a luminous new world of the mind, has instead opened the minds of medical researchers to a dark world of hitherto unsuspected dangers.... " (September 15, 1967). They referred to the symposium as an "emergency meeting of top geneticists," thereby intensifying the alarm and emphasizing the credibility of the scientists involved. *Newsweek* included two photos in the middle of their story. The top photo showed a young woman, evidently having a bad trip, drawing herself into a fetal position in some sort of institutional setting. Beneath her another frame displayed three microscopic images of broken chromosomes. The "breaks" look like little notches in the sausage-shaped chromosomes, and are subtle enough to require arrows for identification. The message is far from subtle, though: a young woman who uses LSD risks both her own mind and her baby's body. *Newsweek* concludes with another rhetorical jab at hippies: as research continues into possible birth defects, "the hippie term 'freak out' becomes sicker every day."

The Saturday Evening Post published a cover story by Bill Davidson on "The Hidden Evils of LSD." Above a photograph of a young man struggling against attendants in a hospital, a banner reads, "If you take LSD even once, your children may be born malformed and retarded." Lacking definitive proof of causal links between LSD and genetic damage, The *Post* used looser logical and rhetorical strategies. "In Oregon, a young mother brought her newborn baby in to be examined. The child had a defect of the intestinal tract and its head was developing grotesquely—one side growing at a much faster rate than the other." The mother had at some point in her life tried LSD, the story continues: readers are thereby invited to make the fallacious connection between the drug and the defect. Later, the story draws an analogy between LSD and Thalidomide, the most notorious teratogen in recent history. If the link between LSD and birth defects has not yet been proven, Davidson argues, we must remember that "it took some time to get proof of what Thalidomide could do to unborn babies, but when the ghastly proof came, it was as irremediable as it was convincing." Elsewhere, Davidson mentions a young man who had tried LSD and was later "found to have a chromosomal abnormality that seems to be identical with the first stages of leukemia, the incurable blood cancer that proliferated in Hiroshima after the bomb fell." Through this rhetorical sleight of hand, Davidson links LSD, widely associated with flowers and peace, with nuclear war.

Newspapers, network newscasts, and documentaries similarly relied on analogies with Thalidomide and other rhetorical devices to shore up the weaknesses of the scientific case. They spread their message so effectively that the connection between LSD and damaged chromosomes still lingers in the public mind decades after the science was retracted.

Cirque du Soleil. This Canadian performance group created its psychedelic "Love" show for the Mirage hotel in Las Vegas starting in 2006 (see *Mirage*). "Love" presents the music of the Beatles synchronized with spectacular visual effects and acrobatics: psychedelic colors, strobe lights, video and photos projected onto huge screens, and 60 acrobatic and aerial performers. Guy Laliberté, co-founder of Cirque du Soleil, first conceived of a Beatle-themed show in conversation with his friend George Harrison (see *Harrison, George*). Although Harrison did not live to see the results, his widow Olivia Harrison attended a special performance in 2007 along with Yoko Ono and the two surviving Beatles, Paul McCartney and Ringo Starr. Original Beatles producer George Martin and his son Giles reworked the recordings with state-of-the-art technology (see *Martin, George*). The show's aesthetic features and choice of songs emphasize the Beatles' psychedelic period; "Love" contains several songs associated with the use of LSD, including "Lucy in the Sky with Diamonds," "Strawberry Fields Forever," and "Tomorrow Never Knows." See *Beatles*.

Clark, Walter Houston. Clark was a prominent religious scholar who wrote about LSD and other psychedelics as agents for facilitating spiritual experiences. He became friends with Timothy Leary and Walter Pahnke (see *Leary, Timothy; Pahnke, Walter*) and studied ritual use of organic hallucinogens. Clark described psychedelic drugs as "an auxiliary which, used carefully within a religious structure, may assist in mediating an experience which ... cannot be distinguished psychologically from mysticism." Citing spiritual insights recorded in Masters and Houston's *The Varieties of Psychedelic Ex-*

perience, he wrote in *Chemical Ecstasy* that LSD poses "a challenge to the established churches. Here is a means to religious experience that not only makes possible a more vital religious experience than the churches can ordinarily demonstrate, but the regeneration of souls." See *Religion.*

The Clash. One of the most admired and influential punk bands, The Clash was co-founded by Joe Strummer (born John Graham Mellor), who had roots in psychedelic culture. Strummer attended a London art school in 1970 but was expelled for using LSD. The documentary film *The Future Is Unwritten* shows Strummer and other members of The Clash taking acid. In 1978, in reaction to the LSD arrests known as "Operation Julie" (see *Operation Julie*), The Clash released "Julie's Been Working for the Drug Squad": the lyrics mock the police action and begin with an allusion to "Lucy in the Sky with Diamonds" (see *Lucy in the Sky with Diamonds*). After The Clash broke up, Strummer eventually formed another band known as the Mescaleros. He continued to write songs that made LSD references, including "Get Down Moses" and "Coma Girl." In a feature article from 1999, Strummer told a reporter that occasional acid trips were beneficial, and that a good label for his new music would be "acid punk" (*The Globe and Mail,* Nov. 2, 1999). See *Punk.*

Coburn, James. Actor Coburn volunteered to take part in psychiatrist Oscar Janiger's LSD studies in 1959 (see *Janiger, Oscar*). On his application, Coburn wrote that he hoped "to gauge present consciousness (where I am to where I can possibly go)." Janiger accepted him and supervised his first acid trip. Many years later, Coburn reflected on the importance of his psychedelic experience: "It was phenomenal. I loved it. LSD really woke me up to seeing the world with a depth of objectivity." He also said that the drug helped him as an actor, because it "stimulates your imagination. And it frees you from fears of certain kinds."

Eight years later Coburn played the part of a psychiatrist with psychedelic interests. *The President's Analyst* tells the story of Dr. Sidney Schaefer, chosen to serve as psychoanalyst to the President. Schaefer becomes overwhelmed by stress and surveillance; he escapes from the White House and joins a psychedelic band to hide from his pursuers. During his stay with the band, he wears a hippie wig, plays a gong, and enjoys an LSD trip filmed with typical psychedelic visual effects. Producers first offered the role of hippie musician to Jerry Garcia, but he declined, and Barry McGuire played the part instead.

Cohen, Sidney. Cohen was a Los Angeles psychiatrist who experimented with LSD as a therapeutic tool. He wrote two of the earliest papers assessing risks and complications. In the first, "LSD: Side Effects and Complications," Cohen analyzed information gathered from 44 psychiatrists who had used LSD in their practice. Overall, he concluded that the drug was "safe" when taken under professional supervision. In the second paper, "Complications Associated with LSD," Cohen expressed more concern, especially because "a black market in the drug exists," and people were taking LSD outside the clinical setting. Cohen cited four complications: "prolonged psychotic reactions," "acting out" (anti-social behavior), "multi-habituation" (LSD is not addictive, but may link users with addictive drugs), and "abuse of euphoriant property." This last complication related directly to Cohen's concerns about the increasing use of LSD for recreational rather than medical reasons. See *Psychiatry.*

Condrau, Gion. Swiss psychiatrist Condrau, who earned doctorates both in medicine and in philosophy (as a student of Martin Heidegger), was one of the first to explore therapeutic uses of LSD. See *Depression.*

Connery, Sean. After his success as James Bond in *Dr. No* and *Goldfinger,* Connery had trouble dealing with the pressures of celebrity. His wife, Diane Cilento, had read about the psychedelic methods of psychiatrist R.D. Laing, and she persuaded him to go in for therapy (see *Laing, R.D.*). Laing agreed to treat Connery in exchange for a hefty fee, use of a limo, and a bottle of premium Scotch. According to Cilento's autobiography *My Nine Lives* (2006), Connery had an exhausting psychedelic session with Laing. Both men were tripping on acid, and both talked about their difficult upbringing in working-class Scottish families. Afterwards, Connery was so drained that he rested in bed for days.

Coulter, Ann. Although it seems an unlikely match, the controversial conservative commentator was once an ardent fan of the Grateful Dead (see *Grateful Dead*). She attended some 67 shows, and although she never took an acid trip, she once admitted to an interviewer, "No drug has ever tempted me *except* LSD. When I'm in the nursing home some day…" (Gurley).

Country Joe and the Fish. This rock band was responsible for the false report that smoking dried banana skins could produce LSD-like effects (see *Bananas*).

Coyote, Peter. Coyote was one of the founding members of the Diggers, the countercultural group that sponsored social experiments in San Francisco during the Summer of Love (see *Diggers; Summer of Love*). In a 1998 interview with Terri Gross, Coyote described how LSD "offered you a kind of insight into a world which was so much vaster and had so many more options than you could possibly imagine." He also said that ultimately "the trick was to learn how to get there without drugs," and he studied Zen for a time in an attempt to do so. Coyote went on to a successful career as an actor in films.

Cream. Cream took a psychedelic turn in their second album, *Disraeli Gears* (1967). *Disraeli Gears* won critical praise and sold well both in England and America. The band's psychedelic phase was particularly influenced by their association with Jimi Hendrix. Cream guitarist Eric Clapton started using heavier wah-wah and distortion effects, and during concert tours, producers and promoters encouraged him to take longer solos. Colleagues Jack Bruce and Ginger Baker had also begun taking LSD regularly. "We did a lot of acid, took a lot of trips," Clapton has said. "We did play on acid a couple of times" (Sandford).

Disraeli Gears has all the essential features of a psychedelic album, including a day-glo cover collage by Martin Sharp (see *Sharp, Martin*) and trippy, surreal lyrics. The album title follows an informal convention for psychedelic band names in which an adjective and noun are paired incongruously (e.g., Iron Butterfly, Ultimate Spinach). The phrase "Disraeli Gears" actually came from a roadie's malapropism for the "derailleur gears" on a bicycle Clapton wanted to buy, but it passed for psychedelic sublimity. The lyrics for songs on *Disraeli Gears* touch on common psychedelic themes, including sensory alteration and journeys to paradise (see *Psychedelic Rock*).

Creasy, William. General Creasy, head of the Army Chemical Corps in the late 1950s, believed that LSD could be used as a weapon to incapacitate the population of a whole city. Creasy speculated that the drug might be sprayed from the air or dissolved in the water supply (see *Water Supply*). He told Congress that LSD was so powerful that it would get them all "dancing on the desks, or shouting Communist speeches." Despite Creasy's enthusiasm, he never received permission to test LSD on an American city. "I was attempting to put on, with a good cover story, to test to see what would happen in subways, for example, when a cloud was laid down on a city. It was denied on reasons that always seemed a little absurd to me" (Lee and Schlain). Scientists eventually informed Creasy that his plan was unfeasible, because LSD could not be disseminated in aerosol form.

Crick, Francis. In August of 2004, shortly after Crick died, reporter Alun Rees made a startling suggestion: Crick may have been high on LSD when he came up with the double helix structure of DNA. Rees heard the story decades later and at two removes of hearsay. Although the report spread quickly, no corroborating evidence has emerged; moreover, James Watson's *The Double Helix*, a candid inside account of the DNA discovery, makes no mention of LSD use by anyone. According to Watson, the only drug in play during Crick's eureka moment was English ale. Crick was drinking with a colleague in a pub when something "clicked in his head." He had attended "an evening talk by the astronomer Tommy Gold on 'the perfect cosmological principle.' Tommy's facility for making such a far-out idea seem plausible set Francis to wondering whether an argument could be made for a 'perfect biological principle' .... He popped out with the idea that the perfect biological principle was the self-replication of the gene." The idea comes suddenly, from cosmic inspiration, and Watson even uses "far-out" in his description of it. But that's as close as *The Double Helix* gets to a psychedelic moment.

"Crimson and Clover." This 1969 hit by Tommy James and the Shondells became one of the best-selling psychedelic songs, although rock critics generally held it in low regard compared with more ambitious psychedelic music. See *James, Tommy*.

Crow, Sheryl. Crow took LSD on only one occasion, but that trip led to her first hit single, "Leaving Las Vegas." In 1992, following the failure of her first effort to make an album, Crow joined the "Tuesday Night" group of musicians who collaborated to create songs at a producer's home studio in Pasadena, California. Among the musicians were Kevin Gilbert and David Baerwald. According to biographer Richard Buskin, one night Baerwald brought in the galley proofs of John O'Brien's novel *Leaving Las Vegas;* he proposed that the novel's title should be their "shining phrase for the evening." Gilbert had brought hits of acid to stir their creative

spirits. A few of the musicians took the drug, including Baerwald and Crow. As the song started to develop, notes Buskin, Crow found inspiration: "In her headphones she hears the rhythm track that will end up on the finished record; in her mind she hears colors courtesy of the hallucinogen that she's ingested ... and as the LSD kicks into overdrive, the singing just gets better." Crow later told *Q* magazine, "That's the only time I dropped acid. We only did one take of that song and I tried to go back and re-sing it, but I couldn't do it again. I couldn't recreate the energy" (quoted in Buskin).

Crumb, Robert. Crumb was working as a graphic artist for American Greeting Cards in Cleveland when he started taking LSD in 1965. Many years later, he recalled the experience in a drawing. Colored tentacles pulse left and right from a central spine that bisects a dissolving face. "When I was young I took a lot of LSD," he writes above the drawing. The accompanying caption reads, "I'll never be the same. Whoaaa. Infinity frightened the hell out of me."

Despite his early psychedelic fright, Crumb's LSD experiences inspired and transformed his art. As Robert C. Harvey records in *The Art of the Comic Book*, Crumb was particularly influenced by one trip on what he described as "fuzzy" acid: afterwards, he "spent days drawing in his sketchbooks, creating the entire cast of characters that would populate his comics for years— Mr. Natural, Flakey Foont, Schuman the Human, the Snoid, Eggs Arkley, and the Vulture Demonesses." Crumb referred to this acid trip as "a once in a lifetime experience, like a religious vision." Crumb admitted that he was unable to draw while tripping on LSD; he would get ideas from his trips, but do the drawing afterwards. Eventually his altered consciousness spawned *Zap Comix*, first published in February, 1968 (see *Zap Comix*). According to Crumb, "At first, the hippie shopkeepers on Haight St. looked down their noses at it.... It had none of the stylings of your typical psychedelic graphics—the romantic figures, the curvy, flowing styles. It took a while to catch on."

It was the content of Crumb's work more than the visual codes that made it psychedelic. He said that taking LSD gave him access to repressed unconscious materials that informed his work thereafter. His cartoons are filled with images of idiosyncratic sexual fantasies and anxieties (many of which involve women with larger than normal bodily features). Once he characterized his acid visions as releasing "the psychotic manifestation of some grimy part of America's collective unconscious." Elsewhere, Crumb gave a softer and less psychoanalytical description of his psychedelic creations: *Zap Comix* reflected a "sweet, optimistic, LSD-inspired mystic vision drawn in the loveable big-foot style that everyone found so appealing." Crumb drew some memorable figures with disproportionately large feet, his signature psychedelic look; his famous "Keep on Truckin'" cartoon shows four characters cheerfully following their own big feet as they make their daily journeys to nowhere in particular.

For all the influence LSD had on Crumb's life and work in San Francisco, he said that he "wasn't really a hippie. I didn't get out there and play my bamboo flute and dance in my bare feet in Golden Gate Park with the rest of the hippies. I just wanted to sit in my room and jump on big women if there happened to be any around." One of Crumb's first and most enduring characters, Mr. Natural (a bald man with a robe and big feet), presents himself as a sort of guru, but Mr. Natural's Zen-like pronouncements tend more to satirize than to support the notion of psychedelic enlightenment. Those seeking his wisdom often end up with profane dismissal.

Crying of Lot 49. One of the first and most influential novels that featured LSD was Thomas Pynchon's *The Crying of Lot 49* (1966), set in "San Narciso" during the early days of California psychedelia. Pynchon at the time was developing a reputation as the most important young American novelist. *The Crying of Lot 49* was his second novel, written between *V* and *Gravity's Rainbow*. The three books share a flair for dark comedy and an ambitious intellectual agenda aimed at radical critique of American culture. Despite his countercultural inclinations, Pynchon was not at all sympathetic to the cause of LSD. Unlike Ken Kesey, who found inspiration from psychedelic drugs both for his fiction and his life (see *Kesey, Ken*), Pynchon satirized LSD and its surrounding pretensions. *The Crying of Lot 49* portrays acid-heads as ridiculous and morally bankrupt.

LSD enters *Lot 49* in its psychiatric mode. Oedipa Maas, heroine of the novel, has been getting therapy from a psychiatrist named Dr. Hilarius. Oedipa's specific diagnosis is never spelled out, but she suffers from an existential listlessness that would probably be classified as mild depression. Dr. Hilarius wants her to join his experimental group for LSD therapy. He works with "a large sample of suburban housewives" in a treatment program he has nicknamed "The Bridge": "the bridge inward," he explains. Oedipa wants no part of it. She's certain it would get her "hooked"; she says she "would be damned if she'd take the capsules he'd given her. Literally damned." Oedipa, an intelligent but pre-psychedelic graduate of Berkeley, assumes that LSD is an addictive drug. Her hostility to LSD is so sharp and unchecked that it suggests a deep authorial conviction.

The novel's anti–LSD message returns near the end of *The Crying of Lot 49* in much greater detail. Oedipa's husband, Wendell "Mucho" Maas, has started taking the capsules provided by Dr. Hilarius. Mucho Maas also suffered from existential depression: in both of his jobs, as a used car salesman and a disc jockey, he was sickened by the fraudulence and tedium of American consumer culture. After he has taken acid several times, however, Mucho turns into a cheerful enthusiast. Songs that had previously seemed bland and trivial now resonate with cosmic meaning. Oedipa listens in horror to her husband's acid-driven foolishness. *The Crying of Lot 49* scorns the pseudo-revelations generated by LSD because they trick people like Mucho into joining rather than resisting mainstream culture. Ironically, at a time when LSD was beginning to inspire a generation of young Americans to question and stand outside their inherited culture, Pynchon wrote a novel in which LSD had the opposite effect.

"Dark Star." This early song by the Grateful Dead came to be seen as the epitome of their psychedelic style. See *Grateful Dead.*

Davis, Adelle. Davis became famous (and controversial) as an early advocate for reform of American eating habits. Her bestselling books, including *Let's Eat Right to Keep Fit,* argued that many American health problems stemmed from an emphasis on processed foods and from cooking habits that ruined nutritional value. Davis was interested not only in bodily but in spiritual health—and not only in food, but in drugs, especially LSD. When she filled out an application to take part in Dr. Oscar Janiger's LSD studies (see *Janiger, Oscar*), in response to the question, "Why do you wish to take lysergic acid," she wrote, "In hope of overcoming spiritual poverty." Elsewhere she answered the question more whimsically, "To get chemical Christianity."

Davis took LSD five times in 1959–60 under Janiger's supervision. She agreed to write an account of her experiences with the drug as she searched for spiritual fulfillment. *Exploring Inner Space: Personal Experiences under LSD-25* came out in 1961, but Harcourt Brace balked at publishing it under her name: they did not want to jeopardize the credibility of a bestselling author. Instead of Adelle Davis, it was "Jane Dunlap" who experimented with LSD and wrote the first psychedelic book by a woman.

Davis's quest for spiritual fulfillment mirrored her quest for nutritional reform.

In her food books, she had argued that although Americans lived in a land of plenty, they were radically undernourished. In matters of religion, although Americans attended church and professed belief in God, their "spiritual hungers and longings are both widespread and acute." Davis confessed that her own spiritual development "was so pitifully inadequate that I sometimes felt consumed with an empty yearning." When she took LSD, she found the spiritual nourishment she had been craving. Davis wrote about several new convictions, "most of them religious in nature, which are so strong that it makes not one iota of difference whether anyone agrees with me or not.... My lasting gratitude goes to the Sandoz Pharmaceutical Laboratories which not only discovered and produced LSD-25 but are spending millions of dollars on its research. I feel that they have given me a magnificent gift of a mirror in whose lovely depth one sees the reflection of all humanity."

Some passages from *Exploring Inner Space* record exotic mystical visions. During her fourth trip, for example, she saw a giant cobra that served as a spiritual guide. The cobra led her back in time to visit Buddha, Jesus, and Muhammad. Later the cobra reprimanded her for excessive attachments to the material world. On LSD, "Jane Dunlap" found the deep, intimate connection with God that she had longed for. But as Adelle Davis, she continued to write books about the material world of food and cooking, where her advice made a greater impression.

"Day in the Life." The final song on *Sergeant Pepper's Lonely Hearts Club Band,* "A Day in the Life" had clear psychedelic implications and won high critical praise. See *Beatles.*

Delysid. Delysid was the trade name of LSD when Sandoz made it available for use by psychiatrists and medical researchers. Sandoz chemist Albert Hofmann had discovered LSD a decade earlier and suggested its trade name when his company made the drug public. Sandoz decided to provide Delysid to qualified researchers, in exchange for access to results.

The drug came in the form of pills (25 micrograms) or ampoules (100 micrograms). LSD contained in an ampoule could either be diluted and taken orally, or injected (for quicker effect). In the prospectus, Sandoz explained that Delysid had two primary uses. As an aid to psychotherapy, it will "elicit release of repressed material and provide mental relaxation, particularly in anxiety states and obsessional neuroses." Delysid will also facilitate "experimental studies on the nature of psychoses," by allowing psychiatrists to "induce model psychoses of short duration in normal subjects." Sandoz encouraged psychiatrists to take Delysid themselves "to gain an insight into the world of ideas and sensations of mental patients." Sandoz listed only one precaution for Delysid, but a very serious one: the drug may intensify "pathological mental conditions." "Particular caution is necessary in subjects with a suicidal tendency and in those cases where a psychotic development appears imminent." Delysid was to be used only under careful medical supervision. Delysid was available from 1947 until the mid-1960s, when research with LSD began to encounter public controversy and legal obstacles. In a letter dated August, 1965, Sandoz director Dr. A. Cerletti wrote, "In spite of all our precautions, cases of LSD abuse have occurred from time to time in varying circumstances beyond the control of Sandoz. Very recently this danger had increased considerably and in some part of the world has reached the scale of a serious threat to public health.... Sandoz has decided to stop immediately all further production and distribution of LSD." See *Psychiatry*; *Hofmann, Albert*; *Sandoz*; *Stoll, Werner*.

Denver Dog. In fall of 1967, Chet Helms opened a Denver branch of the Family Dog, the group that sponsored psychedelic concerts on San Francisco (see *Helms, Chet*; *Family Dog*). The Denver Dog closed after only three months, however, largely because Denver police acted aggressively to prevent their city from becoming another hippie center.

Depression. In the early years of experimental LSD psychotherapy, one of the first trials was conducted on patients suffering from depression. Swiss psychiatrist Gion Condrau had noticed the drug's euphoric effects on some subjects and thought it might alleviate depressive symptoms. His 1949 study, however, indicated otherwise: he observed no clear therapeutic results, and in several cases the LSD seemed to aggravate the condition. As Stanislav Grof summarized in *LSD Psychotherapy*, "Similar results were reported by other authors who used either Condrau's model of daily medication with LSD in depressive patients or isolated administrations of medium doses of LSD with the intention to dispel depression.... Clinical studies clearly indicated that LSD does not *per se* have any consistent pharmacological effects on depression that could be therapeutically exploited, and this approach has been abandoned." See *Condrau, Gion*; *Grof, Stanislav*; *Psychiatry*.

Dick, Philip K. Dick was a prolific and innovative writer of science fiction novels during the prime psychedelic years. His plots often include drugs, hallucination, disorientation, and visions of alternate realities—all elements suggestive of LSD experience. Although Dick took LSD and acknowledged the connections between his fiction and the psychedelic experience, in retrospect he discounted the influence of LSD on his work. He commented on this subject most explicitly in a 1974 interview with Arthur Cover. When asked, "What effect has LSD had on your writing," Dick replied, "I don't know of any. It's always possible that it's had an effect I don't know about. Take my novel *The Three Stigmata of Palmer Eldritch*, which deals with a tremendous bad acid trip, so to speak. I wrote that before I had ever seen LSD. I wrote that from just reading a description of the discovery of it and the kind of effect it had. So if that, which is my major novel of a hallucinogenic kind, came without my ever having taken LSD, then I would say even my work following LSD which had hallucinations in it could easily have been written without acid."

In the same interview, Dick went on to talk about two other works from the 1960s with apparent psychedelic implications: the novel *Martian Time-Slip* and the short story "Faith of our Fathers." Dick admits that *Martian Time-Slip* "suggests it might have been written with acid," but he says he wrote it before he had taken LSD. When Cover asked about "Faith of our Fathers"—wasn't it "inspired by or written under the influence of acid?"—Dick again minimized the connection: "That really is not true. First of all, you can't write anything when you're on acid. I did one page once while on an acid trip, but it was in Latin. Whole damn thing was in Latin and a little tiny bit in Sanskrit, and there's not much market for that."

Earlier in his career, he had embraced the psychedelic muse more willingly. He told Cover, "I'm amazed when I read the things I used to say about [LSD] on the blurbs of my books. I wrote this myself: 'He has been experimenting with hallucinogenic drugs to find the unchanging reality beneath our delusions.' And now I say, 'Good Christ!'" Despite his latter-day embarrassment about the blurb, Dick's fiction was indeed navigating the borderlands between "reality" and "delusions" in ways that suggest psychedelic perception. In all three acid-resonant works that he discussed in the 1974 interview, a character struggles with recurring visions of semi-mechanical beings. These visions are always disturbing, whether the character interprets the beings to be godlike or subhuman. In *The Three Stigmata of Palmer Eldritch*, the mechanical being is Palmer Eldritch, whose "stigmata" consist of a robotic hand, artificial eyes, and steel teeth.

Protagonist Jack Bohlen of *Martian Time-Slip* suffers periodic schizophrenic episodes when people around him appear mechanical instead of organic. And in "Faith of our Fathers," a bureaucrat in a totalitarian society discovers that their leader is not a human being, but some sort of demiurge; for those who use drugs to see past the illusion, the nice old man becomes a clanking machine, or some other non-human form.

Dick told Cover that he didn't take "that much" LSD, and the trips were not pleasant. "All I ever found out about acid was that I was where I wanted to get out of fast. It didn't seem any more real than anything else; it just seemed more awful." He added, "I've had friends who dropped acid and became permanently psychotic." Dick himself suffered from psychotic episodes. Given the risk of LSD triggering underlying mental problems, Dick had good reason to fear the drug—even as his fiction kept revisiting ontological complexities suggestive of psychedelic consciousness.

Diggers. A group of activist performers known as the Diggers played a critical role in the psychedelic counterculture of Haight-Ashbury. They took their name from English radicals of the seventeenth century who protested laws of enclosure: instead of obeying new restrictions on the use of common land, they "dug" on these lands to provide for the needs of the general public. Like their early namesakes, the Haight-Ashbury Diggers envisioned a society liberated from private property and surrounding capitalist systems. They came up with a manifesto that they tacked onto the door of the San Francisco Mime Troupe. Their basic principles were expressed in the slogan, "Everything is free, do your own thing."

As tens of thousands of young people poured into San Francisco in 1967, the Diggers provided free food, clothing, shelter, and medical care. They also arranged free concerts by the city's top psychedelic bands, including Grateful Dead and Jefferson Airplane (*Grateful Dead; Jefferson Airplane*). The Diggers embraced LSD as one means by which young people could step outside the assumptions and values of the world they had inherited. Diggers expressed this concept literally when they built a large orange structure that they called "Frame of Reference." Anyone who wanted free food had to walk through the Frame to the other side, symbolizing their changed perspective. Later the Diggers handed out small replicas of the Frame for hippies to carry around. They hoped that acid trips would help them recognize the strangeness of normal games and roles, and especially in a concert setting, offer an example of something better. For the Diggers, LSD was important as a catalyst for revolutionary political change; if the psychedelic experience merely facilitated private goals of therapy or enlightenment, it was self-indulgent. Digger Peter Berg said that "LSD can be about starting over. If you go through the mind bath of heavy psychedelic experience, then what do you start over with? What's important?" Digger Peter Coyote summed up the experience as "a four-year performance art piece designed to trigger a fundamental dialogue about power and money and class and status and who owned what in American society."

Even as the Diggers were facilitating the Summer of Love with material support and social organization, they lamented that hippie counterculture was focusing on self-indulgent transcendental mysticism, and becoming increasingly commercialized and distorted by media attention. Digger Emmett Grogan was particularly disturbed by what he saw as a huge marketing coup: he complained that the hippie movement had been co-opted by the world of fashion-driven commerce. In October of 1967 they expressed this discouragement with a public event called "The Death of Hippie." Diggers carried through the streets a coffin inscribed, "Hippie—Son of Media." They wanted to warn psychedelic utopians that the Summer of Love brought peril as well as opportunity, as hippie ideas were assimilated and neutralized by mainstream culture. See *Coyote, Peter; Grogan, Emmett; Berg, Peter; Summer of Love*.

DiPrima, Diane. Poet DiPrima, associated with both Beats and hippies, lived for a time at Timothy Leary's Millbrook estate in New York (see *Leary, Timothy; Millbrook*). While there she tripped, wrote, and published some of Leary's writings; she also took care of her family, and for several weeks she cooked all meals for the fifty people staying at Millbrook. In her essay "Holidays at Millbrook," DiPrima recalled one day in 1966 when the domestic and psychedelic aspects of her Millbrook life coincided most strangely. It was Thanksgiving, and DiPrima had spent most of the day cooking turkeys and vats of cranberry sauce and yams. All seemed well until one Millbrook visitor, a Canadian reporter, started "howling and cursing" from the effects of his inadvertent first acid trip. The reporter had helped himself to a glass of sherry, not knowing that Leary had spiked it with LSD. His wild reaction upset the holiday mood until Allen Ginsberg settled him down by chanting mantras (see *Ginsberg, Allen*). Meanwhile, Leary had absented himself from the Thanksgiving table to take a huge dose of LSD from the same bottle of sherry. When DiPrima went upstairs to check on him, she found him remote and troubled but able to summon a holiday wish: "Tim looked at me from a million light years away, from a place of great sadness and loneliness and terrible tiredness, and after a long time he formed the one word 'Beloved.'"

DiPrima later moved to San Francisco and became involved with the Diggers of the Haight-Ashbury scene (see *Diggers; Haight-Ashbury*).

Disney, Walt. In the late 1960s and early 1970s, Disney executives took advantage of the popularity of LSD to re-market two of their classic animated films to a psychedelic audience. See *Alice in Wonderland; Fantasia*.

Doblin, Rick. Doblin founded the Multidisciplinary Association for Psychedelic Studies in 1995 and continues to serve as its president (see *MAPS*). Doblin wrote a doctoral thesis at Harvard's Kennedy School of Government in which he argued for the resumption of research using LSD and other psychedelic drugs, and proposed regulations to control their use.

Dolphins. One of the most ambitious experiments with LSD and animals involved the administration of the drug to dolphins. American psychoanalyst John C. Lilly directed these experiments during the 1960s (see *Lilly, John C.*). Lilly, best known for his work with sensory deprivation tanks, also did considerable experimentation with hallucinogenic drugs. He conceived of an extended research project in which dolphins were given doses of LSD and monitored for behavioral changes.

Lilly administered doses of LSD ranging from 100–300 micrograms, levels that would be considered low to average strength for humans. He paid careful attention to controlling and varying the setting for the dolphins' LSD experiences. Lilly observed dolphins tripping while they were out of water, in shallow water, and in deep tanks; he tried having them trip alone, with another dolphin, and with a human. Lilly concluded that dolphins on LSD showed increased "vocalization activity" in all settings, especially when they had company: "If a person enters the tank, the vocalization index goes up and stays up with LSD. It rises only briefly without LSD. If you put a second dolphin in with the first (with the LSD), the vocalization index rises and stays up right around 70 per cent for the full three hours. In other words, an appropriate exchange takes place." Lilly hoped that these experiments would sharpen his understanding of dolphin communication, and improve chances for interspecies conversation between dolphins and humans.

Lilly's work with LSD and dolphins also focused on prospects for psychotherapeutic results. He reported on one case in which a traumatized dolphin, who had been shot with a spear gun, restored her relationship with humans:

> In our pool she would stay on the far side away from anybody that was there. If you tried to approach her, she would shoot away from you. We decided to use her as one of our controls, using LSD-25. As the LSD effect came on, forty minutes after of the injection of 100 micrograms, the dolphin came over to me. She had not approached me before. She stayed still in the tank with one eye out of water looking me in the eye for ten minutes without moving. She followed me right around the edge of the tank. It is a very amazing change in behavior. She will now come within five feet of me instead of staying twenty feet away [quoted in Abramson].

Psychoanalysts using LSD therapy were aiming for similar results with human patients who suffered from trauma, depression, or other forms of social dysfunction.

Donovan. Scottish singer-songwriter Donovan Leitch recorded some of the earliest pop music that showed the influence of psychedelic drugs. He began taking LSD at roughly the same time that his friends from The Beatles did, and although he did not trip as frequently as John Lennon and George Harrison, his LSD experiences altered his style and imagery. By 1966 he was producing music that blended psychedelic elements into the traditional folk music that was his foundation. Several songs contained fairly overt references to drug use, and he recorded them with new instrumental textures. Donovan said that the distinctive sound of "Sunshine Superman"—harpsichord, flute, congo drums—came to him on an acid trip, as he watched raindrops falling from leaves. He was also among the first to use a sitar as part of his instrumental mix.

Donovan's psychedelic lyrics come to the fore on two albums from the late 1960s, *Sunshine Superman* and *Mellow Yellow*. The most obvious LSD-related song is "The Trip," which he wrote after an acid trip in Los Angeles: the lyrics include references to Alice in Wonderland, kaleidoscopes, Zen, and Bob Dylan. Another obvious example is "Fat Angel," with a chorus about the pleasures of tripping. Two other songs suggest more oblique psychedelic references. Because the title of "Sunshine Superman" contains two brand names for LSD (Orange Sunshine and Superman blotters), many listeners have assumed that he was making a direct reference to doses of acid; however, Donovan's song pre-dated both Orange Sunshine and Superman blotters. The lyrics of "Sunshine Superman" describe a person with sensory superpowers, but the only literal reference to tripping involves a decision *not* to trip. Still, the song sounded trippy enough for The Beatles to feature it in a promotional video for their psychedelic masterpiece, "A Day in the Life": the camera focuses on a turntable spinning "Sunshine Superman." Another Donovan song, "Mellow Yellow," quickly became associated with the myth that bananas contain a natural hallucinogen. In fact, Donovan wrote that song before the rumor about psychedelic bananas. The "electrical banana" of "Mellow Yellow" actually referred to a vibrating sex toy (see *Bananas*).

Doors. The Doors took their name from Aldous Huxley's *The Doors of Perception,* which Jim Morrison had read and liked (see *Huxley, Aldous*). Morrison also read and liked the poetry of William Blake, where Huxley had found his title: "If the doors of perception were cleansed, every thing would appear as it is, infinite" (*The Marriage of Heaven and Hell,* 1790). All four members of the band took acid, but Morrison's tripping had the greatest impact on their music. The Doors flourished in the prime years of psychedelic culture and acid rock, from late 1966 to early 1969. Morrison's use of other drugs, especially alcohol, led to his withdrawal from the band and his early death in 1971 at age 27.

Record executives took note of The Doors in 1966 when they were playing reg-

ularly at the Whiskey a Go Go in Hollywood. Elektra signed them shortly before the Whiskey fired them: Morrison had taken the stage high on LSD and delivered a performance of "The End" that the club owners considered unruly and indecent. This moment of psychedelic excess cost them a job, but "The End" found a place on their first album, *The Doors,* which made them stars in the world of psychedelic rock. "The End" gives a good picture of Morrison's psychedelic lyricism, which was The Doors' most distinctive contribution to music of that era. His style suggests French symbolist poetry, with images expressing his particular blend of sexual energy, emotional chaos, and death wish. In "The End," all of these elements are present, but the most striking (and controversial) lyrics depict a Freudian scene: Morrison imagines someone killing his father and copulating with his mother. Morrison, like many other LSD enthusiasts, linked acid trips with psychotherapeutic catharsis. If the Freudian plot of "The End" seems fairly straightforward, the song otherwise creates an eerie apocalyptic atmosphere. Francis Ford Coppola borrowed "The End" for the famous opening sequence of *Apocalypse Now.* Many other songs by The Doors are not as self-consciously psychoanalytic and archetypal, but they usually contain hints of psychedelic content. "Break on Through," for example, invokes a gate to another world, where normal time and perception might give way to something more exciting.

Oliver Stone made the 1991 film *The Doors* in an attempt to tell Morrison's story and to capture the spirit of the psychedelic era. Surviving members of the band, especially keyboard player Ray Manzarek, criticized Stone for overemphasizing Morrison the drunkard and missing his humor and intellectual liveliness. In 2009, Manzarek and the other Doors cooperated with filmmaker Tom DiCillo on the documentary *When You're Strange,* which they believed would present a more balanced portrait.

Dosage. LSD doses are measured in micrograms, not milligrams: acid is more potent than mescaline and psilocybin by a factor of one thousand. Doses as low as 25 micrograms will have a psychotropic effect. In what was termed "psycholytic" therapy, psychiatrists gave patients doses ranging from 25 to 75 micrograms; a stronger "psychedelic" dose was typically 200 to 300 micrograms (see *Psychiatry; Psycholytic; Psychedelic*). Street acid of the 1960s usually came in psychedelic doses, with standard Owsley tablets delivering 250 micrograms (see *Owsley*). Informal surveys suggest that typical doses from later decades tended to be less powerful. With blotter acid, users could choose a low dose or heavy dose by ingesting one or several blotter squares (see *Blotter Art*). No human death has been indisputably attributed to LSD overdose, and a number of people have survived huge overdoses. Although an elephant died after receiving a massive dose in a psychiatric experiment, it is not clear that the LSD directly caused the death (see *Elephant*).

Dragnet. Jack Webb's television series presented two anti-LSD episodes in the late 1960s. The most famous of these is "The LSD Story" (1967), more commonly known as "Blue Boy" (see *Blue Boy*). The other is "The Big Prophet" (1968), which features a fictional version of Timothy Leary named "Brother" William Bentley. Brother William leads a psychedelic sect called the Temple of the Expanded Mind, suggestive of Leary's League for Spiritual Discovery (see *League for Spiritual Discovery*). By the end of the show, police arrest Brother William for dealing drugs to school children. At one point, Sergeant Friday lectures Brother William on the difference between alcohol and LSD. Friday admits that alcohol impairs judgment, but good judgment returns when a person sobers up; with LSD, judgment is permanently endangered. In his summation, Friday traces the probable course for young drug victims. LSD is more dangerous for Friday than any other drug: "Too many kids that begin with pot end up on heroin, then on to LSD. Pot is the flame, heroin is the fuse, LSD is the bomb."

Drake, Betsy. The third wife of actor Cary Grant, Drake underwent LSD psychotherapy in 1958 with Dr. Mortimer A. Hartman of Beverly Hills (*see Hartman, Mortimer A.*). She took the drug 31 times during the course of her therapy. She later told an interviewer for *Look* magazine that "LSD therapy is certainly not easy," but that the process led her to discover "true reality in myself for the first time." When she recognized the benefits of her therapy, she suggested that her husband try the same thing; Grant began his own LSD therapy and reported excellent results (see *Grant, Cary*). Both of them credited the therapy for saving their marriage.

Dulles, Allen. Dulles was the CIA director in the early 1950s who started the covert drug testing program called MK-Ultra (see *MK-Ultra*). He was concerned that American prisoners in the Korean War had been subjected to mind-manipulating drugs, and he wanted to test the strongest such drugs for possible use by the American military and intelligence community. LSD was one of the drugs he found particularly interesting. Under the guidance of Dulles and chief research chemist Sidney Gottlieb (see *Gottlieb, Sidney*), the CIA obtained batches of LSD from Sandoz and encouraged American pharmaceutical companies to improve techniques for producing the drug (see *Sandoz; Lilly, Eli*).

Dunlap, Jane. Nutritionist Adelle Davis published *Exploring Inner Space: Personal Experiences under LSD-25* under this pseudonym. See *Davis, Adelle*.

Dying. When Aldous Huxley was dying of cancer in November, 1963, he asked his wife to inject him with LSD. He thought that the drug would help him get through the final stages. She complied, and Huxley died a few hours later, apparently peacefully, still under the influence of the drug. Laura Huxley did the same thing for someone else, but the results were different. "For Aldous, it was very good," she told an interviewer. "For the other person, it wasn't" (see *Huxley, Aldous; Huxley, Laura*).

The Huxleys' improvisational use of LSD as therapy for the dying had some basis in clinical science. As an outgrowth of studies in psychedelic psychotherapy, researchers in the early 1960s began to investigate whether LSD might ease the pain and anxiety of terminally ill patients. Overall, these studies showed the drug to be effective as an aid to the dying in roughly two-thirds of the experimental population. The first major study, published in 1964 by E.C. Kast and V.J. Collins, determined that LSD worked better than Demerol against pain (see *Kast, Eric*). Further studies by Kast in 1966 indicated that LSD did more than simply reduce physical pain: patients who took the drug found an improvement in their emotional well being. They were less subject to depression and anxiety, and less inclined to withdraw from social interaction. Kast noted that some of these effects were difficult to quantify, because they had to do with spiritual insights emerging from the LSD experience. Terminally ill patients often came away from psychedelic therapy better able to accept death as part of the big cosmic picture, and more ready to focus on the life remaining rather than the upcoming death. Studies continued through the 1960s and early 1970s, with researchers confirming the generally positive results with LSD and other hallucinogens. Researchers emphasized the necessity of administering the drug under carefully controlled conditions, with an appropriate psychiatric foundation having been laid beforehand; and the usual risks of LSD use were still present, including panic reactions and the triggering of underlying mental disorders. Among the leading investigators were Walter Pahnke of the Good Friday project (see *Harvard*) and Stanislav Grof (see *Grof, Stanislav*).

Experimental use continued in Europe past the 1970s, but mainly in private practices, with anecdotal reporting. American research on LSD and the dying was effectively discontinued in the early 1970s due to legal complications. In 1970, LSD was reclassified as a Schedule I drug—meaning that it carried great risk of abuse and no valid medical uses (see *Laws*). It was technically still possible to conduct experiments with LSD, but the conditions were so restrictive that research became impractical.

In the early years of the new century, however, some researchers resumed experimentation with psychedelics as therapy for the terminally ill. Studies by Roland Griffiths of Johns Hopkins and Charles Grob of UCLA used psilocybin and reported generally favorable results. In June, 2008, Swiss researchers reported the beginnings of a clinical trial using LSD.

Dylan, Bob. Dylan first took LSD in April of 1964 after giving a concert at Amherst College. Biographer Bob Spitz heard the story from Paul Rothchild, who was with Dylan at the time. Dylan and two friends were relaxing at agent Albert Grossman's house at the end of a long concert tour. They were smoking marijuana, one of two drugs that Dylan used regularly (the other was amphetamines). One of the friends went to the refrigerator for snacks and found some tabs of LSD wrapped in foil; they decided to give it a try.

Critics and biographers have offered differing opinions about the influence of LSD on Dylan's work. Joyce Carol Oates assumed that LSD contributed significantly to his lyrics in the period from late 1964 through 1966: "Dylan clearly anticipated the formal, aesthetic, and tonal limitations of folk music, even as, by way of LSD experimentation, he explored the myriad possibilities of bending music as one bends one's mind, toward the surreal, the fantastic, the phantasmagoric" ("Dylan at 60," 2002). Biographer Clinton Heylin is more cautious about the influence of LSD. Heylin points out that well before Dylan first took acid, he had told friends of his admiration for French poet Arthur Rimbaud, whose poetry was inspired by "a long, prodigious, and rational disordering of the senses." Dylan said that "Rimbaud's where it's at. That's the kind of stuff means something. That's the kind of writing I'm gonna do." In other words, the surreal, symbolist complexity of Dylan's lyrics was germinating in advance of any LSD experience. "The drugs-explain-inspiration brigade would doubtless prefer" a post-acid date of composition for "Mr. Tambourine Man," Heylin asserts, but Dylan actually began writing that song in February.

Dylan offered a few specific comments about LSD in two interviews. He told Nat Hentoff in 1965 that "LSD is a medicine. You take it and you know ... [that] you don't really have to keep taking it all the time." By 1978, he was more cynical about the medicinal value of the drug: "People were deluded into thinking they were something they weren't: birds, fire hydrants, whatever." Dylan's lyrics from 1964–1966—what most critics consider his greatest period—hint at the influence of psychedelia, but also show signs that he was not a true believer in the Leary gospel. "Mr. Tambourine Man," which he began in February but finished and recorded in the months after his first acid trip, contains imagery that suggests a pleasantly psychedelic reordering of the senses. On the other hand, "Stuck Inside of Mobile with the Memphis Blues Again" includes a mind-altering "cure" that sounds like a bad acid trip, inducing alienation and temporal distortion.

LSD had some influence on Dylan's imagination, but he was by no means a psychedelic enthusiast. Amphetamines had a more palpable effect on his work than psychedelics. As Heylin notes, Dylan "insisted that the drugs *never* prompted a song: they only kept him 'up' long enough to pump them out."

Easy Rider. This low budget film that became a countercultural icon includes a thought-provoking scene in which the main characters take LSD. The three stars of *Easy Rider*—Peter Fonda, Dennis Hopper, and Jack Nicholson—had earlier collaborated on *The Trip*, and all of them had experience with real LSD trips as well as fictional ones (see *Trip; Fonda, Peter; Hopper, Dennis; Nicholson, Jack*).

The acid trip comes late in *Easy Rider*, near the end of the journey undertaken by Wyatt (Fonda) and Billy (Hopper). Wyatt and Billy take the LSD with two prostitutes they have met in New Orleans. Up to this point, the main drugs of *Easy Rider* have been marijuana, alcohol, and cocaine. Marijuana is the daily recreational drug for Wyatt and Billy, alcohol for their friend George (Nicholson). Wyatt and Billy began the film by selling a big load of cocaine they had acquired in Mexico; we never see them use cocaine, and Wyatt seems to feel uneasy about the way he makes a living. Wyatt's guilt becomes more pronounced near the end of the film, when he tells Billy that "We blew it." On their trip across the West to New Orleans, he and Billy encounter two families—a Western rancher with many children, and a hippie commune—both of which appeal to Wyatt as alternatives to the life he has created for himself. As Wyatt is about to leave the commune, his friend there offers him a square of LSD with this advice:

> MAN: "When you get to the right place, with the right people, quarter this. You know, this could be the right place. The time's running out."
> WYATT: "Yeah, I'm hip about time. But I just gotta go."

LSD thus enters *Easy Rider* not just as one more illegal drug, but as an elixir or sacrament. Wyatt places it on the tongues of the two women in a gesture resembling Communion. The ensuing acid trip resonates with Catholic imagery for Wyatt as he moves around a cemetery. Cinematically, the montage effects are complex and disorienting. For the only time in the film, Wyatt overflows with emotion: he confesses deep secrets about his relationship with his mother, in a therapeutic process that delivers no real therapy. The trip is also intense and confessional for one of the women, who weeps about her body and her job, longs for a child, and panics about dying. Only Billy stays pretty much a pleasure tripper. He enjoys the aesthetic novelty—"We're all aglow, man!"—and for him, the trip is mainly an occasion for sexual play, in contrast with the angst happening all around him. As accompaniment to the chaotic imagery of Wyatt's emotions, a female voice can be heard reciting the Apostles' Creed. Wyatt stares at crucifixes, embraces a statue and sobs, "Oh, Mother, why didn't you tell me? Why didn't anybody tell me anything? What are you doing to me now? Why did you leave like that? Oh God how I love you. You're such a fool, Mother, and I hate you so much." As his speech ends, the film cuts abruptly to the next day with Wyatt and Billy back on their motorcycles, about to die.

Peter Fonda has said that the acid scene in *Easy Rider* was stressful for him psychologically. As he began to improvise Wyatt's confessional agony about his mother's betrayal, Fonda was tapping into emotions surrounding own mother's suicide when he was young. Director Hopper encouraged him to vent for the camera. In this interesting convergence of cinema and psychiatry, a simulation of psychedelic therapy stood in for the real thing.

Ecstasy. MDMA, a psychedelic stimulant nicknamed "ecstasy," became popular in the 1980s among people attending raves. Although ecstasy has significant differences from LSD—its psychedelic effects are milder and of shorter duration, it produces more predictable euphoric feelings, and use of the drug may bring unpleasant side-effects associated with stimulants—the popularity of ecstasy is one of the main reasons cited for the dramatic decline of LSD use over the last three decades. As Preston Peet reports, "Those familiar with the drug culture claim that there has been a clear shift in focus from acid to ecstasy. The shift was most visible at the 2000 New Year's festival put on by Phish, called Big Cyprus. There for the first time, say concert goers, ecstasy had flooded the market, while acid was difficult to find. Since Big Cyprus, shows at which acid once seemed to be given away at the door have become centers for the sale of ecstasy." Ecstasy is much easier to produce than LSD, and it fetches a higher price for its producers and distributors—typically $25 to $30 dollars per dose, compared with $5 to $10 per dose for LSD. Use of ecstasy by adolescents peaked around 2001 and has declined steadily since, in part because of well publicized health warnings.

"Eight Miles High." This 1965 song by the Byrds is considered one of the earliest examples of psychedelic rock. See *Byrds*.

Electric Kool-Aid Acid Test. New Journalist Tom Wolfe published this detailed account of Ken Kesey and the Merry Pranksters in 1968 (see *Kesey, Ken; Merry Pranksters*). Wolfe drew on extensive interviews with the people involved, and his book attempted to describe the psychedelic experience from an insider's perspective. *The Electric Kool-Aid Acid Test* became a bestseller and spread the Pranksters' story to a broad reading public. Wolfe came to the Pranksters during their latter days, and very much as an outsider. Early in the book, Wolfe teased himself about his outsider status. When a Prankster named Black Maria called him "too solid for a Pisces," he reflected, "But I know she means stolid. I am beginning to feel stolid. Back in New York City, Black Maria, I tell you, I am even known as something of a dude. But somehow a blue silk blazer and a big tie with clowns on it and ... a ... pair of shiny lowcut black shoes don't set them all to doing the Varsity Rag in the head world of San Francisco." Another Prankster, Doris Delay, urged him "to put some more ... well, *color* ... into my appearance." Later, when Wolfe suggested to Kesey that the Acid Tests resembled what Andy Warhol was doing, Kesey gently put him down: "'No offense,' said Kesey, 'but New York is about two years behind.'"

Wolfe tried as best he could to catch up with the California avant garde. In his "Author's Note" at the end, he wrote, "I have tried not only to tell what the Pranksters did but to re-create the mental atmosphere or subjective reality of it. I don't think their adventure can be understood without that." To convey the "subjective reality" of a mind on an acid trip, Wolfe deployed a number of stylistic eccentricities. He leans heavily on surrealistic metaphors: for example, "And rrrrrrrrrrrush those fantastic neon bubbles rushing up out of the heart square into the human squash and bursting into—*skull mirrors!*" With other tricks of style, Wolfe tries to mimic the temporal and spatial distortions common in acid perception. He occasionally stretches words ("rrrrrrrrrrrush"), and frequently he stretches sentences well beyond normal expectations of length. Such distortions are enhanced by various eccentricities of punctuation. Wolfe loads his prose with dashes and ellipses, to stitch together little patches of perception. Ellipses indicate a boundary of sorts but keep the sentence going; they gesture at closure but resist it. He invents a new punctuation mark, the multiple colon:

> Oh yes, Major, it was the drug, you understand—and yet—he was fully into the bare Halusion Gulp of the moment out there and there ::::: was the Power and the Call and this movie is big enough to include the world, a cast of millions, the castoff billions ... Control Tower to Orbiter One
> CONTROL

The multiple colon interrupts the flow of syntax, as if to signal that something inexpressibly important is happening, something that can't be conveyed by mere words. He uses capital letters here and elsewhere for emphasis, along with an unusual density of italics and exclamation points. All of these devices brighten up and defamiliarize ordinary words, just as LSD brightens and defamiliarizes ordinary objects.

If Wolfe's style seems an appropriate way to mimic psychedelic perception, to

some degree that style pre-dated his interest in LSD. Many of the devices he used for acid prose appear in the two books he wrote before *Electric Kool-Aid:* long sentences, ellipses in lieu of traditional closure, italicized words and exclamation points all over the place, even moments of more exotic punctuation. The acid prose of *Electric Kool-Aid* adapts a style Wolfe invented to jazz up a number of cultural topics. When Wolfe turned his attention to the Pranksters, a writing style found LSD as much as LSD found a writing style.

Elephant. Although no human has ever died from physical causes associated with LSD, an elephant died in 1962 shortly after he was given a massive dose of the drug in a scientific experiment. The elephant, named Tusko, was a young male adult living at the Lincoln Park Zoo in Oklahoma City. He was in the early stages of sexual maturity at the time of the experiment; he had a mate at the zoo, Judy, who tried to support him when his legs buckled after the LSD injection.

The scientist in charge was Louis Jolyon (Jolly) West, then head of the Department of Psychiatry at the University of Oklahoma Medical Center (see *West, Louis Jolyon*). He administered the LSD with an injection fired from a rifle. The object was to see whether the drug would induce "musth," a state of unusually aggressive behavior that male elephants exhibit from time to time. If LSD induced musth, West could study relevant glands and excretions to find out what he could about the biochemistry of the process. Because Tusko died, West had the opportunity to supervise a necropsy and investigate even more thoroughly. In the end, he did not see any of the "dark brown fluid" he had hoped to find in the elephant's temporal gland.

He published the results in *Science* only a few months after the experiment. The article begins with West praising elephants as an unusually advanced species, which makes the upcoming narrative all the more poignant: "Because of his remarkable intelligence, his extended life span, his capacity for highly organized group relationships, and his extraordinary psychobiology in general, the elephant is an animal of great interest to the zoologist and the comparative psychologist." In his conclusion to the *Science* article, West acknowledged the loss of such a creature and editorialized about the dangers of LSD:

> It appears that the elephant is highly sensitive to the effects of LSD—a finding which may prove to be valuable in elephant-control work in Africa. The death of Tusko suggests the nature of the danger, and the most likely case of death should a lethal overdose be taken by a human. Despite efforts by its manufacturer to prevent misuse of the drug, LSD has been increasingly and sometimes irresponsibly administered to humans as a putative adjunct to psychotherapy. The possibility of suicide or even homicide by LSD cannot be ignored.

West's experiment came at a time when LSD research had a dual focus: to estimate its value as a weapon, and to facilitate psychotherapy. His concluding remarks affirmed LSD's potential as a weapon for controlling minds of elephants (or humans), but warned about the reckless use of the drug in therapy.

Because he ended up killing Tusko accidentally, West took pains in *Science* to justify his methods. To calculate the appropriate dosage, he extrapolated from earlier experiments on smaller mammals. For several years, other scientists had been testing LSD on mice, rabbits, cats, and monkeys, in order to find out how much was needed to produce certain neurological effects (such as temporary blindness)—and how much it took to kill the animal (usually from respiratory arrest). He cited one such researcher, Edward Evarts, who concluded that monkeys and cats needed a hefty dose of LSD to cause dramatic effects:

> Proportionately much larger doses have been required to obtain comparable results in lower animals. In order to produce in the rhesus macaque a sensory blockade sufficient to cause loss of position sense and temporary blindness, Evarts gave doses as large as 0.5 to 1.0 mg/kg. Similar doses must be given to produce a similar effect in the cat. The effecting of even a transient rage reaction in the cat usually requires intravenous administration of at least 0.15 mg/kg. Doses up to 6.5 mg/kg given intravenously are required to kill a cat.

The scientific prose is jarring—high doses "are required to kill a cat"—but West's point here is clinical and detached: he decided to give the elephant a dose comparable to non-lethal but effective doses given to cats, adjusted for body weight. The dose he gave Tusko was 297 milligrams, or roughly 1000 times an ordinary dose for a human. In the years following Tusko's death, other scientists have pointed out potential flaws in West's method. Comparing dosages across species can be complicated and risky, because there are so many important variables besides body weight.

Beyond the question of dosage, another problem clouds the experiment. After Tusko collapsed and went into *"status epilepticus,"* West decided to administer a big dose of Thorazine, the anti-psychotic sedative. After another hour or so, when the situation looked dire, he injected Tusko with Nembutal, a barbiturate. Scientists looking back at the experiment have speculated that these other two drugs contributed substantially to the death of Tusko.

Eleusinian Mysteries. In ancient Greece, a sacred and secret ritual took place at Eleusis, not far from Athens. Participants were initiated into their culture's most profound religious truths. The overall goal was to guide initiates through a process in which they came to know their spiritual essence and to transcend the fear of death. Many of the most influential figures from Greek history took part in the Eleusinian rituals, including Plato, Aristotle, and Sophocles. Because of the immense importance of Greek philosophy and religion in the formation of Western thinking, scholars have been very curious about details of the ceremonies at Eleusis. One crucial element was a sacramental drink called *kykeon*, prepared by priests and given to all participants. There has been much recent speculation that *kykeon* delivered a psychedelic high from a natural source of lysergic acid.

The link between *kykeon* and lysergic acid was first proposed by Albert Hofmann, the discoverer of LSD (see *Hofmann, Albert*). Hofmann was not the first to speculate that *kykeon* contained a psychedelic component; in the mid 1950s, Gordon Wasson had suggested hallucinogenic mushrooms as the likely ingredient (see *Wasson, R. Gordon*). Hofmann theorized that a more likely candidate was ergot, a fungus that grows on grasses and grains, including barley (see *Ergot*). Ergot contains the alkaloid ergotamine (d-lysergic acid amide), which is sometimes referred to as "natural LSD." If the ancient Greeks found a way to process the ergot in order to maximize its psychedelic effects and minimize its unpleasant effects— and Hofmann's research suggests that it would not have been difficult to do so—then ergot could well have been the secret ingredient in the *kykeon* recipe. Hofmann, Wasson, and classical scholar Carl Ruck collaborated on *The Road to Eleusis: Unveiling the Secret of the Mysteries,* a comprehensive presentation of the psychedelic *kykeon* theory (see *Ruck, Carl A.P.*). Although skeptics remain, the theory has gained some scholarly support. In his review of the second edition of *The Road to Eleusis* (1998), Johns Hopkins classicist Georg Luck concluded that the book made "an excellent case for the use of a hallucinogenic drug in one of the ancient world's most venerable rituals.... The real breakthrough, as I see it, is due to Albert Hofmann.... We may never know what the psychoactive element in the *kykeon* was, but Hofmann is probably right."

Ellis, Dock. On June 12, 1970, Ellis pitched a no-hitter for the Pittsburgh Pirates when he was high on LSD. No one knew it at the time—including his catcher, Jerry May. After the game he told reporters that it was "the easiest game he ever caught." The box score does not support May's claim. Ellis walked eight batters and hit another with a pitch. Years later he admitted to a journalist that "sometimes he couldn't see the hitter. Sometimes he couldn't see the catcher. But if he could see the hitter, he'd guess where the catcher was" (*Dallas Observer*). Furthermore, Ellis and May gave up three stolen bases to the Padres, a poor baserunning team. Since May was an excellent defensive catcher, the Padres must have figured out that the pitcher was simply not paying attention.

Ellis first told the story to Donald Hall only a few years later, when Ellis was collaborating with Hall on a book about his baseball career. Ellis didn't come out with the story in public until 1984. Over the years, as the story became more widely known, he continued to give accounts of what he remembered about the game—in 1987 for an article in *High Times,* in 2005 for *The Dallas Observer,* and again that year in an HBO feature. When *Dock Ellis In the Country of Baseball* came out in 1976, Hall told the story of the no-hitter but disguised it. At Ellis's request, Hall replaced "LSD" with "vodka"— thereby turning an astonishing story into something routine. Ellis and his girlfriend tripped from Thursday night into Friday morning. Around noon on Friday they realized that he was scheduled to pitch at 6:00 that evening in San Diego. At this point he "took another half tab" before making last minute arrangements to grab a flight to San Diego. Ellis told Hall that he took Dexamyl and Benzadrine before the game to try to straighten up (or in the bowdlerized version, "coffee: a lot of coffee"). Ellis's memory of the no-hitter is faulty enough to suggest that he remained spaced out for the duration. The most obvious memory problem within Hall's original account comes as Ellis tries to remember a close call in the eighth inning: "The other man [to hit it hard] was Clarence

Gaston. No, it wasn't Clarence Gaston, because Clarence Gaston didn't play. It *was* Clarence Gaston, because Ollie Brown didn't play. One of the two. He hit a line drive that was knuckling at Matty Alou." Ellis got Matty Alou right, but the hitter was neither Clarence Gaston nor Ollie Brown: it was Nate Colbert.

If Ellis tried to give Hall the impression that he wasn't really that high during the game, he was more candid years later. He mentioned that his fingers tingled, and the ball felt alternately too big and too small in his hand. *High Times* described his memory of the first strike he threw: "It was no ordinary pitch. The ball burst from Dock's hand and left a blazing, comet-like tail that remained visible long after the ball was caught." Although he "felt wobbly on the mound," "the comets kept bursting across the plate. All he had to do was steer the ball down the multicolored path." When HBO dug up a video of the press conference held immediately after the game, Ellis showed it to members of a drug rehab group he was leading; they found it hilariously obvious that he was high.

Entheogen. One of the names given to the class of drugs that includes LSD, "entheogen" comes from Greek roots meaning "generating the God within." Those who endorse the name believe that LSD and other entheogens help people discover profound spiritual truths (see *Religion*). The term was first used in 1979 by a group of researchers that included Gordon Wasson, specialist in mushrooms, and Carl Ruck, the classics scholar who collaborated on theories about drugs and the Eleusinian mysteries (see *Eleusinian Mysteries*). "Entheogen" has established a place in the language but has not displaced its more common synonyms, "psychedelic" and "hallucinogen." See *Psychedelic; Hallucinogen*.

Ergot. Ergot is the familiar name of *claviceps purpurea*, a fungus that grows on various grasses and grains, including rye, wheat, and barley. The ergot produces powerful changes in the neurochemisty of any herbivore that consumes it; the fungus thereby benefits both itself and its host by discourging insects and animals from eating the grain or grass. Because ergot has powerful effects on the nervous system and circulation, food contaminated by ergot can cause a number of symptoms: most seriously, gangrene and stillbirths, but more commonly, convulsions and hallucinations.

Albert Hofmann was working on potential medical benefits of ergot's circulatory effects when he discovered LSD-25. Ergot contains the alkaloid ergotamine (d-lysergic acid amide), sometimes known as "natural LSD," which Hofmann used to synthesize lysergic acid. Hofmann's synthetic compound of lysergic acid diethylamide proved to be much stronger in its psychotropic effects than natural ergot. However, ergot has been linked by some scholars with outbreaks of supposed demonic possession, as well as with culturally approved religious ceremonies. Historian Linnda Caporael has made plausible connections between periods of ergot-friendly weather and incidents of witch hunts or other forms of public demonization. (Symptoms of ergotism, especially convulsion and hallucination, led people to infer supernatural causes.) Researchers Gordon Wasson and Carl Ruck, along with Albert Hofmann, have speculated that ergot may have been the key ingredient in *kykeon,* the drink consumed by initiates during rituals surrounding the Greek Eleusinian mysteries (see *Eleusinian Mysteries*).

Esalen. As Jeffrey Kripal has chronicled, this Big Sur spa became a haven for intellectuals who were exploring how LSD (among many other drugs and practices) might catalyze human evolution and alter social and political behaviors. Co-founders Michael Murphy and Richard Price hired none other than Hunter S. Thompson to guard the property when Esalen started up in 1961 (see *Thompson, Hunter S.*). As the institute flourished in the 1960s, it hosted a number of LSD celebrities, including Timothy Leary, Gregory Bateson, Terence McKenna, and George Harrison (see *Leary, Timothy; Bateson, Gregory; McKenna, Terence; Harrison, George*). During these years, the use of LSD and other drugs was very common at Esalen. The institute remains open today for seminars in alternative thinking, although all guests are now warned that Esalen strictly bans illegal drugs.

Exploding Plastic Inevitable. This was the psychedelic name of Andy Warhol's New York show that resembled Acid Tests. See *Warhol, Andy; Velvet Underground; Acid Test*.

Family Dog. Family Dog Productions was a loosely organized group of hippie friends who lived communally in Haight-Ashbury and organized dance concerts at the Avalon Ballroom. Chet Helms was a leading figure in the group, which also included poster artist Alton Kelley. See *Avalon Ballroom; Helms, Chet; Kelley, Alton*.

Fantasia. Disney's 1940 film, which presented elaborate animated images to accompany various pieces of classical music, did not make money from its original release—or from several re-releases—until it struck gold with a psychedelic audience in 1969. Young adults came in great numbers to see a film that seemed a psychedelic classic *avant la lettre*. According to David Koenig, Disney executives "asked the theaters to promote the film not as typical Disney fare, but 'now you sell *Fantasia* as you did *Easy Rider*. Hip youngsters come to see it as a special kind of trip.'" Koenig also found a studio promotional kit that quoted the following underground review: "Disney's *Fantasia*: A Head Classic: Representation of sound as color does resemble tripping on STD, LSD, THC and various other letters of the alphabet." Disney advertised the 1969 re-release with a poster that might have been designed for a Fillmore concert, with dancing mush-

rooms, flying horses, and a towering pagan demon. The marketing strategy paid off, but as Koenig notes, "Conservative groups began picketing movie theaters for screening Disney's animated 'drug fantasies.'" Disney had nothing to do with the next connection between *Fantasia* and LSD: a popular issue of blotter acid with a picture of Mickey Mouse as the Sorcerer's Apprentice.

Fear and Loathing in Las Vegas. New Journalist Hunter S. Thompson first published this wild narrative in the pages of *Rolling Stone*, where readers welcomed his reflections on LSD and a host of other psychotropic drugs. See *Thompson, Hunter S.*

Feilding, Amanda. Feilding (Lady Neidpath) created and directs the Beckley Foundation near Oxford to support research into potential benefits of LSD and other mind-altering drugs (see *Beckley Foundation*). In a speech she gave at the Basel symposium marking Albert Hofmann's 100th birthday, Feilding recalled her first LSD trips in 1965: "I thought, this is what I've been looking for! With LSD I could better experience the subtle energies and the interconnectedness of all things, from my inner world to the pulsating, living universe." She took LSD regularly to "psychoanalyze myself—I found that on LSD I could be both doctor and patient simultaneously." Feilding also maintained that LSD improves the flow of blood to the brain and thereby enhances intellect and creativity.

Ferlinghetti, Lawrence. Beat poet and co-founder of City Lights Booksellers in San Francisco, Ferlinghetti welcomed the early hippie community and tried LSD on two occasions. He enjoyed a trip he took in Big Sur, but not the second one, when he dropped acid along with Allen Ginsberg at the Human Be-In (see *Ginsberg, Allen; Human Be-In*). In 2007 he told Jesse Hamlin of *SFGate.com*, "It was terrible. It's not a good idea to do it in a crowded place." In 1968 Ferlinghetti published *The Secret*

Meaning of Things, a long poem that includes a section called "Imagining LSD."

Feynman, Richard. A Caltech theoretical physicist who won a Nobel Prize and became one of the best known personalities in American science, Feynman experimented with LSD in the 1960s. Feynman, whose boldness was legendary, displayed an uncharacteristic reluctance to publicize the fact. According to James Gleick's biography, "Feynman experimented with LSD during his professorship at Caltech. Somewhat embarrassed by his actions, Feynman sidestepped the issue when dictating his anecdotes; consequently, the 'Altered States' chapter in *Surely You're Joking, Mr. Feynman* described only marijuana and ketamine experiences at John Lilly's famed sensory deprivation tanks, as a way of studying consciousness" (see *Lilly, John C.*).

Fillmore. Music entrepreneur Bill Graham founded three of the most famous concert sites for psychedelic music: Fillmore Auditorium, Fillmore West, and Fillmore East (see *Graham, Bill*). The original Fillmore Auditorium was located on Fillmore Street in San Francisco. Graham took over the smallish theater in 1966 to present shows primarily by local psychedelic bands. Well known San Francisco bands that performed there included the Grateful Dead, Jefferson Airplane, Big Brother and the Holding Company, Moby Grape, and Quicksilver Messenger Service. Prominent psychedelic bands from elsewhere also played the Fillmore Auditorium, including the Doors, Jimi Hendrix, Pink Floyd, and Cream. Graham shut down operations at the original Fillmore in the middle of 1968 and moved to a different location in San Francisco, a dance hall then called The Carousel. He renamed it Fillmore West, to pair it up with the Fillmore East concert hall he had opened in New York City's East Village a few months earlier. At Fillmore East Graham booked many of the same psychedelic bands who played in San Francisco.

During their prime years, Fillmore concerts took on certain distinctive psychedelic features. Shows were advertised with posters designed by the most famous psychedelic artists, including Wes Wilson, who served as house artist for the Fillmore until mid–1967. When Wilson resigned after a dispute with Graham about compensation, he was replaced by Bonnie MacLean (see *Wilson, Wes; MacLean, Bonnie; Psychedelic Posters*). Sometimes handbills of concert posters were distributed to patrons as souvenirs. Liquid light shows animated surfaces behind the bands on stage (see *Light Shows*). The relatively cozy dimensions and casual set-up of Fillmore theaters encouraged dancing. At the end of a concert, Graham or staff members would pass out apples from a tub near the exit doors.

Graham closed both Fillmore West and Fillmore East by 1971, when changing economic conditions in the music industry made them impractical. But he felt such nostalgia for the original Fillmore Auditorium that he longed to fix it up and bring it back to life someday. After he died in a helicopter crash in 1991, his friends fulfilled his wish. The Fillmore Auditorium reopened in 1994 with a Smashing Pumpkins concert.

Firesign Theater. A Los Angeles comedy troupe founded in the psychedelic era, Firesign Theater playfully subverted mainstream culture in radio sketches and records, and their performers contributed to psychedelic counterculture. Peter Bergman of Firesign invented the term "Love-In" and organized the first such event in Los Angeles. Some 50,000 people showed up in Griffith Park for a celebration similar to the Human Be-In (see *Human Be-In*). In 1971, members of Firesign wrote the screenplay for *Zachariah,* the first psychedelic Western (see *Zachariah*).

Fisher, Gary. Psychiatrist Fisher used LSD experimentally in the 1950s and early 1960s to treat childhood schizophrenics, including patients labeled as autistic (see *Schizophrenia;*

Autism; Psychiatry). Fisher's most extended clinical trial began with twelve such patients; after nine months of treatment, he judged that five of them showed substantial potential for improvement, and he continued intensive LSD therapy with the smaller group. Fisher was aided by a core of assistant therapists, all of whom had considerable experience with psychedelic drugs. In 1963, however, political pressure mounted against the use of LSD, and Fisher's trial was closed down. Reflecting back on that disappointment, he wrote, "The abandonment of these children was an extremely painful experience for all of us. We were very surprised and touched with how supportive and accepting the children were of our departure when we said our good-byes." Fisher also spent time with Timothy Leary at Millbrook (see *Leary, Timothy; Millbrook*).

Flashbacks. "Flashbacks" are the popular name for HPPD: Hallucinogen Persisting Perception Disorder. (The condition was formerly called PHPD, Post Hallucinogen Perception Disorder.) LSD flashbacks are the most commonly reported type. According to the *Diagnostic and Statistical Manual of Mental Disorders* (American Psychiatric Association), "The essential feature of HPPD (Flashbacks) is the transient recurrence of disturbances in perception that are reminiscent of those experienced during one or more earlier Hallucinogen Intoxications." Visual disturbances may include the appearance of geometric forms, flashes of intense color, stroboscopic effects, and halos around objects. "The abnormal perceptions associated with HPPD occur episodically and may be self-induced (e.g., by thinking about them) or triggered by entry into a dark environment, various drugs, anxiety or fatigue or other stressors." People experiencing HPPD retain proper "reality testing": in other words, they recognize that their perceptions are being caused by drug-related changes in sensory processing, not by any changes in the objective world. Although the *DSM* uses

"flashbacks" as a synonym for HPPD, a semantic distinction is sometimes made between the two terms. HPPD refers to milder, recurring perceptual disturbances, and flashbacks to more intense episodes of psychological distress. The more intense flashbacks have been linked with the broader condition of post-traumatic stress disorder. HPPD/flashbacks are rare enough that only limited research has been conducted on causes and consequences.

The condition was recognized back in the 1950s and early 1960s during the period of psychedelic psychotherapy, but flashbacks were not considered sufficiently common or dangerous to constitute a serious side effect. During later years when LSD use became more widespread, warnings about flashbacks intensified. Documentaries and journalistic accounts portrayed flashbacks as a serious risk. A 1966 cover story in *Life* magazine referred to "instances where LSD symptoms have resumed weeks after taking it, leading the victims to believe they were losing their sanity" (see *Life* magazine). The real deaths of two public figures were blamed on LSD flashbacks: Frank Olson of the CIA, and Diane Linkletter, daughter of television personality Art Linkletter (see *Olson, Frank; Linkletter, Diane*).

Flower Power. Although Allen Ginsberg is widely credited with coining the phrase "Flower Power," it was a 1967 photograph entitled "Flower Power" that publicized the hippie slogan most strikingly. Bernie Boston of the *Washington Star* took the photo at an antiwar protest near the Pentagon. A young man is shown inserting carnations into the barrels of soldiers' rifles. Boston captures the incongruity between the threat—a harmless looking young man with a handful of flowers—and the military response: nine shiny helmets ringing the flower man, with gun barrels aimed at his turtleneck. Flower Power came to mean not only a philosophy of non-violence and resistance to war, but more generally, a set of values associated with hippies. These hippie principles included a preference for organic over industrial products, a faith in the benevolence of nature, and an emphasis on beauty and love more than utility and achievement. Hippies wore flowers in their hair, scattered them at concerts, painted them on vans, grew them in plots of disputed city land, and named children after them.

As a central element of hippie culture, LSD certainly belongs within the constellation of Flower Power referents. Indeed, one connection between LSD and Flower Power is not simply figurative but literal: hallucinogens occur naturally in several flowering plants. The flowers with chemical properties most similar to LSD are Morning Glories. Certain Morning Glory varieties have seeds that contain ergot-like alkaloids (see *Ergot*), close to LSD in chemical structure. Morning Glory seeds have been used sacramentally in some cultures, including the Zapotec. It takes hundreds of seeds to produce a hallucinogenic effect, because the natural alkaloid that resembles LSD is much weaker than its synthetic cousin. Commercial Morning Glory seeds have been treated with preservatives or other chemicals that render them unfit for consumption. Still, some American varieties of ergot-active Morning Glories have nicknames that sound appropriately psychedelic: Heavenly Blue, Pearly Gates, Blue Star, Flying Saucer.

Fonda, Peter. Although his sister Jane became more notorious as a political figure during the Vietnam era, Peter Fonda starred in two LSD-related movies that earned him iconic status within the counterculture of the late 1960s. In Roger Corman's *The Trip* (1967), he played a television director who takes his first acid trip (see *Trip*). In 1969 he produced, co-wrote, and starred in *Easy Rider,* a low budget but hugely successful film that includes an important scene depicting an acid trip (see *Easy Rider*). Fonda took LSD in real life with various Hollywood friends, including Dennis Hopper and Jack

Nicholson, both of whom collaborated on *The Trip* and *Easy Rider*. Both films deliver ambiguous messages about LSD: it is portrayed both as a therapeutic aid with spiritual implications, and a cause of psychological confusion and distress. In an interview given many years after the films were made, Fonda offered similarly mixed comments about LSD. "It was an abused drug," he said, and "most of the people who tried LSD did it for the wrong reasons." But he also said that LSD "was designed for you to look inside yourself. Quite a liberating experience, if you can pull it off" (*Time.com*).

Fool. Named for a Tarot card, "The Fool" was a group of Dutch artists who designed psychedelic clothing and other artifacts, most notably for the Beatles (see *Beatles*). Among other projects, the Fool designed clothes worn by the Beatles in their 1967 television production "All You Need Is Love," painted a psychedelic mural at the Beatles' Apple Boutique in London, and decorated cars and guitars for George Harrison and John Lennon.

Ford, Gerald. During his political career, Ford had three awkward events associated with LSD. The first was a close call with LSD-spiked coffee. A few hours after he gave a speech in Chicago, a pot of electric coffee was discovered backstage; according to newspaper accounts, "six stagehands who drank the coffee became lightheaded and giggly and were hospitalized" (AP, May 15, 1974). Lab tests confirmed the presence of LSD in the coffee. A spokesman for the Secret Service said that they would investigate the case, but he "seriously doubted that anything had been done to injure the Vice President." Two other incidents occurred during Ford's presidency. After documents came out exposing the CIA's secret testing of LSD (see *MK-Ultra*), Ford met the family of the late Frank Olson at the White House and offered an official apology for the CIA's misconduct: Olson had been given LSD without his knowledge and apparently committed suicide as a result (see *Olson, Frank*). The second incident involved a member of the Manson family, all of whom took LSD under Manson's direction (see *Manson, Charles*). Lynette "Squeaky" Fromme, disguised as a nun, approached Ford with a pistol and pulled the trigger, but the firing chamber was empty. She nevertheless received a life sentence for the crime.

Foucault, Michel. The influential French poststructuralist philosopher took LSD for the first time in 1975, when he was nearly fifty. Foucault was visiting California at the invitation of Berkeley professors; he took his trip in the dramatic setting of Death Valley, with music of Stockhausen as background. According to biographer David Macey, "rumours abound about the acid trip" and its effects on Foucault's intellectual life, but Foucault's only comment on record came in conversation with a friend: "Foucault spoke nostalgically to Claude Mauriac of 'an unforgettable evening on LSD, in carefully prepared doses, in the desert night, with delicious music, nice people, and some chartreuse.'"

Funkadelic. This African-American band grew from the doo wop group known as the Parliaments. George Clinton, leader of the Parliaments, gradually added musicians to the original vocal group, and in 1968 he changed their name to circumvent a legal dispute. Bass player Billy Nelson invented "Funkakelic" as a portmanteau word combining "funk" and "psychedelic."

Funkadelic's first three albums all had prominent psychedelic elements, inflected with a distinctive urban hipness. The second of these albums, *Free Your Mind, and Your Ass Will Follow* (1970), delivered their most audaciously psychedelic production. According to George Clinton, it was an experiment "to see if we can cut a whole album while we're all tripping on acid," and they ended up recording all six tracks in a single day. The title song, which takes up about one third of the album, sets out a psychedelic manifesto accompanied by an extreme psy-

chedelic soundscape. Lead guitarist Eddie Hazel plays in a style reminiscent of Jimi Hendrix, and the songs unfold with a variety of spacy effects and heavy doses of feedback. The lyrics call for an evolution of consciousness that will take the place of political revolution. Like many psychedelic songs, "Free Your Mind, and Your Ass Will Follow" expresses discontent with the social status quo and imagines finding relief through a liberating mental journey. In several lyrics from the album, Funkadelic samples bits of Christian scripture and prayer for their own rhetorical purposes—whether to criticize social injustice, or to emphasize the spiritual aspects of psychedelia.

The psychedelic elements of Funkadelic became less prominent after their third album, *Maggot Brain* (1971), although they continued to thrive and to define the nature of "funk" for music of the 1970s. Their early psychedelic music remains influential, however; in the early 1990s, En Vogue enjoyed a hit when they borrowed a Funkadelic title, albeit with one polite revision: "Free Your Mind, and the Rest Will Follow."

Gamblers. This surf group recorded the first song with a reference to LSD: the B-side of their 1962 single "Moon Dawg" was titled "LSD-25." Songwriters Sam Taylor and Derry Weaver plucked the name from a magazine story about therapeutic uses of the new drug. Despite its provocative title, "LSD-25" was a conventional surf-style instrumental.

Garcia, Carolyn. Born Carolyn Adams and later nicknamed "Mountain Girl," Garcia joined the Merry Pranksters when she was a teenager. She traveled from her home in Poughkeepsie to Palo Alto in 1964, where she met Neal Cassady, Ken Kesey, and the rest of the circle that was developing into the Pranksters (see *Merry Pranksters; Cassady, Neal; Kesey, Ken*). She had a child with Kesey named Sunshine, but their romantic relationship was short-lived. After a short marriage to another Prankster, George Walker, she began a relationship with Jerry Garcia and eventually married him in 1981 (see *Garcia, Jerry*). Carolyn and Jerry Garcia had two daughters and lived together for several years, but the marriage finally broke up. When Jerry died in 1995, his new wife, Deborah Koons, disputed Carolyn's right to the portion of Jerry's estate that he had given her by informal contract. The resulting trial was shown for weeks on the Court TV channel, where viewers heard interesting but often muddled testimony from psychedelic veterans. In the end, the judge ruled in favor of Mountain Girl.

Garcia, Jerry. The lead guitarist for the Grateful Dead acquired the nickname "Captain Trips" because of his fondness for LSD. Garcia first took LSD in 1964, at a time when he and his friends were playing conventional country and rock music in bars. As he told Reich and Wenner in a 1972 *Rolling Stone* interview, "Along came LSD, and that was the end of the whole world. The whole world just went kablooey." Garcia said that LSD dramatically changed both his life and his music. The experience "freed me because I suddenly realized that my little attempt at having a straight life and doing that was really a fiction and just wasn't going to work out." LSD also transformed his music. When his band moved from bars to Acid Tests (see *Acid Test*), he was able to "stretch out" and improvise: "So our trip with the Acid Test was to be able to play long and loud ... as long and loud as we wanted and nobody would stop us." When Charles Reich asked for elaboration, Garcia added, "Of course we were improvising cosmically, too. Because being high, each note, you know, is like a whole universe. And each silence.... When you're playing and you're high on acid in these scenes it is like the most important thing in the world. It's truly cosmic." After a while, Garcia tapered off in his use of LSD, especially when he was performing. Garcia admitted, "You don't play that well when you're really high. But

you learn a lot. So it's like there are times when it's groovy to get real high and play because you learn a lot but it's not necessarily groovy to perform that way or to play really well together."

Garcia later struggled with addiction to heroin and died of a heart attack at a rehab clinic in 1995. His death, which brought an end to the popular Grateful Dead concert scene, is one of the main reasons cited for the decline of LSD use in the later 90s. See *Grateful Dead; Psychedelic Rock*.

Gates, Bill. Like his rival Steve Jobs at Apple, Gates participated in the psychedelic scene surrounding the early computer industry. Jobs candidly acknowledged the importance of LSD in his life (see *Jobs, Steve*), but Gates was more evasive. The subject came up in a *Playboy* interview (Rensin):

> PLAYBOY: Ever take LSD?
> GATES: My errant youth ended a long time ago.
> PLAYBOY: What does that mean?
> GATES: That means there were things I did under the age of 25 that I ended up not doing subsequently.
> PLAYBOY: One LSD story involved you staring at a table and thinking the corner was going to plunge into your eye.
> GATES: [Smiles.]
> PLAYBOY: Ah, a glimmer of recognition.
> GATES: that was on the other side of that boundary. The young mind can deal with certain kinds of gooping around that I don't think at this age I could. I don't think you're as capable of handling lack of sleep or whatever challenges you throw at your body as you get older. However, I never missed a day of work.

Gates did not deny using LSD, but unlike Jobs, he dismissed it as youthful silliness. It was "errant," a wrong path, and at least on one occasion, a cause of anxiety. The respective acid personae of Jobs and Gates coordinate with the corporate images of Apple and Microsoft: the cool guy versus the square. Jobs recalled his psychedelic enlightenment, while Gates bragged about his perfect attendance at work.

A few years after this interview, Bill

Gates and Microsoft had another awkward experience with LSD: this time not the drug itself, but a group of Polish security researchers who called themselves LSD, for "Last Stage of Delirium." The LSD group warned Microsoft of a serious vulnerability in their system—a flaw that would later be exploited for the "Blaster" worm. The four Polish researchers chose their pseudonym cleverly. By naming themselves LSD, they managed both to signal a dire threat to the Microsoft computer brain, and to tease Bill Gates about his errant youth.

Gathering of the Tribes. The Human Be-In held of January, 1967 also went by this name. See *Human Be-In.*

Ginsberg, Allen. Poet Ginsberg first took LSD in 1959 when he volunteered for experiments being conducted in Palo Alto by the Menlo Research Institute. Although his first acid trips were far from pleasant, Ginsberg eventually took LSD in more congenial settings and experienced much better results. He tripped with Timothy Leary and Ken Kesey, among many other psychedelic celebrities. Ginsberg became an advocate for the use of LSD by the general public, and he envisioned a grand remaking of society that would emerge from psychedelic revelations. He worked with Leary to publicize the benefits of LSD; he attended Kesey's Acid Tests (see *Acid Test*); he helped to organize a 1965 poetry reading at the Royal Albert Hall that catalyzed the London psychedelic scene; and he was a conspicuous figure at events in San Francisco during the Summer of Love.

Ginsberg expressed his thoughts about LSD most tellingly in two pieces of writing, both of which he composed while tripping on acid. The first is "Lysergic Acid," a poem he wrote in 1959 during one of his Palo Alto experimental trips. "Lysergic Acid" records the spiritual anxiety Ginsberg felt in this early psychedelic experience. The poem is dominated by images of spider webs and other fibrous networks of energy. For the most part, these webs induce a cosmic malaise, although the poem becomes more hopeful at the end, with flowers supplanting images of death and entrapment.

Almost twenty years after he wrote "Lysergic Acid," Ginsberg took a latter-day acid trip and recorded his thoughts in prose. He took the LSD to mark a special occasion: he would be flying to California for the 1977 Santa Cruz conference on "LSD: A Decade Later." While tripping on the plane, he wrote down some reflections on the drug that had been so important in his life ("Preface and a Trip [LSD]," in *Deliberate Prose*). This Ginsberg trip is much mellower than the early one. In "Preface and a Trip," he explains how his training in Buddhist meditation has helped him steer clear of "Anxiety Alley" while high on LSD. Meditative practice "has the built-in advantage of continually 'letting go' of thought-forms instead of clinging to them or solidifying them; thus hope and fear are dissolved." Ginsberg concludes that "LSD is OK because it teaches one not to cling to anything, including LSD." His acid trips, "charming as they are," will be "infrequent" for the maturing poet.

Go Ask Alice. This anti-drug classic was published in 1971 and quickly became a bestseller on the Young Adult shelf. The book, which took its title from Grace Slick's "White Rabbit" (see *Slick, Grace; "White Rabbit"*), was presented as the work of an anonymous teen diarist. The diarist's life had been ruined as a result of taking LSD and other drugs. Eventually, it became clear that out that the real author was not an anonymous high schooler but Beatrice Sparks, a middle-aged woman with credentials in counseling and a knack for writing pseudo-nonfiction in the voice of troubled teens. *Go Ask Alice* nevertheless remains a popular book as originally packaged.

Of all the drugs the diarist takes (listed chronologically: LSD, speed, barbiturates, tranquillizers, marijuana, heroin), LSD is the most important, both because it was her first drug and the one that delivered the most powerful altered state. On acid she had her most terrifying nightmares as well as her most uplifting visions. Indeed, Sparks takes a bit of a risk with the girl's first acid trip, which sounds quite pleasant. She marvels at the beauty all around her. She appreciates the aesthetic complexity of ordinary objects in the room, in the manner of a less articulate Aldous Huxley: "I looked at a magazine on the table, and I could see it in 100 dimensions." As she listens to music, "Never before had anything ever been so beautiful. I was a part of every single instrument, literally a part. Each note had a character, shape and color all its very own." Her new powers also enable her to transcend the limits of ego, and overcome insecurities that had hindered her teenage life: "Was I the table or the book or the music, or was I part of all of them, but it didn't really matter, for whatever I was, I was wonderful."

The diarist's last acid trip delivered quite the opposite experience: an epic bummer. As she babysat for a neighbor, she ate several chocolate-covered peanuts that had been coated with LSD by a school enemy. In her hallucinogenic panic, she saw her flesh crawling with worms and other disgusting signs of corruption; she clawed at her arms and face and did considerable damage. She only recovered after an extended stay in the hospital.

Sparks fashioned two endings for the diarist in *Go Ask Alice,* one happy and one tragic. In the first, she came to understand that all these drug experiences were harming rather than helping her efforts to resolve teenage anxieties of life and love. She found comfort in simple pleasures like holding a kitten, an experience that was "a trillion times better" than an acid trip. The second, unhappy ending comes in a brief epilogue, which reports that the young woman died of an unexplained drug overdose shortly after her last entry. With the mysterious death of the protagonist, *Go Ask Alice* thereby retains

its monitory force, even after it has shown a path away from LSD and back to normal life.

Golightly, Bonnie. Author of several titillating mass market novels in the 1950s and 1960s (e.g. *Wife Swapping, A Breath of Scandal*), Golightly co-wrote *LSD: The Problem-Solving Psychedelic* with Peter Stafford in 1967 (see *Stafford, Peter*).

Gottlieb, Sidney. Gottlieb was an American chemist who supervised MK-ULTRA, the CIA program that experimented with drugs for use in interrogation, espionage, and warfare (see *MK-Ultra*). Gottlieb's first major project focused on LSD. As reported in the *New York Times* obituary (March 10, 1999), "Mr. Gottlieb was fascinated by the drug, and, a family friend said, took it hundreds of times." Under Gottlieb's direction, the CIA gave LSD to thousands of human subjects. At first the experiments were performed only on Gottlieb's colleagues in MK-ULTRA; then the pool broadened to CIA employees in general. Gottlieb and his group went on to conduct extensive testing on captive populations—prisoners and mental patients—as well as on volunteers, including two subjects who later became psychedelic celebrities: Ken Kesey and Allen Ginsberg (see *Kesey, Ken; Ginsberg, Allen*). Gottlieb is often named as the inspiration for the character "Doctor Strangelove" in Stanley Kubrick's film, although other Cold War scientists also fit the bill.

Gottlieb's tactics in testing LSD led to many lawsuits, and obviously his use of the drug was radically different from the countercultural use that dominated the later 1960s. However, Gottlieb's post–CIA life showed elements of peaceful, hippie-style influences. He lived in India for a time (caring for lepers), moved to a cabin in rural Virginia, tried a communal lifestyle, pursued folk dancing, and herded goats.

Graham, Bill. The most powerful rock entrepreneur of his generation, Graham got his start in San Francisco during the psychedelic era. Graham was born in Germany and narrowly escaped the Holocaust as a child. He moved to San Francisco in the early 1960s and managed the Mime Troupe (see *San Francisco Mime Troupe*). When one of the Mimes faced legal troubles, Graham organized a successful benefit concert that featured Jefferson Airplane. Soon he started producing concerts full time. He arranged for the use of the Fillmore Auditorium, where all of his early concerts took place. At first he teamed up with Chet Helms (see *Helms, Chet*), but the two split up after only a few events: Helms had a laid-back, hippie way of doing things, whereas Graham was a practical and careful businessman. Graham eventually managed two Fillmores, one in San Francisco and the other in New York City, where all the prominent psychedelic bands played (see *Fillmore*). He employed Wes Wilson and later Bonnie MacLean (Graham's wife) to design posters for his concerts, and he gave them artistic leeway to develop the distinctive psychedelic style (see *Psychedelic Posters*). In 1971, Graham closed the Fillmores, but he continued to produce shows elsewhere for the psychedelic bands that remained active, most notably the Grateful Dead.

In later years Graham promoted national tours for major acts like Bob Dylan and the Rolling Stones, and he helped organize many benefit concerts, including Live Aid in 1985. He was inducted into the Rock and Roll Hall of Fame in 1992 (a year after his death). The citation began, "Bill Graham forever changed the way rock and roll is presented. He provided the business and organizational acumen that allowed the anarchic San Francisco scene of the mid-to-late Sixties to flower."

Grahm, Randall. The iconoclastic founder of Bonny Doon Winery projected an image suggestive of psychedelia: he was a student at U.C. Santa Cruz during the psychedelic era (see *Santa Cruz*), set up his winery in the woods nearby, and created labels with artwork by Ralph Steadman and trippy descriptive prose (see *Steadman, Ralph*). In an interview with Connie Blaszczyk, however, Grahm brought up LSD only to speculate how it might compare with fine wine: "I remember drinking the Scharzhofberg, and despite having gone to school and lived in Santa Cruz forever and having long hair, I'm not quite as psychedelic as people would have me, or believe that I am, but when I tasted the Scharzhofberg, I thought to myself, 'This must be what LSD is about. This must be like LSD.' I was thinking, 'This is yellow submarine. I'm in the yellow submarine right now'" (see *Yellow Submarine*).

Grant, Cary. Starting in November of 1958, the actor took LSD dozens of times under the supervision of psychiatrist Mortimer A. Hartman (see *Hartman, Mortimer A.*). Grant would eventually declare that LSD therapy transformed his life: he said that it made him a much happier and better man. He told his story first to *Look* magazine in 1959 and then to *Good Housekeeping* in 1960. It was Grant's third wife, Betsy Drake, who suggested that he try Dr. Hartman's new method (see *Drake, Betsy*). Drake had been undergoing LSD therapy herself in 1958. Their marriage was going the way of Grant's first two, which ended in divorce. According to the *Look* article, he was prone to depression, withdrawn, and had almost no close friends. His three wives all saw him grow emotionally distant from them. Drake first got him to try hypnotic therapy, which helped him curtail smoking and drinking but left the underlying difficulties intact.

The results of Grant's LSD therapy were dramatic. According to *Good Housekeeping*, "Almost at once he began to learn things about himself that he had not known—or, perhaps, had not wanted to know.... He became so excited over what he found out that he could not contain himself. His former aloofness vanished almost at once, for he literally was bowled over." He told a reporter that after the LSD sessions started working, he had "two immediate reactions. His first was, 'Oh, those wasted years; why didn't I do this sooner?' And the second reaction was, 'Oh, my God, humanity, please come on in.'" He realized that his problems stemmed from doubts and self-loathing that he had concealed effectively for so many years. "I was hiding behind all kinds of defenses, hypocrisies, and vanities," he said. "I had to get rid of them layer by layer." The therapy sessions put him in touch with memories and emotions that he had repressed; when he worked through them, he felt like a new man.

Of the two magazine accounts of Grant's therapy, *Good Housekeeping* was more skeptical than *Look* about his drug-catalyzed transformation. Richard Gehman, who wrote the *Good Housekeeping* piece, cautioned that "Grant's reported comments may be likened to those of someone in the early stages of psychoanalysis who, having scraped the surface of insight, may hastily conclude, out of resistance to—and fear of—going deeper, that he has skimmed off all there is to know." Near the end of his article, Gehman warned, "Readers of this magazine are advised emphatically that the use of LSD-25 is still in the experimental stages.... For some people, use of the drug would be dangerous." This caution notwithstanding, the story of Cary Grant gave LSD its first substantial publicity as a psychoanalytic tool.

When Timothy Leary met the actor in 1962, Grant reaffirmed the importance of LSD in his life, and he mentioned to Leary that "there was nothing he would rather do than a movie about LSD." All he needed was the right script: "Put on paper the grandeur and the splendor and the romance and the revelation of LSD, and then I'll be begging for a part in the movie."

Grateful Dead. During the height of San Francisco hippie culture, and for decades thereafter, the Grateful Dead was the quintessential psychedelic rock band. Living communally in a Victorian house on Ashbury St. (see *Haight-Ashbury*), they played concerts at all the famous San Francisco venues and most of the signature hippie events. Posters designed for their concerts became some of the most enduring psychedelic icons (see *Psychedelic Posters*). Core members of the band included lead guitarist Jerry Garcia, rhythm guitarist Bob Weir, bass player Phil Lesh, drummer Bill Kreutzmann (later joined by Mickey Hart), and keyboard player Ron "Pig Pen" McKernan (succeeded by a handful of others).

At first they played traditional music as "Mother McCree's Uptown Jug Champions." When they started taking LSD, Garcia said, everything changed dramatically: "The whole world went kablooey" (see *Garcia, Jerry*). The band changed their name to The Warlocks and began playing electric music. In 1965 and 1966 The Warlocks—soon to be renamed the Grateful Dead—played at nearly all of the Acid Tests (see *Acid Test*). Their performances at the Acid Tests fundamentally shaped what became their signature psychedelic style. According to Bob Weir, "The Acid Tests were complete chaos with little knots of quasi-organization here or there that would occur and then dissipate.... There was a lot of straight-ahead telepathy that went on during those sessions. We learned during those sessions to trust our intuitions.... We learned to start improvising on just about anything" (*I Want to Take You Higher*). Typical Dead concerts consisted of songs from a wide variety of genres, including traditional blues and folk songs and early rock and roll standards. Often the Dead performed these songs with extended improvisational interludes. Many sets included medleys of two or more songs woven together. The band did not go into concerts with fixed plans for what they would play; as Garcia said, "We'd rather work off the tops of our heads than off a piece of paper." At the Acid Tests, the Dead were high on LSD when they played. Over the years they moderated and eventually discontinued their use of

LSD during performances. The drug crucially influenced their musical style, but as Garcia admitted, it usually hurt the quality of their performances.

A few of the Dead's original songs have lyrics with clear links to the psychedelic scene. Most of these lyrics were written by Robert Hunter, a poet who first took LSD in the Menlo Research Institute experiments (see *Hunter, Robert*). "That's It for the Other One," for example, refers to the Pranksters' bus and driver Neal Cassady (see *Merry Pranksters; Cassady, Neal*). Other songs have lyrics that are gently surreal in a way that is typical of acid rock, such as "China Cat Sunflower." "Dark Star," which combines both the surreal lyrical style and some of the Dead's most extended musical improvisations, became known among fans as their most ambitious attempt at psychedelic sublimity. The Dead performed countless versions of "Dark Star," often drawing it out to a length of half an hour. Singing the lyrics would take up only a minute or two of this time; for the rest of the performance, the Dead would improvise melodic riffs around the song's simple structure, try out different rhythms and instrumental tones, and experiment with digressive passages. In later years, as performances of the song became less frequent, Deadheads would hold up signs that said, "___ days since last Dark Star." When Jerry Garcia was asked by Charles Reich what "Dark Star" meant, he declined to answer: "I have a long continuum of Dark Stars which range in character from each other to real different extremes. 'Dark Star' has meant, while I'm playing it, almost as many things as I can sit here and imagine" (*Rolling Stone* interview). If the musical meanings of "Dark Star" are too various to be pinned down, the song's lyrics offer some hints. The title and many other images suggest a paradoxical world where light and knowledge mix with darkness and dissolution. The lyrics evoke a feeling of psych-edelic disorientation that is both attractive and scary. Hunter's chorus invites listeners to take one of those romantic adventures that come up frequently in psychedelic music. The destination is a transfigured other world, with dark stars reimagined as diamonds. However, the emphasis is on transitional threshold rather than destination. In "Dark Star," the vehicle for making this transition is the music improvised by the Dead, continually changing from performance to performance.

Loyal cohorts of fans ("Deadheads") followed the band for decades after psychedelic culture had passed its prime. The Grateful Dead and Deadheads kept that culture alive through concert tours, tapes of live shows, tie-dyed memorabilia, and a communal spirit that amounted to an ongoing, small-scale reincarnation of Woodstock. The Dead concert scene also contributed to keeping LSD in circulation. Experts have suggested that a marked decline in the availability and use of LSD in the later 1990s can be attributed to the death of Jerry Garcia in 1995 and the dissolution of the Grateful Dead.

Graves, Robert. The English poet, novelist, and translator—known best for *I, Claudius* and studies of classical mythology—tripped on Mexican hallucinogenic mushrooms in 1954. He was friends with Gordon Wasson, one of the first to write about mushroom rituals (see *Wasson, R. Gordon*). Unlike the American banker Wasson and fellow English man-of-letters Aldous Huxley (see *Huxley, Aldous*), Graves soon lost his appetite for psychedelic exploration. He never tried LSD. In an interview from the 1960s he sharply denounced LSD: "First of all it's dangerous, and secondly ergot, from which LSD is made, is the enemy of mankind.... LSD reminds me of the minks that escape from mink farms and breed in the forest and become dangerous and destructive. It has escaped from the drug factory and gets made in college laboratories" (Kersnowski).

Grey, Alex. One of the best known contemporary psychedelic artists, Grey first took

LSD in 1975 when he was 21 and attending art school in Boston. In an interview with David Ian Miller (*SFGate.com*, March 24, 2008), Grey described that first trip. A professor "offered me a bottle of Kahlua laced with a high dose of LSD. I drank a good deal of it. Tripping that night I experienced going through a spiritual rebirth canal inside of my head. I was in the dark, going towards the light, spinning in this tunnel, a kind of an opalescent living mother-of-pearl tube. All paradoxes were resolved in this tunnel— dark and light, male and female, life and death." Grey and his wife Allyson continued to take acid trips for many years in search of spiritual and artistic inspiration. He told Miller about one such trip when, blindfolded and listening to Bach, they discovered the "universal mind lattice": "Our identity with the physical body melted down into a kind of fountain and a ball of light that was connected with an infinite expanse of very similar balls of light; it seemed like the same kind of energy was running through all of us, and every other being and thing in the universe was one of these balls of light." Many of Grey's paintings show the influence of his LSD trips: they present translucent, brightly colored figures, archetypal symbols, and rays of light connecting all the images within the frame.

Griffin, Rick. One of the most important poster artists during the peak years of San Francisco psychedelic culture, Griffin moved to San Francisco shortly after he attended an Acid Test in Watts (see *Acid Test*). His graphic art attracted the attention of people organizing the Human Be-In (see *Human Be-In*), and they commissioned him to do a poster for the event. Soon he was creating concert posters for the Avalon Ballroom and other psychedelic venues. He also contributed artwork to the *Oracle* and *Zap Comix* (see *Oracle; Zap Comix*). Griffin's work was notable for its highly wrought lettering. Like other San Francisco poster artists, he tested the limits of legibility: the letters were read-

able, but only to initiates whose eyes had adjusted to psychedelic fluidity (see *Psychedelic Posters*). Griffin's letters were particularly challenging, as he elaborated the serifs and sometimes merged them with images on the poster. His images resonated with symbolic complexity. For example, in a design that became the album cover for the Grateful Dead's *Aoxomoxoa*, Griffin put a skull and crossbones at the focal center, but elsewhere drew smaller symbols of life—eggs, seeds, and squiggly solar flares that look like spermatozoa. Jimi Hendrix liked his image of a winged eyeball so much that he wanted to adopt it as a personal symbol. Griffin was a perfectionist who labored over every detail of his designs, and this painstaking process took its toll. According to fellow artist Randy Tuten, "Rick had more demons than all of us put together." In the 1970s he converted to Christianity and did religious artwork, including an illustrated version of the Gospel of John.

Grof, Stanislav. Freudian analyst Grof moved from Czechoslovakia to the U.S. in 1967 and became an advocate for the use of LSD in psychotherapy (see *Psychiatry*). In 1980 he published a major book on the subject, *LSD Psychotherapy: Exploring the Frontiers of the Hidden Mind.* In Grof's model, LSD lowers defenses and facilitates access to unconscious materials, especially memories of birth and early childhood. His therapeutic goal is to help patients process these materials and thereby alleviate neurotic symptoms. As work with LSD became impractical due to legal restrictions, Grof experimented with drug-free methods for achieving the therapeutic effects of LSD, mainly through controlled breathing and meditation. His first American appointment was at Johns Hopkins, but he later moved to positions in less traditional academic settings, including the Esalen Institute and the California Institute of Integral Studies.

Grogan, Emmett. A founding member of the Diggers, Grogan became their most cynical prophetic voice: he complained that the hippie movement had been co-opted by mainstream media and commerce. See *Diggers; Summer of Love*.

Gunn, Thom. When he came to San Francisco in the middle of the 1960s, Gunn had already established himself as one of the most accomplished young poets in England. In San Francisco, he participated enthusiastically in the acid counterculture of the city. Gunn credited LSD with enriching his poetry, his life, and his knowledge of himself. In 1965 he began to write a series of poems, later published in a collection entitled *Moly*, which reflected the influence of LSD on his poetic imagination. The title refers to the magical plant given by Hermes to Odysseus. Circe had turned his men into swine, and moly would protect Odysseus from the same fate. The parallel is clear enough: like moly, LSD has magical powers to elevate consciousness, to prevent against entrapment in a lower state of being. In *The Occasions of Poetry* (1982), Gunn recalled the excitement of the 1960s in San Francisco. He felt that life had suddenly become fuller, "crowded with discovery both inner and outer": "We tripped at home, on rooftops, at beaches and ranches; some went to the opera loaded on acid, other tried it as passengers on gliders, every experience was illuminated by the drug. These were the fullest years of my life, crowded with discovery both inner and outer, as we moved between ecstasy and understanding. It is no longer fashionable to praise LSD, but I have no doubt at all that it has been of the utmost importance to me, both as a man and as a poet."

A few of the *Moly* poems refer to LSD directly, but most of them leave the connection implicit. One poem that does mention LSD is "At the Centre," the most ambitious poem in the collection. Gunn develops a latter day Romantic ode with echoes of Wordsworth, Shelley, and Yeats, as well as Milton and Genesis. Focusing on the neon sign for Hamm's beer that hangs over San Francisco, he reflects on an ineffable presence that manifests itself to the tripping poet. He eventually returns from these moments of inspiration and sublimity to a comfortable gathering of friends around the kitchen table. Having glimpsed the cosmic center that is everywhere, he returns to a home where he feels newly centered. As a postscript to the poem, Gunn acknowledges his muse: "*LSD, Folsom Street.*"

Haggard, Merle. In 1969, Haggard wrote and performed "Okie from Muskogee," a catchy country song that rejected LSD and the unpatriotic hippies who were tripping on it. The song became a huge hit and won country music's top award. Two years later the Youngbloods replied with "Hippie from Olema," a defense of hippie values that never caught on. At about the same time, the Grateful Dead made gestures toward a reconciliation of psychedelic and country music: they began to play some of Haggard's songs, most notably "Mama Tried," which became part of their regular repertoire. In one 1971 concert, they even performed "Okie from Muskogee."

Haight-Ashbury. The San Francisco neighborhood named for the intersection of Haight St. and Ashbury St. became the capital of hippie counterculture during the psychedelic era. The area was full of Victorian houses that had fallen into decline during the 1950s, which provided a cheap and colorful supply of housing for the psychedelic community that began to gather there in the mid–1960s. Charles Perry has described Haight-Ashbury of that time as "basically the biggest LSD party in history." As stories about hippie life proliferated in the national media, tens of thousands of young people traveled to Haight-Ashbury in hopes of joining an anti-establishment utopia. For them, the Haight stood for a carnival-like exemption from normal identity and conventions, and offered opportunities for subversive political theater, free love, good music, and plenty of mind-altering drugs (especially marijuana and LSD).

The original Haight counterculture of a few thousand neo-Beats proved too attractive for its own good: the so-called "Summer of Love" in 1967 drew so many young people with so little means of support that the resources of Haight-Ashbury were overwhelmed (see *Summer of Love*). Living conditions deteriorated and crime increased, in part because many of the new inhabitants were using addictive drugs like speed and heroin. Although many of the original hippies chose to move away from Haight-Ashbury when conditions declined, the Diggers continued their efforts to supply food and other social services (see *Diggers*). Dr. David Smith founded the Haight-Ashbury Free Clinic to provide medical care for those who would otherwise have none (see *Smith, David*). In post-psychedelic decades, Haight-Ashbury saw changes resulting from gentrification, but it has retained a bohemian atmosphere. Various boutiques, restaurants, and bars keep alive the memory of the few years when the neighborhood was synonymous with countercultural dreams of a new order. At the actual intersection of Haight and Ashbury, hippie-friendly entrepreneurs Ben and Jerry opened up one of their ice cream shops (see *Ben and Jerry's*); this was the place where Grateful Dead fans gathered to mourn Jerry Garcia in 1995, only a block away from the Victorian house where the Dead lived communally from 1966 to 1968.

Hair. This controversial Broadway musical from the psychedelic era featured a tribe of New York City hippies who sang about Aquarian values, pacifism, and their appreciation for mind-expanding drugs, including LSD. In one scene, a character takes a trip as the others act out his psychedelic visions, accompanied by the song "Walking in Space." *Hair* had a successful original run starting in 1968 and won a Tony Award when it was revived on Broadway in 2009.

Hallucinogen. Although Humphry Osmond and Aldous Huxley objected to calling LSD a "hallucinogen" because it emphasizes a pathological symptom, this label for LSD and similar drugs remains in common use. See *Psychedelic*.

Harrison, George. Harrison's dentist gave him his first dose of LSD at a dinner party in 1966. Without telling anyone, he spiked the coffee he served to Harrison, John Lennon, and their wives (see *Beatles*). Although this first trip was inadvertent, it turned him into a psychedelic enthusiast. As he recalled many years later, LSD dramatically changed his life. He had been suffering from the pressures of celebrity, and his psychedelic experience offered immediate psychological help: "The whole world opened up and had a greater meaning. Up until LSD, I never realized that there was anything beyond this state of consciousness. I had such an overwhelming feeling of well-being, that there was a God, and I could see him in every blade of grass. It changed me, and there was no way back to what I was before" (DeCurtis). Harrison's changes were musical as well as psychological. He developed an interest in Hindu philosophy and Indian culture, which began to influence his music. For his major contribution to *Sergeant Pepper's Lonely Hearts Club Band* (1967), "Within You Without You," Harrison joined Indian musicians playing sitar and related percussive instruments. The song's lyrics reflect Hindu ideas that resonated with Harrison's psychedelic revelations, especially the idea that our normal perceptual world is an illusion.

Hartman, Mortimer A. Hartman and partner Arthur Chandler were psychiatrists practicing in Beverly Hills who experimented extensively with LSD as an aid to psychotherapy. In 1960 they published a study in *Archives of General Psychiatry* which tracked dozens of their patients, including actor Cary Grant and his wife (see *Grant, Cary; Grant, Betsy*). In the study published by Hartman and Chandler, they concluded that LSD helps to "release repressed material" and to "increase insight." Of 110 patients treated with LSD, only 22 showed no notable improvement. Patients who were "closest to 'normal' emotional health to begin with" fared particularly well, as did alcoholics. Hartman and Chandler did list some disadvantages with LSD therapy. The most mundane disadvantage was a matter of time and money: these sessions last longer and cost more. A more intangible disadvantage involved "Philosophical Insights," with patients claiming to know profound truths about life and love. They warned about one version of post-session "acting out," when the patient "feels that he has discovered the answer to everything, that he has acquired philosophical insights into the meaning of life, the nature of the universe, etc." These practical psychiatrists dismissed as a distraction all the cosmic sublimities that would become staples of psychedelic culture only a few years later.

Harvard. Harvard University has a strong claim as the birthplace of American psychedelia. Timothy Leary arrived at Harvard in 1959 as a full-time lecturer (see *Leary, Timothy*). His colleague Frank Barron told him about their predecessors in Harvard psychology who worked in some fashion with altered states of consciousness (see *Barron, Frank*); as Leary writes in *Flashbacks,* he got the feeling that he "was being initiated into a secret order of Cambridge Illuminati." At the time Leary got there, one prominent Harvard psychologist was Henry Murray, a former military intelligence officer who classified various elements that influence states of mind and psychological outcomes (see *Murray, Henry*). Intrigued by Leary's project, Murray himself took LSD in 1961, out of "curiosity and the envisaged possibility that I might revel in a little efficacious lunacy." He took the subject seriously enough to sponsor the research group to which Leary was attached. That research group met in a building called "Morton Prince House," in honor of another Harvard psychologist. Prince was more eccentric than Murray, but he was influential in the earlier twentieth

century for his work on special states of consciousness. And back one more generation, Harvard housed the great William James, pillar of American pragmatism and one of the founders of modern psychology. James was born too early for LSD, but he did try peyote once; his delicate stomach betrayed him on that occasion, but he had more success with nitrous oxide: he inhaled the drug and found the mental effects immensely interesting. Like Leary many decades later, James encouraged his colleagues to experiment with psychotropic drugs for the intellectual exhilaration. "I strongly urge others to repeat the experiment," he wrote. "With me, as with every other person of whom I have heard, the keynote of the experience is the tremendously exciting sense of an intense metaphysical illumination. Truth lies open to the view in depth beneath depth of almost blinding evidence."

Generations later, Harvard nurtured Leary's psychedelic research group. Michael Hollingshead recalls the gist of the Harvard Research Project (see *Hollingshead, Michael*): it consisted of some forty faculty and graduate students "who had sensed in the psychedelic experience a new tool with which to shape and extend their awareness of the world and the other people in it. And their claims on behalf of LSD were highly articulate, and perhaps tinged with a fervor usually associated with religious belief." The more traditional guardians of Harvard's reputation suspected that their research was lightweight and their purpose as much recreational as scholarly. One of the most vocal critics was David McClelland, the psychology professor who had appointed Leary in the first place: "Many reports are given of deep mystical experiences, but their chief characteristic is the wonder at one's own profundity rather than a genuine concern to probe deeper into the experience of the human race in these matters."

Before they got rid of Leary, one of his graduate students conducted a daring experiment with psychedelic drugs and "deep mystical experiences." Walter Pahnke, a graduate student in theology at the Harvard Divinity School, devised a double-blind experiment to test the entheogenic properties of hallucinogens. Pahnke gathered a group of twenty divinity students, none of whom had ever taken a hallucinogen. On Good Friday, 1962, in the setting of a chapel service, he gave ten of them psilocybin and the other ten an active placebo. The Good Friday Experiment produced the results that Pahnke and Leary had anticipated: among the students who received psilocybin, nine out of ten reported a significant spiritual experience and were eager to try it again (see *Pahnke, Walter; Religion*).

Leary's supervisors at Harvard were not impressed. McClelland linked the Leary group with what he considered the failings of Indian culture: "It is probably no accident that the society which most consistently encouraged the use of these substances, India, produced one of the sickest social orders ever created by mankind in which thinking men spent their time lost in the Buddha position under the influence of drugs exploring consciousness, while poverty, disease, social discrimination, and superstition reached their highest and most organized form in all history." In 1963 Harvard ousted Leary, who moved elsewhere to promote his psychedelic version of Buddhism.

Head. This 1968 movie starring the Monkees satirized psychedelic themes in contemporary music. See *Monkees*.

Headaches. In 2006, two researchers from Harvard Medical School conducted a study of LSD and psilocybin as possible remedies for the condition known as cluster headache. Cluster headache is rare but causes recurring episodes of debilitating pain. John Halpern of Harvard took up the subject after one of his colleagues committed suicide because of suffering caused by such headaches. Halpern and Andrew Sewell studied 53 people with the condition who had tried LSD or psilocybin in an attempt to treat their headaches. Because LSD and psilocybin are classified as Schedule I drugs (see *Laws*), Halpern and Sewell could not conduct a clinical trial; instead, they studied a group of subjects who had previously self-medicated with the illegal hallucinogens. These people had heard or read anecdotal evidence that psychedelics might help. Halpern and Sewell published the results in *Neurology*, where they offered the following conclusion: "Our observations suggest that psilocybin and LSD may be effective in treating cluster attacks, possibly by a mechanism that is unrelated to their hallucinogenic properties." Although they caution that their study "should not be misinterpreted as an endorsement of the use of illegal substances for self-treatment," they considered the results promising enough to apply for a proper clinical trial.

Health Risks. Although LSD brings no significant threats to physical health and is not addictive, use of the drug has been associated with various risks, most of them psychological in nature. One demonstrated physical risk relates to uterine contractions. Early testing by Sandoz (see *Sandoz*) indicated that LSD may stimulate contractions and should be avoided by pregnant women. Four other categories of risk have been studied: chromosome damage, flashbacks, bad trips, and LSD psychosis. Of these four, only chromosome damage has been effectively dismissed as a danger. Early experiments linking LSD use with chromosome breakage were corrected in subsequent, more careful studies, and there is no current evidence to suggest that LSD causes birth defects or increases the risk of cancer (see *Chromosomes*).

Flashbacks are the popular term for "Hallucinogen Persisting Perception Disorder" (see *Flashbacks*). *DSM-IV* defines HPPD as "the transient recurrence of disturbances in perception that are reminiscent of those experienced during one or more earlier hallucinogen." Visual disturbances may include the appearance of geometric forms, flashes of intense color, stroboscopic effects, and halos around objects. "The abnormal perceptions associated with HPPD occur episodically and may be self-induced (e.g., by thinking about them) or triggered by entry into a dark environment, various drugs, anxiety or fatigue or other stressors" (*DSM-IV*). People experiencing HPPD retain proper "reality testing": in other words, they recognize that their perceptions are being caused by drug-related changes in sensory processing, not by any changes in the objective world. HPPD episodes can be minor and brief, with minimal disruption of a person's life, or severe and persistent. Estimates vary considerably regarding how many people are affected by HPPD, with suggestions ranging from 10 percent to 50 percent of LSD users. No definitive studies have been done.

Bad trips, known colloquially as "bummers" (see *Bummer*), are the most common risk associated with LSD use. Even people who have experienced several pleasant acid trips can find themselves suddenly in the midst of a bad one. Bad trips can develop from any number of circumstances of set and setting, and may revolve around various themes of distress, but they usually bring an intensification of anxiety, paranoia, or depression. People experiencing bad trips may find themselves panicking and unable to stop the emotional acceleration overwhelming their common sense. Perceptual alterations caused by LSD, including visual and auditory distortions or even hallucinations, often aggravate the negative emotions. Trippers' panic and perceptual confusion may lead to poor judgments that put them at physical risk. Contrary to legend, however, LSD trippers have not shown an inordinate tendency to jump out windows or blind themselves by staring at the sun.

In his 1960 study of LSD risks, Dr. Sidney Cohen (see *Cohen, Sidney*) suggested that two types of subjects were more vulnerable to bad trips: "those with excessive initial apprehension," and those who have "rigid but brittle defensive structures or considerable subsurface guilt and conflict." Medical authorities recommend two types of treatment for people in distress from a bad acid trip. The simplest therapy is to have a companion offer comfort—to assure them that there is no threat to their physical well being, that their distress is being created by their minds and can be reshaped with a little help from a friend, and that the trip will be over in a few hours. Many LSD veterans recommend that a trip "guide" or "babysitter" be appointed to serve as counselor for anyone who starts showing signs of a bad trip. A second form of therapy is to counteract the effects of LSD with a strong sedative or antipsychotic drug. Thorazine (chlorpromazine) has given way to Risperdal (risperidone) as the preferred antipsychotic for this purpose.

A fourth risk is loosely called "LSD psychosis": these are episodes of serious mental dysfunction following an LSD experience, with more long-lasting effects than a simple bad trip. Studies indicate that such episodes are rare, and that the people affected are likely to have either a history of or genetic predisposition for serious conditions like schizophrenia or bipolar disorder. Experts believe that LSD does not "cause" these psychotic episodes in a strict sense, but it may trigger a condition that had been latent up to that point. Psychiatrists who used LSD in therapy recommended that patients be screened for such vulnerabilities and carefully supervised during the psychedelic sessions. Sidney Cohen and several of his colleagues worried that the unsupervised, recreational use of the drug during the later 1960s would increase the likelihood of serious psychological consequences. There were two incidents in which a public figure apparently committed suicide as a result of LSD psychosis: Frank Olson, a CIA scientist, and Diane Linkletter, daughter of television personality Art Linkletter (see *Olson, Frank; Linkletter, Diane*). In both cases, the linkage between LSD and suicide remains controversial, and studies of psychiatric subjects have shown no definitive correlation between LSD use and an increased risk of suicide.

Heard, Gerald. Heard was an English intellectual who became one of the early experimenters with LSD in the 1950s. He learned of the drug from psychiatric researchers; when he took it himself, he came to believe not only in its therapeutic value but its potential to catalyze the mental evolution of humanity. He and friend Aldous Huxley tripped together and theorized about LSD's psychological and philosophical implications (see *Huxley, Aldous*). When freelance researcher Michael Hollingshead approached Huxley for information about LSD, Huxley warned him that "it is much more potent than mescaline, though Gerald and I have used it with some quite astonishing results really" (quoted in Hollingshead; see *Hollingshead, Michael*). Heard wrote several books on topics related to psychedelic consciousness and evolution.

Hell's Angels. In 1965, Hunter S. Thompson introduced Ken Kesey to the notorious Hell's Angels motorcycle gang (see *Thompson, Hunter S.; Kesey, Ken*). Thompson had been associating with the Angels as he gathered information for *Hell's Angels*, his first book. Kesey liked the Angels he met and decided to invite the whole group to one of his Prankster parties at his house in La Honda, California (see *Merry Pranksters*). As Thompson pointed out, Kesey's invitation was risky, given his recent drug arrests: "His association with the Hell's Angels was not calculated to calm his relationship with the forces of law and decency, but he pursued it nonetheless, and with overweening zeal."

On the day of the party, the Pranksters hung a big sign over the gate to Kesey's property: "THE MERRY PRANKSTERS WELCOME THE HELL'S ANGELS." The Angles rolled into La Honda on their motorcycles. Their presence attracted the attention of local police, who parked just outside the property and watched. What they saw was a typical Prankster psychedelic party supplemented by some thirty bikers who were taking acid for the first time. "Contrary to all expectations," Thompson wrote, "most of the Angels became oddly peaceful on acid. With a few exceptions, it made them much easier to get along with. The acid dissolved many of their conditioned reflexes." Poet Allen Ginsberg described the event in "First Party at Ken Kesey's with Hell's Angels": he ends the poem by folding the four police cars into the party landscape, their revolving lights just another psychedelic decoration. The police annoyed but did not deter the Angels, many of whom became dedicated acidheads. Thompson theorized that they were attracted to the drug as "a cure for boredom, a malady no less prevalent among Hell's Angels than any other segment of the Great Society."

Eventually the Angels drifted away from the Pranksters, although they remained a part of the psychedelic scene. At the Altamont music festival in 1969, which was held in the Bay Area not long after Woodstock, members of the Hell's Angels acted in some semi-official capacity to guard the stage (see *Altamont*). The Angels used roughhouse tactics with concertgoers, punched a member of the Jefferson Airplane, and ended up killing a man whom they thought had threatened them. The documentary film *Gimme Shelter* (1970) chronicles the event and tries to sort out the violence sparked by the Angels' presence. Altamont was seen by many as the tragic counterpart of Woodstock, marking an end of the utopian innocence associated with the earlier hippie festival.

Helms, Chet. Helms was one of the leading figures in the psychedelic music scene that developed in San Francisco during the later 1960s. Helms came to San Francisco in 1962, having hitchhiked from Texas in the spirit of Kerouac and the Beats. Helms lived in Haight-Ashbury, where he met up with several proto-hippies like himself; soon he began organizing informal dance parties in the basement of an old Haight-Ashbury house. By the beginning of 1966, Helms and his friends were calling themselves "Family Dog Productions" and sponsoring concerts at the Avalon Ballroom (see *Family Dog; Avalon Ballroom*). At first, Helms teamed up with Bill Graham to produce concerts at the Fillmore Auditorium (see *Graham, Bill; Fillmore*), but Helms soon left the Fillmore to Graham and settled at the Avalon. Helms and Graham had very different styles as promoters. Graham was a practical and careful businessman; Helms, in the words of Grateful Dead's Mickey Hart, "was a hippie. He hated to charge for the music." The Avalon venue was small, security was lax, and the concerts had the feel of large hippie parties.

Helms hosted all of the major San Francisco bands at the Avalon, along with many lesser known local acts. He founded Big Brother and the Holding Company and persuaded his Texas friend Janis Joplin to come sing for them. Like Graham, he employed poster artists to advertise his shows in high psychedelic style (see *Psychedelic Posters*). At the end of 1968, Helms ceased operations at the Avalon. Although it was Graham whose concert business flourished well beyond the peak years of Haight-Ashbury, Helms was held in high regard by the bands and their audiences. According to Barry Melton of Country Joe and the Fish, Helms "wasn't just a promoter, he was a supporter of music and art. He really made the scene what it was."

Helms, Richard. Helms conceived of the drug testing program that became MK-Ultra (see *MK-Ultra*). In the early 1950s, he and other CIA officials worried about Soviet and Chinese use of mind-altering drugs to brainwash prisoners or intelligence agents. They heard about LSD and decided to test its potential as a weapon for the Cold War. In a 1978 interview with David Frost, Helms recalled, "We had learned that something

called LSD had been discovered in Switzerland by a scientist named Hofmann. It was tasteless, odorless, and colorless and taken even in small quantities created a kind of schizophrenia.... We felt it was our responsibility not to lag behind the Russians or the Chinese in this field." MK-Ultra continued until the mid 1960s. When Helms was CIA Director in 1973, he ordered the destruction of all documents related to the program; however, enough survived to fuel the 1975 Congressional investigations that exposed MK-Ultra .

"Helter Skelter." LSD Svengali Charles Manson interpreted several Beatles' songs as sending him clues about the apocalyptic racial war to come (see *Manson, Charles*). Foremost among these songs was "Helter Skelter" from the White Album in 1968. Manson heard the title as a reference to the imminent war, and thereafter he used the phrase as his code name for the conflict. As Manson understood the song, the Beatles were confirming the impending chaos and directing him to the place where he and his followers should retreat for safety: Death Valley, the lowest point in the United States. Saner listeners recognized that the Beatles were referring to an amusement park slide, but Manson's charismatic hermeneutics persuaded his family. Another Beatles' song that he fixed on was "Yellow Submarine," which inspired the psychedelic movie that came out at the same time as "Helter Skelter" (see *"Yellow Submarine"*). Manson and his family moved into a yellow house in southern California that he dubbed "Yellow Submarine"; as with Death Valley, this would be a place where they could hide beneath the surface world and avoid detection. When the Manson murders were committed in 1969, one of the family wrote "Healter [sic] Skelter" in blood on the refrigerator in the victims' kitchen.

In a 1971 interview with *Rolling Stone*, John Lennon shrugged off Manson's craziness but compared his interpretive approach to that of earnest fans: Manson "is balmy, like any other Beatles-kind of fan who reads mysticism into it. We used to have a laugh about this, that, or the other, in a light-hearted way, and some intellectual would read us, some symbolic youth generation wants to see something in it." See *Beatles*.

Hendrix, Jimi. Hendrix had a significant influence on psychedelic music in the U.S. and the U.K. Although he warily down-played his use of LSD when questioned by interviewers, Hendrix took LSD frequently, and his music as well as his performance persona helped to define psychedelic style. In concert, his outfits exemplified high psychedelic fashion (see *Fashion*): velvet suits, brightly colored shirts, patterned waistcoats, and exotic accessories—including a pink feather boa that he wore at the Monterey Pop Festival in 1967. He did tricks with his guitar on stage, sometimes smashing or burning it at the end of a concert. Above all, Hendrix played guitar with rare virtuosity. He used extreme bending of notes, heavy wah-wah pedal and reverberation, and controlled feedback to produce a complex sonic texture that set the standard for psychedelic guitar work.

Hendrix' first album, *Are You Experienced?* (1967), quickly rose near the top of the charts, bested only by the Beatles' *Sergeant Pepper* (see *Beatles*). The hit single "Purple Haze" was particularly linked with his use of psychedelic drugs. This association derived in part from Hendrix' use of an acid named "Monterey Purple," which Owsley distributed at the Monterey Pop Festival (see *Owsley*). Soon enough "Purple Haze" became a slang term for this brand of LSD. Hendrix claimed that his inspiration for "Purple Haze" came from a dream he had of walking along the ocean floor, surrounded by a purple haze; the dream had been influenced by a science fiction novel he had been reading that used the phrase "purplish haze." Whatever the circumstances of his inspiration, the lyrics are suggestive of an acid

trip, with an emphasis on mental transformation and altered perceptions of space and time.

The double album *Electric Ladyland* (1968) has earned widespread praise as Hendrix' masterpiece. It was the only album over which he had complete creative control. "Electric" in the title implies not only the musical tools but the psychedelic drugs he was using (as in "electric kool-aid"). The title song, "Have You Ever Been (to Electric Ladyland)," proposes a trip to a psychedelic paradise where erotic pleasures abound. "1983" presents another version of psychedelic paradise, this time framed as an escape from apocalyptic ruin. *Electric Ladyland* includes a performance of "Voodoo Chile" in which Hendrix takes a simple blues pattern and transforms it with surreal lyrics and swirling guitar improvisations.

Hendrix' death at age 27 had nothing to do with his use of psychedelic drugs; like several of his contemporaries, he died from the effects of very different drugs, alcohol and barbiturates.

Hippie. Also spelled "hippy," this term for a member of the psychedelic counterculture derives from the adjective "hip." Although several ingenious theories about the etymology of "hip" have been proposed—including one associated with opium—scholars have found them unpersuasive, and the word's origin remains unknown. "Hip" or "hep" dates to the early twentieth century and was frequently used in reference to performers and devotees of jazz. "Hippie" amounts to "hip" with a diminutive suffix, as if to indicate a lesser version of hip coolness. The earliest uses of "hippie" date from the 1950s, as a variation of "hipster," a common term for Beatniks. In the later 1960s, it quickly caught on as the label for a new version of Beatnik bohemianism, the young people influenced more by psychedelic rock than jazz. As psychedelic culture faded, the derogatory slang term "hippie-dippie"—formed as a nonsense rhyming pair—referred to naïve or pretentious adherence to countercultural ideals.

Hitchcock, William Mellon. A nephew of Andrew Mellon, Billy Hitchcock used some of his resources to support Timothy Leary and the production of LSD. Hitchcock gave Leary the use of his estate in Millbrook, New York after Leary had been dismissed from Harvard (see *Leary, Timothy*). At the huge main house, Leary gathered a group of psychedelic pilgrims who lived communally and tripped frequently on the grounds of the estate. Hitchcock was loosely attached to the group but lived in a separate cottage and continued to work as a stockbroker. After Leary's group left in 1967, Hitchcock helped finance and organize an operation to manufacture LSD in California and Colorado: he underwrote Tim Scully and Nick Sand's LSD labs that produced Orange Sunshine, and helped arrange distribution through the Brotherhood of Eternal Love (see *Scully, Tim; Sand, Nick; Brotherhood of Eternal Love*). By 1973, law enforcement agents were closing in on the operation. When they threatened Hitchcock with prison on charges of tax evasion, he gave testimony that helped convict Scully and Sand.

Hoch, Paul. In 1959, the first major conference was held on the topic of LSD in psychotherapy. Prominent researcher Paul Hoch chaired the conference and was the most influential voice in shaping its skeptical conclusions about the utility of the drug. Although several psychiatrists reported promising results with LSD due to patients' enhanced self-awareness, Hoch maintained that the drug was fundamentally psychotomimetic, not psychedelic. As Lee and Schlain note, Hoch considered LSD an "anxiety-producing drug," likely to "stir up the patient's symptoms": "Dr. Hoch was incredulous when other participants in the Macy conference reported that their patients found the LSD session beneficial and personally rewarding and were usually eager to take the drug again. 'In my experience,' Hoch announced, 'no patient asks for it again.'" See *Psychiatry*.

Hoffer, Abram. Hoffer was a Canadian psychiatrist who worked with Humphry Osmond on clinical experiments with LSD (see *Osmond, Humphry; Psychiatry*). Starting in the 1950s, Hoffer and Osmond tried LSD therapy on patients with various symptoms; their most striking results came with alcoholics (see *Alcoholism*). Advocates of more orthodox methods disputed their claims, and Hoffer and Osmond found themselves increasingly marginalized in the psychiatric world.

Hoffman, Abbie. Political activist Hoffman regarded LSD as a tool for unsettling the establishment. "Aldous Huxley told me about LSD back in 1957," Hoffman recalled, "and I *tried* to get it in 1959," but was thwarted by a long line of volunteers for LSD testing at a San Francisco clinic (Stafford). He finally took his first trip in 1965. After his conviction in the trial of the Chicago Seven, when given a chance to address the court before sentencing, Hofmann recommended that Judge Julius Hoffman try LSD. He even offered to set the judge up with a dealer. The gesture did him no good at the hearing, although an appeals court later overturned his conviction. In 1970, Jefferson Airplane singer Grace Slick brought Hoffman as her date to a White House reception (see *Slick, Grace*). She had been invited to a reunion of Tricia Nixon's classmates. Slick and Hoffman plotted to smuggle in powdered LSD and spike the President's tea, but the Secret Service managed to turn the couple away without incident.

Hofmann, Albert. A scientist with the disposition of a mystic, Hofmann was well suited to discover LSD. He first synthesized LSD in 1938 at Sandoz Laboratories, hoping to find a drug that would improve circulation (see *Sandoz*). When tests on animals showed nothing promising, Sandoz abandoned LSD as a useless compound. But Hofmann's mystical side came out five years later to override this scientific decision. He said he felt a "premonition" that LSD was important; he used the German word *Vorgefuhl*, from the root for "feeling," as opposed to reasoning. When he made the chemical again, he accidentally gave himself a mild dose. He passed into "a dreamlike condition, in which all of my surroundings were transforming. My experience of reality had changed and it was rather agreeable" (interview with Stanislav Grof, 1984, MAPS website).

A few days later he deliberately took a larger dose. This second experience was much more intense and complex. Hofmann felt tremendous temporal and spatial disorientation as he bicycled home. He recalled for Grof, "I was in a very, very bad condition. It was such a strange reality, such a strange new universe which I had entered, that I believed I had now become insane." Eventually his panic abated, and his trip turned euphoric: "It was a very, very happy feeling and a very beautiful experience. After some time, with my eyes closed, I began to enjoy this wonderful play of colors and forms, which it really was a pleasure to observe. Then I went to sleep and the next day I was fine. I felt quite fresh, like a newborn.... I had the feeling that I saw the earth and the beauty of nature as it had been when it was created, at the first day of creation."

The world's first full-dose acid trip revealed the opposite poles for the psychedelic experience: the altered world as insanity, the altered world as paradise. Hofmann initially felt the insanity, which crucially influenced his ideas about LSD. He recognized how dangerous this drug could be for the wrong person in the wrong circumstances. But the very thing that made LSD dangerous also made it valuable as a tool for psychotherapy. Hofmann and his colleagues at Sandoz began testing it for this purpose, and they marketed it to psychiatrists as "Delysid" (see *Delysid*). Hofmann thought that Delysid would give psychiatrists a glympse into the perceptual

world of the mentally ill, and would help patients gain access to unconscious materials.

At the opposite pole, Hofmann's acid trip led to a mystical sense of intimacy with nature. Hofmann believed that LSD could help people reach a comparable state of natural piety. His aspirations for LSD went beyond psychotherapy to spiritual elevation. Near the end of his memoir, *LSD: My Problem Child*, he explained that the "true importance of LSD" lay in "the possibility of providing material aid to meditation aimed at the mystical experience of a deeper, comprehensive reality." In later years, he studied the organic hallucinogens used in various cultures for sacred rituals, and he helped to generate the psychedelic theory of the Eleusinian Mysteries (see *Eleusinian Mysteries*).

As much as Hofmann respected the spiritual potential of LSD, he feared, even resented, its misuse by reckless enthusiasts (most notably Timothy Leary). He told Grob that he hoped LSD and other psychedelic drugs would one day become legal again, "but as long as they continue to be misused, and as along as people fail to truly understand psychedelics and continue to use them as pleasure drugs and fail to appreciate the very deep, deep psychic experience they may induce, then their medical use will be held back."

Hofmann died in 2008 at the age of 102, but not before he had a chance to witness a special celebration of "Bicycle Day," fifty years after he pedaled home while tripping on acid. On April 19, 1993, 25 Swiss bicyclists rode the same route as thousands lined the streets and cheered.

Hollingshead, Michael. Hollingshead is the British freelance researcher who took a huge first dose of LSD in 1960 and spent the next several years promoting and experimenting with the drug. He heard about LSD from Aldous Huxley, who warned him that it was much stronger than mescaline. Hollingshead's friend Dr. John Beresford received a supply of the drug from Sandoz for his own research, and he gave Hollingshead one gram of it—enough for about 5000 doses (see *Beresford, John*). Hollingshead dissolved the powdered LSD in water and added confectioner's sugar to make a paste that looked like icing; he then used a spoon to transfer the paste to a mayonnaise jar. According to his autobiography *The Man Who Turned on the World*, "I should add at this point that I had, like all good chefs, been tasting the preparation during its making with my finger, and must have absorbed about the equivalent of five heavy doses." He tripped for fifteen hours looking out from a New York City rooftop. "I had literally 'stepped forth' out of the shell of my body," he recalled, "into some other strange land of unlikeliness, which can only be grasped in terms of astonishment and mystery, an ecstatic nirvana."

Hollingshead took his electric mayonnaise around America and England to let others share his astonishment. He was the first to give LSD to Timothy Leary (see *Leary, Timothy*), whom he later joined at Millbrook to live in a psychedelic commune. Many musicians, poets, and academics reportedly received their first acid from Hollingshead.

Holy Modal Rounders. In 1964, the folk group Holy Modal Rounders recorded a version of Leadbelly's "Hesitation Blues" with an interesting addition: for the last verse, they substituted "psychedelic" for "hesitation" as the word describing the singer's blues. This was the first use of Humphry Osmond's neologism in popular music (see *Psychedelic*).

Homosexuality. Until 1973, the psychiatric profession classified homosexuality as a form of mental illness. Psychiatrists of the 1950s and 1960s who were experimenting with LSD therapy reported some success in changing the attitudes and behaviors of many patients who had been diagnosed with this supposed illness. In many cases, these psychiatrists emphasized a goal of bringing their patients around to "normal" heterosexuality: in this sense, LSD was credited with helping to "cure" homosexuality. However, psychiatrists recognized that LSD therapy

helped some patients resolve the guilt and uncertainties surrounding their homosexual desires. For these patients, LSD facilitated an acceptance of homosexuality as their natural identity.

Timothy Leary helped to publicize the use of LSD in therapy for homosexuality. As biographer Robert Greenfield explains, "Ignoring his own conspicuous lack of success in using LSD to 'treat' Richard Alpert for homosexuality, Tim posited LSD as a 'specific cure for homosexuality.'" Leary believed that homosexuality was caused by childhood trauma; LSD would help patients gain access to repressed memories and resolve their sexual confusion. Leary had no luck with his close friend Alpert, but he did claim that LSD had "cured" Allen Ginsberg: "The most famous and public of such cases is Allen Ginsberg, who has openly stated that the first time he turned on to women was during an LSD session several years ago."

Despite the strong preference for "cure" in a world that still regarded homosexuality as an illness, psychiatrists recognized the other outcome—patients embracing their supposedly unhealthy sexuality—as a valid therapeutic result. As one group of Canadian psychiatrists wrote about their work with LSD therapy, "Many [homosexuals] have derived marked benefit in terms of insight, acceptance of role, reduction of guilt and associated liabilities" (Stafford and Golightly).

Hopkins, John. Hopkins was a photographer and political activist who played an important role in the development of London's psychedelic culture. Among his many activities, he co-founded two significant countercultural institutions: the underground publication *International Times* and the psychedelic UFO Club (see *UFO Club*). Hopkins considered LSD a useful tool in the struggle for social progress. He said about acid trips, "The effect is to kick your frame of reference and give it a good shake. [Taking LSD] helps us recognize we're all part of the same tribe."

Hopper, Dennis. Hopper began experimenting with LSD while he was working on the 1967 movie *The Trip*, written by Jack Nicholson and starring Peter Fonda as a first-time tripper. Hopper played the supporting role of a druggy acquaintance. In 1969 Hopper co-starred with Fonda and Nicholson in *Easy Rider*, which he also directed. *Easy Rider* includes an important scene depicting an acid trip taken by the Hopper and Fonda characters. See *Trip; Easy Rider; Fonda, Peter; Nicholson, Jack*.

Houston, Jean. Through her interests in psychology and mythic archetypes, Houston became involved with LSD in the mid 1960s. She and husband Robert Masters conducted studies of people who took LSD and other psychedelics (see *Masters, Robert*). In 1966 they co-authored *The Varieties of Psychedelic Experience*, the most thorough account of trippers' experiences then available (see *Varieties of Psychedelic Experience*). Houston and Masters also wrote *Psychedelic Art* (1968). In *Varieties* they expressed their view that LSD could help expand consciousness "beyond its present limitations and on towards capacities not yet realized and perhaps undreamed of." Although she remained active in New Age approaches to human potential, Houston later became disillusioned with psychedelia and what she viewed as the irresponsible promotion of LSD by Leary and others. "Some say it is a shortcut to reality," she said. "But the fact is, it doesn't seem to sustain that reality" (Horgan).

Hubbard, Al. Hubbard was a legendary figure from the early years of LSD who is often referred to as the psychedelic "Johnny Appleseed." He first read about LSD in a 1951 paper by an English scientist who had done experiments with rats; Hubbard contacted the researcher and received a sample for his own use. His first trip left him greatly impressed with the psychological and spiritual potential of the drug. For the rest of his life, he made it his mission to supply LSD to the U.S. and Canada and promote its use in the two countries where he lived and worked.

It is not clear whether or to what extent Hubbard participated in the secret CIA experiments with LSD that began in the early 1950s and continued into the mid–1960s (see *MK-Ultra*, code name for this experimental program). The CIA programs funded much of the clinical work being done with LSD at the time, but their purpose was primarily to determine its usefulness as a mind-control weapon for the Cold War battlefields of interrogation. Hubbard, an enthusiast for consciousness expansion but also a covert employee of the CIA, had affiliations with the two contrary agendas governing experimental work with LSD: acid as an aid to mental health, acid as a tool for manipulating minds. Because many relevant documents have been destroyed, details of his CIA work and any possible connections to MK-Ultra have remained sketchy.

Hubbard took a position at the Stanford Research Institute as part of their "Alternative Futures" think tank of the late 1950s and early 1960s. Although his official title was "security guard," he actually led LSD sessions for the assembled thinkers. Hubbard made an awkward fit with the prevailing left-wing ethos of the SRI. For all his psychedelic enthusiasm, the man some called "Captain Trips" was politically conservative; he once showed up at Leary's Millbrook estate wearing a military uniform with a Colt .45 at his hip. He remained a champion of psychedelia but never embraced the hippie lifestyle. Near the end of his life, in the late 1970s, Hubbard undertook one last mission on behalf of LSD: he tried, unsuccessfully, to persuade the FDA to allow the drug in therapy for terminal cancer patients (see *Dying*). He died in 1982.

Human Be-In. An organized gathering of hippies in San Francisco's Golden Gate Park on January 14, 1967, the Human Be-In set out to mark—and to defy—the new California law making LSD illegal. Owsley provided White Lightning acid free of charge; at one point a man parachuted into the park, tossing handfuls of it into the crowd. The Diggers supplied turkey sandwiches, also free of charge. Somewhere between 10,000 and 30,000 people attended the Human Be-In, and the event served more or less as the starting point for the Summer of Love. David Getz, drummer for Big Brother and the Holding Company, later distinguished between the Be-In and the Summer of Love: "The Human Be-In was a creation from within the San Francisco counterculture. The Summer of Love really was a creation of the national news media that befell San Francisco" (*Los Angeles Times,* Jan. 14, 2007).

The driving force behind the Be-In was painter Michael Bowen, who organized and named the event. He coined the name by analogy with civil rights sit-ins and teach-ins. The most difficult obstacle was getting a permit for tens of thousands of hippies to use the park. Bowen solved the problem by asking a favor of his friend Melvin Belli, the famous defense lawyer. Belli went to city hall and simply requested a permit to use the park for his birthday party. When Belli's "birthday party" turned into the Be-In, San Francisco police were angry, but it was too late. The very first issue of *San Francisco Oracle* spread the word about the upcoming "Gathering of the Tribes for a Human Be-In."

By all accounts, most of the people at the Be-In were tripping on LSD and smoking marijuana, but those were the only laws they broke. This was a peaceful event. Participant Elizabeth Gips recalled "women in lace tablecloths, long dresses of oriental fabric, fantasies from every age and place moved gracefully through the silent crowd. Men in pied patterns smiled at the sky. Everyone shared marijuana, apples, LSD and love.... Through the catalyst of LSD we had scratched through the surface of our separateness and recognized ourselves." Jefferson Airplane, Grateful Dead, and Quicksilver played music; Allen Ginsberg and other Beats-turned-hippies read poetry; and Timothy Leary delivered his

first San Francisco sermon about the virtues of psychedelic consciousness.

At an event that marked the 40th anniversary of the Human Be-In (January 14, 2007), panel discussions and nostalgia replaced the original dancing and love. And rock critic Joel Selvin joked about the LSD: "How many of you are on acid right now?" he asked reunioners. "How many of you are on antacid right now?"

Hunter, Robert. Robert Hunter was an important if unofficial member of the Grateful Dead, the quintessential and most enduring of psychedelic rock bands (see *Grateful Dead*). Hunter wrote lyrics for many of the best known Grateful Dead songs, mainly in collaboration with Jerry Garcia (see *Garcia, Jerry*). It was Hunter who first recommended that Garcia try LSD. Before the Grateful Dead had formed, Hunter participated in the CIA-funded Stanford experiments with hallucinogens. Like fellow writers Allen Ginsberg and Ken Kesey (see *Ginsberg, Allen; Kesey, Ken*), he was happy to alter his mind and get paid for it. His first LSD experience overwhelmed him. Hunter's trip notes were enthusiastic: "Picture yourself swooping up a shell of purple with foam crests of crystal drops soft nigh they fall unto the sea of morning creep-very-softly mist ... and then conglomerate suddenly into a peal of silver vibrant uncomprehendingly, blood singingly, joyously resounding bells. By my faith if this be insanity, then for the love of God permit me to remain insane." When Garcia took a look at his friend's notes, "his reaction was simple: 'God, I've *got* to have some of that'" (McNally).

The first song Hunter wrote in collaboration with the Dead was "Dark Star," which evolved into their signature psychedelic work. Before that, he had sent Garcia lyrics to "China Cat Sunflower"—which he wrote while tripping on LSD—along with a few other songs that became Grateful Dead staples. In his brief author's note to "China Cat Sunflower" from the collection *Box of*

Rain, Hunter coyly alludes to its psychedelic origins: "Nobody ever asked me the meaning of this song. People seem to know exactly what I'm talking about. It's good that a few things in this world are clear to all of us."

Huxley, Aldous. Huxley first took LSD in 1955, when Al Hubbard arranged the trip for him (see *Hubbard, Al*). Two years earlier, Huxley had taken his first hallucinogen, mescaline, under the supervision of psychiatrist Humphry Osmond (see *Osmond, Humphry*). Huxley wrote about his mescaline trip in *The Doors of Perception* (1954). He took the title from William Blake's *The Marriage of Heaven and Hell:* "If the doors of perception were cleansed, every thing would appear to man as it is, infinite." For Huxley, the hallucinogenic drugs enabled an ordinary mind to experience the mystical and artistic insights of extraordinary minds like Blake's. *The Doors of Perception,* usually published with a companion essay, *Heaven and Hell,* became one of the most influential books for the upcoming psychedelic era. The rock band "The Doors" took their name from Huxley's book (see *Doors*).

Huxley also wrote two novels that featured hallucinogenic drugs. In the earlier novel, *Brave New World,* "soma" is a mild hallucinogen made available to the general population as a way of keeping them complacent and obedient within their culture of consumption. The later novel *Island* imagines a hallucinogenic drug administered more carefully and for much nobler reasons. People are given "moksha" (made from mushrooms) at certain critical points of their lives, including when death is near. The drug is supposed to ease anxiety at this ultimate moment of transition, and at earlier moments of stress and transition, moksha acts as an aid to psychological well being. In both uses moksha resembles LSD, which was tested as therapy for the terminally ill and as an aid to psychotherapy generally. When Huxley inscribed a copy of *Island* for Albert Hofmann, he wrote, "To Dr. Albert Hofmann,

the original discoverer of the moksha medicine, from Aldous Huxley."

Huxley met with Timothy Leary in the early 1960s, and the two men agreed that the appropriate use of LSD would improve the human condition (see *Leary, Timothy*). Huxley was more reluctant than Leary to launch a widespread campaign to promote its use, but he was sympathetic with Leary's intentions. Huxley believed that LSD would help to free individuals from the narrow constraints of normal consciousness. In normal minds, Huxley theorized, a "reducing valve" keeps us focused on basic survival and prevents us from experiencing the world as something infinite and wonderful. Huxley acknowledged that psychedelic enlightenment might sometimes look like, or even turn into, a state of madness. But he believed that the benefits of LSD greatly outweighed the risks.

Huxley's last LSD trip came on his death bed. Around noon on December 22, 1963, he wrote a note to his wife Laura: "LSD: Try it: Intermuscular: 100 mm." She gave him the injection he requested, and an hour later, a second injection of equal strength. He died peacefully a few hours later.

Huxley, Laura. Laura Archera married Aldous Huxley in 1956. She and her husband shared an interest in psychedelic drugs as tools for improving psychological health, increasing aesthetic and ethical sensitivities, and reaching spiritual insights. Laura Huxley experimented with LSD in the 1950s and early 1960s. When Aldous was on his death bed in 1963, he asked Laura to inject him with LSD; she did so, and he died while under the influence of the drug (see *Huxley, Aldous*). In 1968 she published a memoir of their life together, *This Timeless Moment.* Her later writings were self-help books focused on strategies for improving happiness and creativity.

Laura Huxley had mixed feelings about LSD: she thought it held great promise, but she also acknowledged its dangers. In an interview with David Jay Brown ("Bridging Heaven and Earth"), she said, "If you take a psychedelic without preparation, it's risky. I know many kids do it, and sometimes it's OK, but then comes a time when it's not OK anymore, and it's difficult for many reasons." She told Brown that she favored continued regulation of LSD: "I think that if we had it all completely free again, abuse and damage would happen." She brought up the fact that twice she had administered LSD to people who were dying—her husband and one other person. "For Aldous it was very good," she said. "For the other person, it wasn't."

Hyde, Robert. Psychiatrist Hyde was one of the first Americans to take LSD. Max Rinkel, his colleague at Boston Psychopathic Institute, had brought back Delysid from Sandoz in 1949 (see *Delysid; Sandoz*). Rinkel asked Hyde to be the first guinea pig. The dose was modest, 100 micrograms, but after a while Hyde began showing uncharacteristic testiness and paranoia. He and Rinkel went on to conduct a full clinical trial. In 1950 they presented the first paper about LSD to the American Psychiatric Association: they theorized that the drug produces "transitory psychotic disturbances."

IFIF. Timothy Leary and Richard Alpert founded the International Foundation for Internal Freedom in 1962 in Cambridge, Massachusetts, shortly before they were both dismissed from Harvard (see *Leary, Timothy; Alpert, Richard; Harvard*). IFIF served as a gathering place for LSD enthusiasts and a non-academic sponsor for clinical psychedelic research. IFIF also published *Psychedelic Review*.

"In-A-Gadda-Da-Vida." This Iron Butterfly single was the most successful rock song of the psychedelic era. See *Iron Butterfly*.

"Incense and Peppermints." One of the most popular rock songs of the psychedelic era, this was the only notable hit for Strawberry Alarm Clock, although the band had reservations about the quality of the lyrics. See *Strawberry Alarm Clock*.

Internet. Timothy Leary was often quoted as saying, "the Internet is the LSD of the 90s." He first elaborated on this insight in a 1977 speech to the Libertarian Party Convention. As attendee Eric Garris recalls, Leary foresaw the rapid evolution of the internet and "said it would be the new revolution against the current social order and stifling status quo. He predicted it would be much, much bigger than drugs in its ability to overthrow the establishment" (quoted in Eisner). Champions of the Internet point to similarities with LSD: both the drug and the web enable a transformed sensorium, empower individuals to shake free from ideological assumptions, and foster a sense of interconnectedness. Recent books by John Markoff and Fred Turner have shown how significantly psychedelic culture influenced the development of computers and information technology. See *Gates, Bill; Jobs, Steve; Brand, Stewart*.

Iron Butterfly. This band was known mainly for one hugely successful song, "In-A-Gadda-Da-Vida," and the album of the same name. Keyboard player Doug Ingle founded and named the band in 1966. The "butterfly" part implied gentle hippie aesthetics and natural piety; "iron" suggested the rougher medium of electric instruments. "In-A-Gadda-Da-Vida" was released as a single in 1968 and stayed on the Billboard charts for nearly three years. The album of the same name, the second one produced by Iron Butterfly, sold so many copies that record executives invented a new category to mark the achievement: *In-A-Gadda-Da-Vida* received the first ever platinum album.

The song was written and sung by Doug Ingle, who founded and played keyboards for Iron Butterfly. There are differing accounts of how the song acquired its odd title, but two core facts are clear: Ingle intended the title to be "In the Garden of Eden," and the new title emerged accidentally—either because Ingle slurred the words, or because someone misheard "In the Garden of Eden" through imperfect headphones. However it came about, the band and record company embraced "In-A-Gadda-Da-Vida" as an attractively mysterious title that hinted of Eastern mysticism. The album version of the song ran over seventeen minutes and took up one whole side. Even cut to seven minutes for the single, "In-A-Gadda-Da-Vida" was unusually long for a song on the radio charts. The lyrics take up only a little of the time. Except for the exotic title phrase, the lyrics deliver an ordinary romantic formula: a man asks for a woman's hand and pledges his faithful love. Once past these lyrics, Iron Butterfly fills out the song with organ, guitar, and drum solos. The drum solo became particularly well known for its length and distinctive sound. Although most rock critics then and now prefer the instrumental inventions of other bands (including Jefferson Airplane, The Doors, and Jimi Hendrix, all of whom used Iron Butterfly as an opening act), "In-A-Gadda-Da-Vida" had the experimental, improvisational feel that characterized most psychedelic rock (see *Psychedelic Rock*). Some critics and performers have credited Iron Butterfly with leading the way toward heavy metal.

Izumi, Kiyo. As he was conducting clinical trials with LSD at a mental hospital in Saskatchewan, Humphry Osmond approached architect Kiyo Izumi with an unusual proposal: he wanted Izumi to take LSD, so that he might better understand what sort of interior spaces would suit the mentally ill (see *Osmond, Humphry*). Izumi agreed, and his psychedelic experience inspired him to redesign the hospital. He argued for a sociopetal design—that is, one that would encourage social interaction rather than walled-off privacy. Izumi also called for greater attention to small details of the patients' environment: "Administrators must be aware that what might be considered irrelevant minutiae of design can have traumatic effects on patients. Because of patients' heightened sensitivity to sensory stimuli and their lessened ability to filter out

or adjust to the effects of such stimuli, they are much more likely to be affected by their surroundings than are healthier people."

Jackson, Phil. The most successful coach in the history of the National Basketball Association, Jackson credited an LSD trip with enlightening him about the nature of team play. He tripped for the first time on the beach at Malibu in 1973, when he was a player for the New York Knicks. In his memoir *Maverick,* Jackson wrote that a "spiritual flash" during his acid trip led him to suppress his ego and recognize the deeper harmonies of a team playing as a unified entity. He later applied his psychedelic inspiration to coaching: in championship runs with first the Chicago Bulls and then the Los Angeles Lakers, he managed the egos of basketball's greatest players—Michael Jordan and Kobe Bryant—and helped them merge effectively with the players around them.

James, Tommy. James co-wrote and sang one of the best-selling singles of the psychedelic era, "Crimson and Clover" from 1969. The song had a distinctive wobbly sound that James produced by using his amplifier's tremolo effects for both guitar and vocals. At the height of the song's popularity, James and the Shondells performed it on the *Ed Sullivan Show* with appropriately psychedelic lighting (see *Ed Sullivan*). Rock critics generally held James's work in low regard compared with more ambitious psychedelic music. See *Psychedelic Rock*.

Janiger, Oscar. Janiger was a Los Angeles psychiatrist who conducted LSD studies from 1954–1962. Known affectionately as "Oz" (as in Wizard), he gave LSD to approximately 1000 people, several of whom were celebrities. Janiger conducted his experiments in a more comfortable setting than was typical for LSD research. Instead of taking the drug in a hospital, a prison, or a sterile medical office, his subjects used a room that opened into a garden. Among the many different types of people to whom he gave

LSD—men and women from all professions and trades, housewives, and college students—Janiger said that his fellow psychiatrist "tended to have negative experiences. The ministers were next. The artists had the most positive experiences" (Brown).

Janiger was particularly interested in the artists. He gave special emphasis in his studies to the effects of LSD on the creative process. In one key experiment, which he performed dozens of times, he asked subjects to draw or paint a Native American Kachina doll twice: once before they had taken acid, then again during their acid trip. In analyzing the results, Janiger "was struck by the fact that the paintings, under the influence of LSD, had some of the attributes of what looked like the work done by schizophrenics" (Brown). Janiger theorized that LSD gave subjects access to a reservoir of unconscious resources—resources that were ordinarily available only to schizophrenics and artists. If artists or LSD trippers successfully manage this influx of unconscious material without losing their grip on normal consciousness, they can reach insights of great psychological and religious significance. Janiger's work with artists was the subject of *LSD, Spirituality, and the Creative Process* (DeRios and Janiger).Janiger took LSD himself thirteen times. He told Brown that the experiences changed his life "profoundly." The acid trips "really took me out of a state in which I saw the boundaries of myself and the world around me very rigorously prescribed, to a state in which I saw that many, many things were possible." He was also among the first to take the hallucinogen DMT.

Jefferson Airplane. When the members of Jefferson Airplane were inducted into the Rock and Roll Hall of Fame, the official citation credited them with a central role in psychedelic culture: "In terms of music and lifestyle, the Jefferson Airplane epitomized the San Francisco scene of the mid-to-late Sixties. Their heady psychedelia, combustible group dynamic and adventuresome live shows made them one of the defining bands of the era.... In a sense, San Francisco became the American Liverpool, and Jefferson Airplane were its Beatles." This comparison with the Beatles exaggerates Jefferson Airplane's popularity, but their music did make more of an impression on the broad listening public than anything else from San Francisco acid rock. Two songs from the album *Surrealistic Pillow* (1967) reached the Top Ten in 1967: first "Somebody to Love," then "White Rabbit," which delivered a striking endorsement of psychedelic tripping. Rock critic Jon Savage has described "White Rabbit" as "explicit drug propaganda and one of the oddest records ever to reach the U.S. top ten." Songwriter and vocalist Grace Slick took elements from Lewis Carroll's books and linked Alice in Wonderland with psychedelic adventures (see *Carroll, Lewis; Alice in Wonderland*). "White Rabbit" does not mention LSD directly—only mushrooms, as in *Through the Looking-Glass,* and unspecified mind-altering pills—but Slick and her Jefferson Airplane colleagues were enthusiastic acidheads at the time. The lyrics describe a subversion of normal sensory perception. Musically, "White Rabbit" does not attempt any psychedelic effects to reinforce the message of its lyrics; the song builds quietly, with understated guitar and a rhythmic structure suggestive of "Bolero." But the climactic call for people to feed their heads confirms "White Rabbit" as a psychedelic anthem. Slick herself claimed many years later that she never intended "White Rabbit" to convey a pro-drug message (see *Slick, Grace*).

Of the five albums produced by Jefferson Airplane from 1967–1969, *Surrealistic Pillow* was the most successful and the most conventional. Besides the lyrics to "White Rabbit" and a few moments of instrumental and vocal complication, the album did not sound especially psychedelic. The next album, *After Bathing at Baxters,* offered much more pronounced psychedelic experimentation.

The title of the album referred to the house in Haight-Ashbury where the group was living communally and taking plenty of LSD. *After Bathing at Baxters* was organized as five "suites" instead of discrete (and more easily marketed) songs. Among its psychedelic risks, the album included a nearly ten-minute long instrumental piece improvised by guitarist Jorma Kaukonen and bassist Jack Casady ("Spare Chaynge"); experiments with feedback and other untraditional sounds; and lyrics that evoked the LSD scene of San Francisco in the Summer of Love ("Saturday afternoon"). *After Bathing at Baxters* annoyed the record company and began a decline in the band's popularity, but it confirmed the Airplane's status as psychedelic leaders.

Jefferson Airplane's last studio album, *Volunteers* (1969), retained elements of their high psychedelic style, but it also hinted at musical changes and the upcoming fragmentation of the band. Kaukonen was returning to his roots in acoustic blues. Songwriter Paul Kantner was moving away from psychedelic surrealism and showing more interest in politics, especially in the title song. Another song satirized hippie pieties associated with natural lifestyles and agrarian utopias. Soon the band split into new entities, including one that took the name "Jefferson Starship." Despite its spacier name, the Starship proved to be more conventional than the Airplane it replaced.

Jesuits. Several Jesuit priests took LSD trips in California during the early 1960s, including prominent theologian John Courtney Murray and Esalen stalwart Don Hanlon Johnson (see *Murray, John Courtney; Johnson, Don Hanlon; Esalen*). According to Jeffrey Kripal, Murray and Johnson were two "among many Jesuits who experimented with LSD to catalyze their thought, meditation, and artistic endeavours." Murray tripped at a Jesuit house in Los Angeles when he returned from Rome between sessions of the Second Vatican Council. One Jesuit told Johnson about a spiritual epiphany he experienced during an acid trip at a UCLA clinic: "The bed suddenly became the universe and he, her lover; the two had joined in cosmic bliss. He said the experience left him with a profound sense of the meaning of Christ's becoming embodied." Johnson's own tripping, however, drove him away from his vocation. After Johnson tripped with Murray, he "came home with a huge erection, and began to witness psychedelic explosions and stars in his head. That was the beginning of the end of his celibacy" (Kripal).

Jobs, Steve. In his study of psychedelia and the early computer industry, John Markoff described the impact LSD had on the Apple co-founder. His experimentation with LSD, Jobs told Markoff, was "one of the two or three most important things he had done in his life." A few years earlier, the film *Pirates of Silicon Valley* had dramatized a Steve Jobs acid trip. Jobs asks his friends to trip with him; when they decline, he complains, "This is like living with a bunch of squares and stiffs." The film then offers up a brief and conventional depiction of an acid trip. Jobs imagines himself in a field of wheat, conducting classical music. As pastel colors tint the field and images swirl in soft focus, he exclaims, "Everything's moving just the way I want it to!"

As Markoff explains, LSD was very much a part of the subculture from which the modern computer industry emerged. Steve Jobs took crucial ideas from a cluster of research groups associated with Stanford in the 1960s. The computer pioneers shared much with Ken Kesey and the Merry Pranksters: a Palo Alto hub, radical politics, experiments with communal living and free love, and the use of acid both for recreation and illumination (see *Merry Pranksters; Kesey, Ken*). The freewheeling, liberal spirit that characterized the early years of computers and the internet owed much to this association with 1960s counterculture. Even Bill Gates, who is often blamed (or credited) with bringing capitalist discipline to the industry, participated in this psychedelic scene (see *Gates, Bill*). Steve Jobs and Apple more than Gates and Microsoft remain aligned with the earlier spirit of counterculture, although Jobs was a canny and practical businessman as well as an acidhead.

Jobs' and Apple's complicated relationship with 1960s counterculture came to light at a corporate event in 1993. As reported in the *San Jose Mercury News* (May 17), Apple invited Ken Kesey to a huge party they were organizing to showcase new products. Kesey drove to the San Jose Convention Center in a replica of the Prankster bus, which he parked in the courtyard. Things went all right until Kesey started talking about LSD. Then it became clear that Apple was not comfortable with the old Prankster:

> About 20 minutes into his monologue, Kesey suggested to the audience that the federal government should have dealt with the Branch Davidian standoff in Waco, Texas, by spraying the compound with LSD instead of bullets. That's when a woman helping to produce the show rushed onstage and told Kesey he was through because of the drug reference.... Kesey and his entourage then got back on their bus and started to leave—only to have the producers insist he couldn't drive it away while the party was going on. They called extra security guards, including one armed with a gun, Kesey said. But Kesey eventually got the bus out, and headed back to Oregon.... A reporter's call to Apple for comment Friday initially was answered by a secretary who asked how to spell Kesey's name—and then asked who Kesey was.

Despite this moment of embarrassment, Apple's nostalgic connection with 1960s counterculture remains intact as a marketing resource. It's one of the reasons that Apple has been able to position itself as cooler and hipper than Microsoft.

Johnson, Don Hanlon. Johnson trained as a Jesuit and took LSD in the early 1960s with other Jesuits, including prominent theologian John Courtney Murray. Johnson soon left the Jesuits and became a stalwart of the Esalen Institute. See *Jesuits; Murray, John Courtney; Esalen.*

Johnson, Warren C. Along with fellow psychiatrist Anthony K. Busch, Johnson published the first study of LSD on hospitalized psychotic patients. See *Busch, Anthony K.*

Joplin, Janis. Joplin sang for Big Brother and the Holding Company and became one of the stars of the San Francisco psychedelic music scene. See *Big Brother and the Holding Company.*

Joshua Light Show. Joshua White, who studied film at USC, found his calling as the most prominent liquid light show artist of the psychedelic era (see *Light Shows*). Bill Graham hired White in 1967 to create light shows for concerts at the Fillmore (see *Graham, Bill; Fillmore*). Doing business as the Joshua Light Show, White and his colleagues perfected techniques of rear projection that made light shows more vivid. In an interview years later, White described their artistic flair: "We were able to improvise on a very large, thirty to forty foot canvas behind the musicians as they performed. We had a knowledge of their music but we weren't following any score, we were just improvising, making something visual using our tools."

Jünger, Ernst. German novelist Jünger, among the most honored and controversial writers of his generation, took LSD with Albert Hofmann in 1951 (see *Hofmann, Albert*). Although Jünger had previously tried mescaline, Hofmann gave him only a very small dose of LSD because "the reaction of such a highly sensitive man as Ernst Jünger was not foreseeable" (*LSD: My Problem Child*). The sensitive man had a pleasant trip but told Hofmann, "Compared with the tiger mescaline, your LSD is, after all, only a house cat." Hofmann soon corrected this impression with subsequent trips at more normal dosage levels. Jünger drew on his LSD experience for the 1952 novel *Besuch auf Gotenholm* (*Visit to Gotenholm*): a tripping man watches incense burning "first with astonishment, then with delight, as if a new power of the eyes had come to him.... No goddess could inform the initiates more boldly and freely. The pyramids with their weight did not reach up to this revelation." Jünger later wrote to Hofmann that drugs like LSD "should only be tried in small circles. I cannot agree with the thoughts of Huxley, that possibilities for transcendence could here be given to the masses."

Kast, Eric. In the mid 1960s, Chicago anesthesiologist Kast published studies of LSD therapy for those dying from cancer (see *Dying*). He gave 128 patients doses of 100 micrograms and evaluated the drug's effect on their physical pain and emotional state. Kast found that LSD proved more effective than Demerol in relieving physical pain. He speculated that LSD caused patients to lose focus on the normally insistent stimulus of pain, as they found themselves distracted by psychedelic sensations. Kast also reported great improvement in patients' emotional well being. He told *Time* magazine that because LSD "impairs anticipation," patients focus on the present moment rather than impending death. Patients also reported feelings of happiness and spiritual comfort after their LSD trips.

Katz, Sidney. Canadian journalist Katz took LSD and wrote the first detailed trip diary for a mainstream publication: "My 12 Hours As a Madman" appeared in *Macleans* magazine in 1953. Katz had heard about experiments being conducted by Humphry Osmond and Abram Hoffer at Weyburn Hospital in Saskatchewan (see *Osmond, Humphry; Hoffer, Abram*); he volunteered to take LSD under their supervision and write about the changes to his consciousness. Katz came into the experiment assuming that LSD would turn him temporarily into a schizophrenic. This "set" or mental precondition significantly colored his experience: for the most part, he described the unpleasant, often terrifying effects of a drug that was making him lose his mind. He reported a number of frightening hallucinations, frequently involv-ing either his own body parts changing size and shape or other people's faces turning monstrous—for example, a woman turning into a Medusa-like figure. His trip guides repeatedly had to reassure him that he was safe and would return to normal consciousness in a few hours. Although his harrowing account emphasized moments of panic and despair, Katz also acknowledged that LSD led him to pleasant, even wondrous visions: "At times I beheld visions of dazzling beauty—visions so rapturous, so unearthly, that no artists will ever paint them. I lived in a paradise where the sky was a mass of jewels set in a background of shimmering aquamarine blue; where the clouds were apricot-colored; where the air was filled with liquid golden arrows, glittering fountains of iridescent bubbles, filigree lace of pearl and silver, sheathes of rainbow light." Finally coming down from his trip, he felt "jumpy and on edge," which Osmond diagnosed as a state of shock. Osmond prescribed "a heavy sugar diet," and Katz complied by consuming "seven chocolate bars, two packages of Life Savers, six Cokes, and two large pieces of cake coated with heavy icing": the first recorded case of psychedelic munchies.

Kelley, Alton. Kelley collaborated with Stanley Mouse on some of the most memorable posters from the San Francisco psychedelic era. Kelley moved to San Francisco in 1964 and helped organize the hippie group known as the "Family Dog." One of Kelley's responsibilities was providing posters to publicize dance concerts at the Avalon Ballroom. When he met Mouse early in 1966, he recognized their complementary artistic talents: Kelley was adept at discovering images and envisioning layouts, and Mouse was more skilled at drawing and coloring. Together, they produced roughly one poster per week, and they invited other artists into their studio to "jam" on side-by-side easels.

For some of their most famous work, they borrowed images from old books, magazines, and advertisements. One of their first posters, for a concert by Big Brother and the Holding Company, featured a reproduction of the Zig-Zag man from the brand of cigarette rolling papers. Kelley has admitted that he feared repercussions: "We were paranoid that the police would bust us, or that Zig-Zag would bust us." Kelley made fun of his own paranoia in fine print at the bottom of the Zig-Zag poster: "What you don't know about copying and duplicating won't hurt you." Mouse and Kelley also created the iconic "Skeleton and Roses" poster for the Grateful Dead, with an image borrowed from a nineteenth-century edition of the *Rubaiyat of Omar Khayyam*. Posters by Mouse and Kelley have hung in museums and fetch high prices in the collectibles market. See *Mouse, Stanley; Posters*.

Kemp, Richard. Kemp was a gifted chemistry student at Cambridge in the late 1960s when he became interested in LSD. He joined a Cambridge group that gathered at the house of American writer and psychedelic enthusiast David Solomon (see *Solomon, David*); among Solomon's guests was Francis Crick, whose presence had attracted Kemp (see *Crick, Francis*). After Kemp received from Ronald Stark a big batch of the LSD precursor ergotamine tartrate (see *Stark, Ronald*), he devised an efficient way to produce LSD of exemplary purity. Along with his friend Christine Bott (see *Bott, Christine*), Kemp produced millions of microdots in a lab located in rural Wales. In 1977, after extensive undercover work, British police arrested Kemp, Bott, and fifteen others in the culmination of "Operation Julie" (see *Operation Julie*). Kemp and Bott pled guilty and received prison sentences of thirteen and nine years respectively. Friends of Kemp and Bott described them as psychedelic utopians. One friend, Garrod Harker, described the couple as "hippie idealists who were completely uninterested in the money they were making" (Rees). Harker explained their particular version of psychedelic philosophy: "They believe industrial society will collapse when the oil runs out and that the answer is to change people's mindsets using acid. They believe LSD can help people to see that a return to a natural society based on self-sufficiency is the only way to save themselves."

Kennedy, John F. Allen Ginsberg once whimsically planned to give LSD to Cold War leaders, including Kennedy; he was confident that their psychedelic insights would prevent nuclear war and change history for the good. Ginsberg never followed through. Rumors have persisted, however, that JFK did try LSD with one of his mistresses, Mary Meyer. Meyer had made visits to Timothy Leary at Harvard during the same period she was seeing Kennedy. Meyer kept a diary that was discovered and later burned after her murder in 1964. One man who looked at the diary, CIA official James Angleton (husband of a close friend of Meyer), claimed that Meyer wrote about taking LSD with Kennedy during a session of lovemaking. No one else who looked at the diary supported his claim. Kennedy biographer Michael O'Brien looked at all the evidence, including material from Nina Burleigh's biography of Meyer. O'Brien summarizes what is known: "During her affair with Kennedy, Mary visited Harvard's Timothy Leary, the high priest of the hallucinogenic drug LSD. There is no confirmation that Kennedy tried LSD with Mary, but, said Burleigh, 'the timing of her visits to Timothy Leary do coincide with the dates of her known private meetings with the President.' If Kennedy did experiment with LSD, his aides knew nothing about it."

Kerouac, Jack. Beat novelist Kerouac took LSD one time and had a miserable experience. His friend Allen Ginsberg had recommended that he try LSD to cure his alcoholism (see *Ginsberg, Allen; Alcoholism*); Kerouac went to Timothy Leary's apartment, where Leary supervised his trip. According to a biographer, "Unprepared for the powerful reaction, Kerouac came out of the trip still an alcoholic, but sadder and more introspective than ever before. For years afterward he told everyone he knew that Leary was a liar, that the effects of LSD were long lasting, and that he had never been right after taking it" (Dittman). A few years later Kerouac was visited by his old friend Neal Cassady while he was traveling with the Merry Pranksters (see *Cassady, Neal; Merry Pranksters*). The visit went poorly. Kerouac had little to say to the acid enthusiasts, and when he noticed their couch covered with an American flag, he removed the flag, folded it neatly, and avoided their company. See *Beats*.

Kesey, Ken. Kesey was the West Coast counterpart to Timothy Leary: these were the acid evangelists who spread enthusiasm about LSD during the years leading up to the psychedelic boom of the late 1960s. Kesey first took LSD in 1959, when he was a graduate student in creative writing at Stanford. He volunteered for CIA-sponsored trials of hallucinogenic drugs at a hospital in Menlo Park. Kesey was amazed by the effects of LSD, even in the sterile setting of the hospital. He tolerated doctors' clinical questions about details of perception, but afterwards he wrote freely about what the new drug was doing to his mental life. Kesey's experience in the Menlo Park hospital inspired his first novel, *One Flew over the Cuckoo's Nest*, in two ways: his impressions of the hospital's mental ward informed the plot, and his use of LSD empowered his imagination. Kesey later admitted, "I would not have been able to write that well without LSD."

Kesey began taking the drug outside the hospital and sharing it with friends. Over time, a small community of psychedelic adventurers gathered around Kesey at his new house in La Honda, California (south of Palo Alto). The house with its six forested acres was suitable for communal living and for tripping. The La Honda group began calling itself the "Merry Pranksters" (see *Merry Pranksters*). Among them were Neal Cassady, already famous as a subject of Beat literature (see *Cassady, Neal*), and several younger people who would become famous later on, including Jerry Garcia and Stewart Brand (see *Garcia, Jerry; Brand, Stewart*). At La Honda, they took acid trips frequently and discussed the drug's potential to alter individual minds as well as society at large. In 1964, they decided to take their psychedelic experiments on the road. Kesey bought an old school bus: they painted it with wild day-glo designs, outfitted it with audio equipment, and began broadcasting music and messages to mainstream America as they rolled from California to New York. At the front of the bus, they indicated their destination as "FURTHUR."

Journalist Tom Wolfe wrote a detailed account of the Pranksters in a bestselling 1968 book (see *Electric Kool-Aid Acid Test*). Kesey is clearly the protagonist of Wolfe's narrative. As Wolfe tells it, many of the Pranksters looked to Kesey as their leader and followed his guidance about when and where and how they should take acid. Some in the group resisted Kesey's efforts to control the trip, however, and they wondered whether egocentrism might be impairing his psychedelic spirit. Still, Kesey largely remained the face of the Pranksters. His rambunctious Western persona—he liked to dress in buckskin—contrasted with the more intellectual Leary, who snubbed the Pranksters when they visited him in New York.

After the bus returned to California, Kesey came up with a new way to spread the psychedelic experience. He decided to hold "Acid Tests" at various public sites (see *Acid Test*): these were loosely organized parties at which LSD was made available to all. Usually the Grateful Dead played, accompanied by light shows and films of the bus trip. Pranksters and guests dressed up in costumes, danced, and expressed themselves however they saw fit. On one occasion, Kesey daringly invited the notorious Hell's Angels to an acid party at La Honda; the Angels and Pranksters tripped together peacefully for the most part, and the two groups temporarily forged an unlikely psychedelic alliance (see

Hell's Angels). At the start of 1966, just before a larger scale Acid Test called the "Trips Festival" (see *Trips Festival*), Kesey was arrested for possession of marijuana. He faked a suicide a fled to Mexico for several months. When he returned to California to face charges, Kesey brought a new message for the Pranksters. He said it was time to move beyond acid—to continue exploring psychedelic effects but without the drug. Many disagreed, including master chemist Owsley, who considered LSD essential to the experience (see *Owsley*). Kesey organized one more event to convey his message, the "Acid Test Graduation," but only a few Pranksters cooperated and the graduation fizzled.

With the Prankster era over, Kesey served a prison term and returned to his native Oregon, where he lived until his death in 2001. From time to time he would revive the Prankster spirit and take his painted bus to concerts or other events to which he had been invited. At one such event, a corporate showcase for new Apple products in 1993, Kesey was quickly ushered offstage when he announced that the government should have sprayed LSD into the Branch Davidian compound at Waco (see *Jobs, Steve*). Although he continued to speak and write about his psychedelic adventures, he resisted attempts to objectify the Pranksters as an historical curiosity: when the Smithsonian tried to buy the "FURTHUR" bus for museum display, he declined (see *Museums*).

Kleps, Arthur. School psychologist Kleps took a mescaline trip in 1960 that changed his life. He was greatly impressed by the visionary experience he had undergone; over the next few years he continued to explore the possibilities of altered consciousness with marijuana and psychedelic drugs, especially LSD. In 1964 he was fired from his job. Kleps moved to the Adirondacks and founded the Neo-American Church, the first church to specify LSD as its sacramental vehicle. He referred to himself as "Chief Boo Hoo, Patriarch of the East,"

wrote *The Boo Hoo Bible: The Neo-American Church Catechism,* and in general set out to satirize the whole notion of organized religion. Eventually a court ruled that Kleps' Neo-American Church did not deserve the religious exemption given to the peyote-based Native American Church (see *Religion*).

Kleps lived for a time at Millbrook estate with Timothy Leary, who referred to him as a "mad monk." Leary and his Millbrook colleagues found Kleps' erratic behavior to be troublesome, and at one point they attempted to address the problem with a massive surprise dose of LSD. Jay Stevens offer this account:

> One of his comrades—Kleps swore it was Hollingshead—placed a few thousand mikes of pure Sandoz in a snifter of brandy beside his bedstand. Before he even rubbed the sleep out of his eyes, Kleps downed the brandy. A few minutes later he realized he was having trouble brushing his teeth. 'I was knocked to the floor as all normal sensation and motor control left my body. The sun, roaring like an avalanche, was headed straight for me, expanding like a bomb and filling my consciousness in less time than it takes to describe it.' ... As he groveled on all fours he got a shot of Thorazine in the rear, but it failed to bring him down. He spent the last hours of the trip sitting in a lotus position. As Kleps told it, a big book appeared, suspended in space about three feet in front of him, the pages turning automatically, every letter illuminated in gold against sky-blue pages.

In later years, Kleps' eccentrism took a darker turn as he entangled himself in anti–Semitic conspiracy theories associated with holocaust history. The government of the Netherlands expelled him for anti–Semitic involvement.

Kool-Aid. At an acid test in 1966 held in Compton, California (see *Acid Test*), the organizers decided to serve LSD dissolved in Kool-Aid. They filled two large trash cans with "electric" Kool-Aid, with one can delivering a heavy dose (for veterans) and the other a light dose (for beginners). Attendees were invited to drink from paper cups. The choice of Kool-Aid was a typically random prank by the Pranksters (see *Merry Pranksters*), but Kool-Aid actually made a good fit with psychedelic style: Kool-Aid came in unnaturally bright colors and was associated with childish innocence and playfulness. Most of those who drank the psychedelic Kool-Aid knew what they were getting, but some did not. Tom Wolfe tells the story of one participant, Clair Brush, who had no idea that her Kool-Aid contained LSD; she went through some unsettling moments but ended up having a good experience.

"Drinking the Kool-Aid" eventually entered the language as a figurative expression, but not because of the Kool-Aid acid test. It was a very different event twelve years later that gave rise to the slang trope. Jim Jones, leader of the People's Temple, laced grape Kool-Aid with potassium cyanide and ordered his followers to drink. The resulting mass suicide generated the current sense of "drinking the Kool-Aid": it means obeying an instruction or conforming to a way of thinking without proper critical reflection. The slang meaning has sometimes been applied retroactively to electric Kool-Aid, by people who regard LSD as something closer to poison than panacea.

Krassner, Paul. Paul Krassner became a member of the Merry Pranksters (see *Merry Pranksters*), whose psychedelic counterculture very much suited his subversive, satirical style. Krassner was equally a journalist, a political activist, and a stand-up comedian. Before joining the Pranksters, Krassner had founded *The Realist,* a magazine that offered sharp political satire. After the Pranksters, he helped create the Yippies (Youth International Party) and participated in the famous protests at the 1968 Democratic convention in Chicago. In 2001 he published *Psychedelic Trips for the Mind,* a collection of LSD tales and reflections. Krassner admitted that he had taken acid trips in some unlikely settings, including a Chicago courtroom when he testified at the 1968 trial, and the

Johnny Carson show, during an appearance as a guest comedian. One of Krassner's most intriguing LSD stories involves Groucho Marx: Groucho had asked Krassner to supervise and accompany him on his first acid trip. See *Marx, Groucho.*

Kubrick, Stanley. Although his film *2001: A Space Odyssey* was marketed to psychedelic fans as "the ultimate trip," Kubrick did not regard LSD as a proper resource for artists. In a 1968 interview with *Playboy,* Kubrick said that psychedelic drugs were "basically of more use to the audience than to the artist. I think the illusion of oneness with the universe, and absorption with the significance of everything in your environment, and the pervasive aura of peace and contentment is not the ideal state for an artist. It tranquillizes the creative personality, which thrives on conflict and the clash and ferment of ideas." See *2001: A Space Odyssey.*

Labs. The manufacture of LSD requires considerable expertise in organic chemistry along with the necessary laboratory equipment. Even with the chemical recipe readily available on the internet, very few people actually make LSD: the technical difficulties are considerable, demand for the drug is fairly low, and the risk of arrest constitutes a major deterrent. In the early years following Albert Hofmann's discovery, the Sandoz corporation controlled LSD production within their Swiss laboratories. When the CIA and the U.S. military became interested, they sponsored experiments in American pharmaceutical laboratories that led to refinements in the process, especially in work done at Lilly (see *Lilly*). LSD became illegal after 1966 and manufacturers took their labs underground. The most famous maker of LSD in the 1960s was Owsley (see *Owsley*), a gifted chemical technician who produced a large percentage of the acid distributed in the Bay Area during the peak psychedelic years. Owsley was arrested in 1967, but other makers filled in. As the use of LSD began to decline in the 1970s and beyond, fewer and fewer people manufactured it. By the turn of the century, LSD production had become so centralized that one huge arrest and seizure substantially reduced the supply of the drug (see *Pickard, William*).

Laing, R.D. Scottish psychiatrist Laing became an intellectual celebrity of the psychedelic era with unconventional theories of mental illness and an enthusiasm for LSD therapy. Laing speculated that people labeled insane might actually be reacting sanely to the stresses of life in traditionally constructed families and societies. He believed that orthodox psychiatric methods tended to aggravate rather than relieve symptoms, and he founded a treatment center where there was no hierarchical distinction between doctors and patients. Laing embraced LSD therapy both for its unsettling of normal behavioral patterns and its ability to level the psychiatric playing field: LSD put doctors as well as patients in a vulnerable state. Often Laing would take LSD himself to accompany a tripping patient. He wrote bestselling books and appeared frequently on television as an influential countercultural voice. He associated with artists, rock stars, and movie stars—including fellow Scot Sean Connery, who came to Laing for psychedelic therapy following his sudden celebrity as James Bond (see *Connery, Sean*). In later years, Laing struggled with depression and alcoholism, and he modified some of his early views about the social construction of mental illness.

Laws. Until the middle of the 1960s, LSD was not illegal in the United States and other countries. As use of the drug became more common, and stories of bad trips and traumatic consequences spread, a few states passed laws prohibiting the manufacture, sale, and possession of LSD. The federal government followed with its own laws. By 1971, most countries had agreed to follow the American lead and make LSD illegal, under the provisions of the United Na-

tions Convention on Psychotropic Substances.

The first two states to adopt anti-LSD legislation were New York and California, the Eastern and Western capitals of American acid culture. New York passed its first law in 1965: anyone arrested in possession of LSD would face a maximum penalty of two years in prison. A year later, New York increased the maximum prison sentence to twenty years. The California State Senate took up a similar bill in 1966. Senator Donald Grunsky argued for an LSD ban using the same stories of abuse that had prompted the New York law. The most striking cases included an accidental ingestion by a five-year-old girl, and a homicide committed by a schizophrenic man while he was tripping. The California legislators had serious reservations about the proposed law, and at first they refused to report it out of committee. Advocates against the law argued successfully that it would make tens of thousands of college students into criminals, simply because they were curious about a drug associated with creativity, spirituality, and expanded consciousness. Political pressures became too intense, however, and California passed the law later in 1966. Congress passed comparable federal legislation early in 1967. The drug had become so notorious by then that the LSD ban was the first bill proposed by President Johnson for that session of Congress. Congress passed an even stronger law in 1968, with increased penalties for manufacture or sale, and for the first time a federal ban on possession. President Nixon later took steps to organize the nation's drug laws under a single piece of legislation, the Federal Controlled Substances Act of 1970, which classified LSD as a Schedule I drug. Schedule I means that a drug meets the following conditions: "1. The drug has high potential for abuse; 2. The drug has no currently accepted medical use in treatment in the United States; 3. There is a lack of accepted safety for use of the drug under medical supervision." The Schedule I classification for LSD stirred controversy among medical professionals, especially psychiatrists, some of whom argued that psychedelic psychotherapy should count as a "medical use" with safe supervisory guidelines. LSD nevertheless remains a Schedule I drug. The Multidisciplinary Association for Psychedelic Studies is a non-profit organization that advocates for the reform of laws against LSD and other psychotropic drugs, in order that valid medical uses might be restored (see *MAPS*). Others have argued that some LSD users should be granted a special exemption if they use the drug for religious purposes (similar to the current toleration of peyote use for sacramental rituals: see *Religion*). The Supreme Court has not yet heard a case that would test such a claim for LSD. The Supreme Court has weighed in on another controversy surrounding LSD laws, having to do with "carrier weight" and mandatory sentencing guidelines. Until the Court ruled that such guidelines were merely advisory, a person caught with only a few doses of LSD on sugar cubes or another heavy medium faced a much longer prison term than someone else holding thousands of doses in pure form (see *Supreme Court*).

LBJ. Anti-Johnson Democrats in 1968 took advantage of parallel three-letter initialisms to construct a memorable campaign button: "LSD not LBJ."

League for Spiritual Discovery. In September of 1966, Timothy Leary founded a religious group called the League for Spiritual Discovery (see *Leary, Timothy*). As its initials clearly indicated, the religion was based on the sacramental use of LSD. Leary founded the League at about the same time LSD became illegal; he was hoping to ensure constitutional protection for members of the League who took acid. Because police and prosecutors had been active around Leary's Millbrook estate, he asked his lawyer to draw up a letter for all League members to carry. "Dear Law Enforcement Agent," it began, "The bearer of this letter is a member of the League for Spiritual Discovery, a religious group incorporated under the laws of the state of New York. Unfortunately, members of the League have been recently subjected to harassment and intimidation.... The group has decided to meet each new incident with legal action." The League's claim to religious protection never reached a Supreme Court test, but a lower court dismissed its validity. In *Leary vs. United States,* a circuit court ruled that Leary's use of illegal drugs was not legitimated by the religious structure he had invented (see *Religion*).

Although Leary decided to limit the League to 360 members, he wrote a pamphlet called "Start Your Own Religion" and encouraged others to form psychedelic sects. The original L.S.D. shut down after a few years, but the League was revived in 2006 as "an open consortium of seekers and groups actively exploring, recruiting, assisting, and spreading the ideas of spiritual discovery and peace" (L.S.D. website).

Leary, Timothy. No one did more than Leary to publicize LSD. He coined the psychedelic era's most famous slogan—"turn on, tune in, drop out"—and did such an effective job of spreading enthusiasm for LSD that Richard Nixon called him "the most dangerous man in America." Leary influenced virtually everyone and everything connected with the use of LSD in the 1960s.

After some rocky experiences in pursuit of an undergraduate degree, Leary eventually earned a Ph.D. in psychology from Berkeley. In 1959 he took a position as lecturer in the Harvard psychology department (see *Harvard*). Shortly thereafter he became fascinated by the effects of psilocybin, and he organized a research group devoted to the study of its therapeutic potential. It was in the middle of his psilocybin work that Leary first tried LSD. British researcher Michael Hollingshead (see *Hollingshead, Michael*), who had acquired thousands of doses from Sandoz, visited Harvard in 1962 and told Leary how impressed he was with the drug.

According to Leary's memoir *Flashbacks*, "Hollingshead tried our cozy know-thyself psilocybin and scornfully dismissed it as just pretty colors compared to the philosophic detonations of lysergic acid." Leary soon took his first acid trip and found it to be "the most shattering experience of my life." He described himself "tumbling and spinning down soft fibrous avenues of light that were emitted from some central point. Merged with its pulsing ray I could look out and see the entire cosmic drama. Past and future. All forms, all structures, all organisms, all events were television productions pulsing out from the central eye.... After several billion years I found myself on my feet moving through the puppet show of reality." Leary's description of his first trip suggests two themes that became central features of his psychedelic philosophy. One theme had to do with the artificial "games" that dominate ordinary social behavior (what he called "the puppet show of reality"). If LSD allowed people to detach themselves from these games, they might alter their behavior for the better. The other theme relates to the evolution of the human species. In his first acid trip, Leary claimed to perceive "all forms, all organisms" from "past and future." For the rest of his life he focused on helping humanity progress in what he defined as the evolution of consciousness. Leary consulted with other intellectuals and artists who had been experimenting with hallucinogenic drugs, including Aldous Huxley and Allen Ginsberg (see *Huxley, Aldous; Ginsberg, Allen*). With Ginsberg's encouragement, Leary decided to reject what he called Huxley's "elitist approach" to LSD and embrace "the American egalitarian open-to-the-public approach" (*Flashbacks*). Leary's freewheeling style would get him fired from Harvard in 1963. The official reason was that he missed too many classes, but his dismissal was widely believed to be connected with his psychedelic research. One of his colleagues, Richard Alpert (see *Alpert, Richard*), was fired shortly afterwards for drug-related improprieties. Leary set up

a new home base at a mansion in Millbrook, New York. At Millbrook, Leary gathered a number of people who wanted to experiment with LSD and see what sort of personal and social changes the drug might stimulate. Leary thought of the Millbrook experience as an attempt to assemble "a social molecule, what Kurt Vonnegut calls a 'karass,' a structure of people whose neural characteristics fit together. We hoped that by living and re-imprinting via LSD with different kinds of people we could develop a hive consciousness, each person contributing a specific function, playing a definite role in the completed family" (*Flashbacks*).

While at Millbrook, Leary and two colleagues (Alpert and Ralph Metzner) wrote a manual for tripping based on the Tibetan Book of the Dead. *The Psychedelic Experience* became his most influential book (see *Psychedelic Experience*). Leary, Alpert, and Metzner drew parallels between a Buddhist priest preparing someone for dying and a psychedelic guide preparing someone for an acid trip. *The Psychedelic Experience* emphasizes comfort and safety for the tripper. Many of the instructions have to do with designing a good "setting"—the surrounding environment, including people, objects, music, and food—and maintaining a good "set," the tripper's state of mind. If a tripper starts to feel anxious, the manual provides scripts for reassurance. Usually the guide counsels a tripper to relax and recognize that everything going on has been created by his or her mind. *The Psychedelic Experience* lists several goals for trips but emphasizes the grandest, most spiritual goal, the "attainment of mystical union."

Some of the young people taking LSD thought that Leary was trying to exercise too much control over the psychedelic experience with his "hive" and his manual. Ken Kesey and the Merry Pranksters offered a rambunctious Western alternative to Leary's Eastern spirituality (see *Kesey, Ken; Merry Pranksters*). When the Prankster bus pulled into Millbrook for a visit, the two psychedelic groups didn't get along well. Leary re-called that Alpert "wasn't too thrilled about the rowdy Prankster trip. To put it mildly" (*Flashbacks*). In Tom Wolfe's account of the visit, the Pranksters scorned Millbrook as "one big piece of uptight constipation."

Nevertheless, Leary continued to have enormous influence on the surging psyche-delic scene. At the Human Be-In in San Francisco (see *Human Be-In*), he set the stage for the Summer of Love by inaugurat-ing his signature slogan: "turn on, tune in, drop out." Newspaper and magazine articles, television news reports, and documentary films repeatedly turned to Leary as spokes-person for LSD and its countercultural themes. Even with LSD now illegal, he made flamboyant gestures to promote it. He founded a religion called the League for Spiritual Discovery, and made no attempt to hide the sacramental basis suggested by its initials (see *League for Spiritual Discovery; Religion*).

Eventually Leary ran into legal troubles he could not dodge. He was convicted on marijuana charges in 1968 and sent to prison in California. Leary escaped from the min-imum security prison and spent a few years abroad as a fugitive. When recaptured in 1973, he was sent to Folsom Prison and put in solitary confinement. His cell neighbor at Folsom turned out to be Charles Manson; as the two conversed through an air shaft, Leary learned that Manson had used LSD heavily and looked upon Leary as a mentor. They "liked each other very much," accord-ing to a prison psychologist, although they disagreed over the essence of the psychedelic experience (see *Manson, Charles*).

After his release, Leary occupied him-self with speaking tours and refining what he called the "eight circuit model" for the evolution of consciousness. He believed that people could use various strategies, including psychedelic trips, to access mental resources that would expand intelligence, lengthen lives, and facilitate migration into space. (In 1997, Leary's ashes were in fact carried into orbit by rocket, along with those of *Star Trek* creator Gene Roddenberry.) He was one of the early enthusiasts for the internet, which he referred to as "the LSD of the 1990s." As he drew near death, Leary made use of the internet for one last "psychedelic" experi-ment: he videotaped his final moments so that the public might see his state of mind as he died.

Lennon, John. Lennon first took LSD in April, 1965 at a dinner party in London, when a dentist slipped the drug into his cof-fee. The dentist also served electric coffee to Lennon's wife Cynthia and to George Har-rison and his wife. The four of them even-tually went out to a discotheque. As Lennon recalled in a 1971 *Rolling Stone* interview with Jann Wenner, they had no idea what they were getting into. Lennon described a psychedelic experience that was by turns ter-rifying and contemplative. At one point, they screamed in panic because they thought an elevator was on fire; they were only seeing an ordinary red sign, but on acid it looked like flames. Along with these moments of "going crackers," as he put it, Lennon did lots of drawing, and he found himself "float-ing" peacefully in Harrison's apartment.

That first acid trip was impressive but daunting, and Lennon didn't take another right away. His second trip—the first inten-tional one—came in Los Angeles several weeks later. This time he tripped with Har-rison and Ringo Starr, David Crosby and Roger McGuinn of the Byrds, and Peter Fonda. He recalled Fonda approaching him to whisper, "I know what it's like to be dead." Lennon soon wove this bit of psyche-delic conversation into "She Said She Said" for *Revolver*, the Beatles' first album to show the influence of LSD. Along with "She Said She Said," which Lennon described in the interview as an "acidy" song, *Revolver* included the more conspicuously psychedelic "Tomorrow Never Knows." "Tomorrow Never Knows" was produced in the Indian style that would soon become associated with psychedelic rock, and the song begins with a quotation from Timothy Leary's manual for tripping (see *Psychedelic Experience*). Lennon went on to take LSD about "a thousand times," by his estimation—"I used to just eat it all the time." After *Revolver,* he wrote other acid-related songs, including the single "Strawberry Fields Forever," and "A Day in the Life" and "Lucy in the Sky with Diamonds" from *Sergeant Pepper.* Lennon maintained that the initials of "Lucy in the Sky with Diamonds" were strictly coincidental, but few believed him; the BBC believed the initials and banned the song from radio play.

After a few years Lennon decided that his extravagant use of LSD was causing psychological damage. He told Wenner, "I was reading that stupid book of Leary's [*The Psychedelic Experience*].... I got the message on acid that I should destroy my ego, and I did, you know. I didn't believe I could do anything. I was just nothing. I was shit." He stopped taking acid and managed to regain his self-confidence. For all the trouble it brought, Lennon credited LSD with initiating a therapeutic process that eventually reshaped his identity. "It wasn't a miracle," he told Wenner. "It was more of a visual thing and a therapy, looking at yourself a bit. It did all that." See *Beatles.*

Life **Magazine.** No single piece of journalism did more to publicize LSD than the *Life* cover story from March 25, 1966. The cover depicted a shadowy hand holding a small white capsule, from which colorful squares seemed to radiate; the headline read, "LSD: The Exploding Threat of the Mind Drug that Got Out of Control." The Editor's Note credited a correspondent and a photographer, both in their twenties, and explained that neither man actually tried the dangerous drug at the center of their story. Nevertheless, these men came to feel sympathetic with the acidheads they researched. "We found ourselves feeling very protective about these people," said correspondent Ger-

ald Moore. The *Life* story accordingly detailed both the risks and the attractions of LSD. LSD has "tantalizing possibilities for good and evil"; it leads "sometimes into a world of beatific serenity and shimmering insight, sometimes to frenzy or terror. In either case the person who has taken this remarkable drug never sees life quite the same way again." One inset feature recorded a teenage girl's bummer ("LSD user meets terror on a bad trip"), but another listed several scientists and religious scholars who found LSD therapeutic or inspiring. As part of the story, Science Editor Albert Rosenfeld addressed a series of questions about LSD. His answers were well informed and balanced. He mentioned risks to psyche and warned about reckless use of the drug, but also explained that LSD had only mild physiological effects, was not habit-forming, did not cause hallucinations in the clinical sense, and might have legitimate medical uses.

Photographer Lawrence Schiller illustrated the story with several images of LSD users, most of them suggesting trouble. He photographed scenes from Acid Tests and other gatherings showing trippers dazed, introverted, dancing awkwardly, clutching at their faces, and sobbing. One photo showed Timothy Leary sitting on the floor next to his sad daughter as he awaited trial on drug charges. Even the photographic portion of the story, however, included some hint of psychedelic benefit. The last page consisted mainly of a large photo showing a respectable-looking young man ruminating in a neat apartment. The caption read, "A San Francisco mathematician takes a trip on LSD with his cat, who is on the drug too. He does this every other week." Neither mathematician nor cat appeared to be in any distress.

Light Shows. At many concerts in the 1960s and 1970s that featured psychedelic rock (see *Psychedelic Rock*), the experience was enhanced by distinctive "liquid" light shows. The basic idea was to project colorful patterns that would swirl in synchrony with the music. Light show artists would pour dyed water into a shallow, lens-like container, and add drops of oil; as they moved a second lens over the first, colors and shapes swirled and changed. Overhead projectors would transmit the play of colors to screens located behind and around the band. Like tie-dye designs on clothing (see *Tie-Dye*), liquid light shows were meant to mimic certain effects of psychedelic perception—especially a heightened sensitivity to colors and patterns. Because light show operators were reacting to the music, the effects were spontaneous rather than programmed. For a given show, there might be only a single operator or as many as ten, and there could be dozens of projectors deployed to create the effects. One of the most prominent light show companies was founded by Joshua White (see *Joshua Light Show*). The first organized light show operation, which created shows for the Charlatans at the Red Dog Saloon (see *Charlatans*), named itself "Light Sound Dimension" in deference to the drug of inspiration.

Lilly. Indianapolis-based Lilly pharmaceuticals became the first American manufacturer of LSD, encouraged by the CIA in the context of Cold War politics. Albert Hofmann and the Sandoz Corporation of Switzerland had received a U.S. patent for LSD in 1948; in their application, Sandoz described it as a "valuable therapeutic product." Sandoz made small quantities of LSD available to researchers who wanted to investigate potential medical and psychotherapeutic benefits (see *Sandoz; Delysid*). In the early 1950s, the Central Intelligence Agency took a keen interest in LSD for very different reasons: they wanted to test its value as a tool for interrogation and a chemical weapon. Because the CIA needed LSD in greater amounts than Sandoz was providing, director Allen Dulles supported American research to develop another source for the drug. Eli Lilly was one of the companies that received

CIA funding to tackle the problem. In 1954, Lilly chemists succeeded: they invented a new process for synthesizing lysergic acid, which had previously been possible only through the use of scarce reagents controlled by Sandoz. This was exciting news for the CIA, because they now had a plentiful and inexpensive supply of LSD for their MK-ULTRA testing program. The program was kept secret, and details did not come out until decades later, when confidential CIA documents were finally released. Lilly received a U.S. patent in 1956 for their new method of preparing lysergic acid amides.

Lilly's new method for manufacturing LSD kept alive the CIA program to test LSD as a Cold War weapon. In a memo written shortly after the Lilly discovery, a CIA official noted the importance of their work: until this moment, "LSD could not be considered seriously as a candidate Chemical Warfare agent for overt use"; thanks to Lilly, however, "LSD can now be produced in quantity and recent technical developments make it possible to disseminate solids in an effective manner" (quoted in Szulc). The drug never worked out as a weapon, but it was disseminated more effectively than the CIA ever imagined. Over the next decade, Lilly's method for making cheap acid enabled the widespread manufacture of the drug by underground producers, who sold it to the growing countercultural market.

Lilly, John C. Lilly was an American psychoanalyst and researcher who experimented with LSD beginning in the 1960s. He was best known for his work with sensory deprivation tanks, which he frequently combined with the use of hallucinogenic drugs, including LSD. He also experimented with LSD and dolphins, in an attempt to detect significant alterations in dolphin behavior relating to vocalization and social habits (see *Dolphins*). Lilly's work attracted the interest of many prominent countercultural intellectuals, including the physicist Richard Feynman (see *Feynman, Richard*). The 1980 film *Altered States* was loosely premised on Lilly's experiments with sensory deprivation and hallucinogens.

Linkletter, Art. After the 1969 suicide of his daughter Diane, which he blamed on LSD, television personality Art Linkletter became one of the most prominent critics of the use of the drug. Linkletter's public campaign served to increase political pressure for stricter anti–LSD laws, and in 1970 Congress passed legislation that classified LSD as a Schedule I drug. See *Linkletter, Diane; Laws.*

Linkletter, Diane. The youngest daughter of television personality Art Linkletter committed suicide by jumping out her sixth-floor window. Her father blamed her death on the effects of LSD flashbacks: "It isn't suicide because she wasn't herself. It was murder. She was murdered by the people who manufacture and sell LSD" (*Los Angeles Times,* October 6, 1969). As the story spread, an urban legend developed that Diane Linkletter had jumped under the psychedelic delusion she could fly.

Barbara Mikkelson conducted a careful review of the evidence in 2005. The legend about flying had no basis in fact. Mikkelson ended up being skeptical of the claim that LSD caused Diane Linkletter's death, although she could not rule it out definitively. The two men who testified in 1969 gave conflicting information about her final night. A friend who spent the night talking with Diane described her as feeling very depressed about her life, but he made no mention of LSD or any other drugs. He was still in the apartment when she jumped at 9:00 in the morning. Her brother Robert told police that Diane had called him early in the morning, shortly before her death; according to Robert Linkletter, his sister was beginning to panic due to an LSD flashback. It was the brother's claim that prompted Art Linkletter's attack on LSD.

Part of the uncertainty surrounding the Linkletter incident has to do with the imprecision of "flashback" as a diagnosis. Flashbacks are usually minor events of perceptual alteration, such as blurring of visual borders; and if flashbacks are implicated in more serious episodes of distress, they are usually considered a symptom of post-traumatic stress disorder, and consequently connected with deeper underlying psychological problems (see *Flashbacks*). Another element to consider in the Linkletter death is the correlation between LSD use and suicide. Although two publicly controversial suicides were blamed on LSD—Linkletter's death, and the death of CIA agent Frank Olson (see *Olson, Frank*)—evidence does not indicate that LSD users face an increased risk of suicide (see *Suicide*). Sidney Cohen surveyed 44 psychiatrists who had used LSD in their practice, in order to investigate possible side effects and dangerous consequences ("Side Effects"). Cohen concluded that suicides "attributable to LSD are indeed rare," and that "all the suicidal acts have been in disturbed patients rather than normal subjects." However, LSD cannot be entirely ruled out as a possible factor in Diane Linkletter's death. In some people, LSD may bring to the surface a latent psychological disorder, or magnify an existing condition such as anxiety or depression. Although Cohen found no appreciable increase in risk of suicide, he noted that, in a "very few instances, a direct connection between the LSD experience and the movement toward self-destruction could be discerned." In a later paper ("Complications"), Cohen expressed even more concern about LSD triggering or aggravating mental symptoms that might lead to suicide. Cohen worried about the increasing use of the drug by young people who were taking it without professional supervision.

Living Theater. Julian Beck and Judith Malina founded this experimental dramatic troupe on principles adapted from Antonin Artaud: they aimed to subvert the conventions of traditional theater and to produce plays that would catalyze social revolution. During the 1960s, Living Theater members lived communally in Europe and America and started using psychedelic drugs. Beck acknowledged that he and his colleagues often went on stage while tripping on LSD. Their dramatic style accommodated LSD well. In productions from the late 1960s such as *Paradise Now* and *Frankenstein,* actors worked largely by improvisation and collage, with members of the audience frequently drawn into the action. Clive Barnes' review of *Frankenstein* described it as "essentially a non-verbal theater" that emphasized "visual rather than intellectual images." Although Barnes found the results "at times repetitious, at times banal," he also recognized Living Theater for creating "a new physical style of theater, raw, gutsy, and vital" (*New York Times,* October 6, 1968).

Love-Ins. This 1967 B-movie aimed both to criticize and to cash in on America's fascination with Haight-Ashbury (its tagline: "The Hippies and Diggers Are Here! With the Way-Out Excitement That's Turning on America Today!"). The plot involves a Leary-like figure who invents a psychedelic slogan—"Be More. Sense More. Love More"—and leads a hippie community. *The Love-Ins* takes a dark view of hippie self-indulgence. In the movie's one psychedelic set piece, a young woman freaking out on acid dances awkwardly with characters from Alice in Wonderland (see *Alice in Wonderland*).

Luce, Clare Boothe. Luce took LSD at the suggestion of psychiatrist Sidney Cohen (see *Luce, Henry; Cohen, Sidney*), and soon recommended the drug to her husband Henry (see *Luce, Henry*). Clare, who served in Congress and as ambassador to Italy, was one of the most influential voices in American conservatism during the Cold War. According to biographer Sylvia Morris, "She had been a fervent convert to Catholicism in 1946 but as her religious enthusiasm waned, she was perhaps looking for a new mystical experience. LSD provided that to some extent because she usually had enjoyable and illuminating trips." After her first trip in 1959, which she took with Gerald Heard (see *Heard, Gerald*), she wrote to Cohen, "Whatever the effects of LSD on the body, the effect on the psyche—my psyche—in any event, were at the time altogether good." Once she had a bad trip: she became preoccupied with death—"Feel all paths of glory lead but to the grave," she wrote at the time, "an almost shattering fact." She started weeping, and noted, "I've paid enough. I am quite gone." For the most part, however, her acid trips were pleasant and therapeutic. Clare more than Henry preferred to keep her psychedelic experiences private, especially when she considered running for president on the Conservative Party ticket in 1964.

Luce, Henry. The publisher of *Time* and *Life*, Luce took LSD at the suggestion of his wife Clare (see *Luce, Clare Boothe*). Henry took at least two acid trips at the start of the 1960s. According to Stephen Siff, during one trip, "he conducted an imaginary orchestra in his back yard, and in the other, 'he claimed to have talked to God on the golf course, and found that the Old Boy seemed to be on top of things and knew pretty much what he was doing,' in the words of biographer Wilfred Sheed." Luce's *Life* published some of the first important articles about LSD (see *Life Magazine*), and as Robert Herzstein observed, "LSD was the only part of 1960s 'counterculture' treated respectfully by *Time*." Luce's LSD use made headlines in 1968 when it became known to the public.

"Lucy in the Sky with Diamonds." Although John Lennon denied the significance of his title's initials, most listeners interpreted it as a reference to LSD. See *Beatles; Lennon, John*.

MacDonald, John D. MacDonald's Travis McGee series included a 1966 novel that featured LSD at its best and at its worst. See *One Fearful Yellow Eye*.

MacLean, Bonnie. MacLean took over as poster designer for Fillmore concerts after Wes Wilson gave up the job in 1967 (see *Wilson, Wes*). MacLean was married to Fillmore promoter Bill Graham, and up to that point, her only artistic work had consisted of chalkboard notices announcing upcoming concerts. She began making posters and quickly established herself as one of the elite psychedelic artists. MacLean's posters shared several features with other examples of the genre, including elaborate, curving letters and vibrant coloring, but she also showed a distinctive style. MacLean's posters often had the look of medieval illuminated manuscripts. She frequently featured human figures that had a faraway look in their eyes—ruminative, even melancholy—that offered counterpoint to the party atmosphere of the events she was advertising. See *Graham, Bill*; *Psychedelic Posters*.

Macleans. In 1953, Canadian journalist Sidney Katz published in *Macleans* magazine the earliest mainstream account of an acid trip. See *Katz, Sidney*.

Magical Mystery Tour. This was the psychedelic album (and accompanying Prankster-like tour) that followed the Beatles' *Sergeant Pepper's Lonely Hearts Club Band*, but did not generate the same interest. See *Beatles*.

Manson, Charles. Manson used LSD as one of his primary tools in forging the "family" that committed the Helter Skelter murders in 1969. The Manson family took plenty of acid as their patriarch conditioned them for the business he had in mind. In Manson's delusional, paranoid view of the world, nonwhites were adversaries to be engaged in an upcoming racial war. Manson interpreted several Beatles' songs as containing oblique clues about the apocalyptic events to come (see *Helter Skelter*). In 1973, while serving his life sentence for the murders, Manson was pleased to welcome Timothy Leary to solitary confinement at Folsom Prison. Leary was beginning his second, more punitive jail term (see *Leary, Timothy*); the authorities put Leary in the cell right next to Manson's, and they were able to discuss LSD through the air shaft.

Leary biographer Robert Greenfield provides details of their interaction. As a cell-warming gesture, Manson sent Leary a few books with religious themes, including Carlos Castaneda's recent sensation *The Teachings of Don Juan:* the story of a student and his psychedelic mentor. At Folsom, Manson got his chance to question his own psychedelic mentor. In their first conversation, Manson told Leary, "I've been waiting to talk to you for years." He had a complaint to air: "We were all your students, you know. When I got out of jail in 1965, there were millions of kids cut loose from the old lies just waiting to be told what to do. And you didn't tell them what to do. That's what I could never figure out. You showed everyone how to create a new head but you never gave them the new head. Why didn't you?" Leary replied, "I didn't want to impose my realities. The idea is that everybody takes responsibility for his nervous system, creates his own reality. Anything else is brainwashing." Despite his aversion to brainwashing, Leary told Manson how impressed he was by his achievement in "programming": "Now, that's amazing. You did what every intelligence agency in the world dreamed of. You programmed people to go out on assassination missions. And they'd probably do it again today." Manson and Leary also talked about the psychedelic "moment of truth" when a tripper confronts the dissolution of normal identity:

> [Manson] wanted to know what Tim called the moment of truth when you took acid and your entire body dissolved into nothing but vibrations, space and time fused, and it all became just pure energy. Bouncing the question right back at him, Tim asked Manson what he had found there. 'Nothing,' Manson said. 'Like death must be. Isn't that what you found?' Having fielded this question many times before, Tim told Manson this was a trip someone else had laid on him. 'It's the moment when you are free from biochemical imprints,' he said. 'You can take off

from there and go anywhere you want. You should have looked for the energy fusion called love.' 'It's all death,' Manson insisted. 'It's all love,' Tim responded.

Despite this sharp difference in psychedelic exegesis, two men got along well. A prison psychologist told Greenfield that Manson and Leary "liked each other very much."

MAPS. The Multidisciplinary Association for Psychedelic Studies is a non-profit organization founded in 1995. MAPS raises and oversees funding for scientific research into the medical and psychological uses of psychedelic drugs, especially LSD, psilocybin, MDMA (Ecstasy), and marijuana. Rick Doblin, president and founder of MAPS, wrote a doctoral dissertation at Harvard's Kennedy School of Government in which he argued for resumption of research on these drugs. Doblin reviewed the history of psychedelic psychotherapy, analyzed the reasons for the termination of that research, and proposed a new regulatory model that would revive such experiments. MAPS offers the following summary of its goals: "With sound research results, psychedelic psychotherapy and medical marijuana research have the potential to help millions of people in alleviating the pain, psychological distress and other symptoms of such illnesses as cancer, AIDS, and addiction."

In its short history, MAPS has funded a few research projects that focus on LSD. One early project revisited and followed up on LSD medical studies conducted in the 1950s and early 1960s. A more recent project resumed one specific area of experimentation: the use of LSD as therapy for anxiety and depression in terminally ill patients (see *Dying*). MAPS helped to fund and legitimize a study in Switzerland with a group of such patients.

Martin, George. Although his production of Beatles' songs was crucial to their psychedelic innovations, Martin never took LSD himself. He worked with Lennon and McCartney to create sounds that mimicked certain features of hallucinogenic perception, especially on songs produced around the time of *Sergeant Pepper's Lonely Hearts Club Band*. Martin's recording tricks included filtered voices, backward tapes, and layered ambient noises. See *Beatles*.

Marx, Groucho. Marx took acid in 1968 to prepare for the role of "God" in Otto Preminger's *Skidoo*. Groucho wanted to find out about LSD because he felt that the movie was implicitly promoting its use (see *Skidoo*). He asked comedian-activist Paul Krassner to provide the drug and accompany him on his trip (see *Krassner, Paul*). According to Krassner, Groucho's LSD experience was mainly upbeat. There were "long periods of silence and of listening to music…. After we heard the Bach Cantata No. 7, Groucho said, 'I may be Jewish, but I was seeing the most beautiful visions of Gothic cathedrals. Do you think Bach knew he was doing that?'" Another time he reflected on his upcoming role: "I'm really getting quite a kick out of this notion of playing God like a dirty old man in *Skidoo*. You want to know why? Do you realize that irreverence and reverence are the same thing?" Groucho's trip also included a few more down-to-earth insights. As he and Krassner shared a snack, Groucho said, "I never thought eating a fig would be the biggest thrill of my life." Groucho's thoughts also drifted back to his "little crush on Marilyn Monroe when we were making *Love Happy:* I remember I got a hard-on just talking to her on the set." Krassner reported only one portion of the trip "when our conversation somehow got into a negative space," but even Groucho's negative thoughts focused on hippie-friendly themes. He complained about restraints on free love (marriage was "like quicksand") and the misdeeds of LBJ ("potato-head").

Masters, Robert. With his wife Jean Houston (see *Houston, Jean*), Masters wrote *The Varieties of Psychedelic Experience* and *Psychedelic Art. Varieties* was an attempt to analyze primary themes of the psychedelic experience, based on reports from numerous trippers. Like his wife, Masters saw LSD as one key to unlocking the potential of human consciousness. In a preface for the 2000 edition of *Varieties,* Masters expressed his continuing enthusiasm for psychedelic drugs and his disappointment over current bans on their use: "We are at a time when existing as well as new and unexplored psychedelics could be providing important understandings and knowledge so urgently needed by our people and our planet. Given the multitude of our problems, how foolish and how tragic it is to deny ourselves such treasures of experience and such vehicles of multifaceted empowerment."

Matrix. At the start of the San Francisco psychedelic rock scene, Marty Balin founded a small club called the Matrix as a showcase for his new band, Jefferson Airplane. The Airplane's Matrix concerts impressed critics and record executives, and soon they outgrew the venue. Although it was overshadowed by the Avalon and Fillmore (see *Avalon Ballroom; Fillmore*), the Matrix remained popular among local musicians; in *Fear and Loathing in Las Vegas,* Hunter S. Thompson recalled nights at the Matrix as a high point of psychedelic culture (see *Thompson, Hunter S*).

Max, Peter. Max created a psychedelic style of Pop Art known as "Cosmic 60s." His paintings and graphic designs used bright Fauvist colors to depict images and themes that resonated with hippie culture. Typical images included flowers, mandalas, clouds, and stars; prominent themes included love, peace, and harmony with nature. Posters of his work caught on quickly with college students of the later 1960s, and soon dozens of American companies engaged Max to design products and ads. He created, for example, a successful line of alarm clocks for General Electric, and a brand of panty hose that promised "to carry irresistible vibrations of love." In the late 1960s and early 1970s his images could be seen all over the country—

on billboards, t-shirts, lunch boxes, in dorm rooms, magazines, even museums. At one point he had commercial ties with 72 companies. He also worked for non-profit organizations such as the American Cancer Society, for whom he created an anti-smoking television commercial (see *Advertising*). Although Max made a well known poster titled "Psychedelic Cloud" and drove "Psychedelic Car," a Rolls Royce decorated with dayglo designs, he said that his inspiration did not come from drugs: he cited as influences contemporary rock music (especially the Beatles) and Eastern spirituality (especially yoga). In post-psychedelic decades he served as unofficial painter laureate, commissioned to paint presidents and to illustrate Olympics and Super Bowls. See *Psychedelic Art.*

Mayonnaise Jar. Michael Hollingshead, the English researcher who introduced Timothy Leary to LSD, converted one gram of the drug into an icing-like paste and stored it in a mayonnaise jar (see *Hollingshead, Michael*). As he took his LSD around with him and spooned out first doses for many artists and academics, his mayonnaise jar took on iconic status as a psychedelic artifact.

McCartney, Paul. Although his colleagues Lennon and Harrison took LSD much more frequently than he did, it was McCartney whose use of the drug became a scandal in 1967. McCartney had answered a newspaper reporter's question truthfully and acknowledged that he had taken LSD. Shortly afterward, when a television reporter pursued the subject, McCartney and the reporter sparred over whose responsibility it was to control public messages about drug use:

> Q. Don't you believe that this is a matter which you should have kept private?
> A. I was asked a question by a newspaper, and the decision was whether to tell a lie or tell him the truth.... I'm not trying to spread the word about this. But the man from the newspaper is the man from the mass medium. I'll keep it a personal thing if he does too.
> Q. Do you think that you have now encouraged your fans to take drugs?

A. I don't think my fans are going to take drugs just because I did.

Q. But as a public figure, surely you've got the responsibility to....

A. No, it's you who've got the responsibility. You've got the responsibility not to spread this *now*. You know, I'm quite prepared to keep it as a very personal thing if you will too. If you'll shut up about it, I will.

McCartney's testy response raised important questions about journalists and celebrities, but he must also have been annoyed by the irony of the situation: Paul was the least appropriate Beatle to take the fall for LSD. He admitted to using it "about four times" (as opposed to hundreds of trips for John and George). According to Lennon, Paul was "a bit more stable than George and I," and did not share their fascination with the psychedelic disruption of normal identity. See *Beatles; Lennon, John; Harrison, George; Starr, Ringo.*

McCloud, Mark. McCloud, a San Francisco artist with academic credentials, became the foremost collector of blotter art (see *Blotter Art*). He put on an exhibition of framed blotters in 1987 at the San Francisco Art Institute, which was also shown in New York and Houston. Despite his contention that the blotters were essentially art, not drugs, McCloud was twice arrested on charges of conspiracy to manufacture and distribute LSD. He was acquitted on both occasions. His lawyer argued successfully that none of the blotter squares retained any chemical potency, because exposure to sunlight had rendered the LSD inert.

McKenna, Terence. New Age philosopher McKenna considered psychedelic drugs the key to human evolution: organic hallucinogens gave humans the edge on apes, he believed, and more powerful psychedelics would show the way to alien dimensions and a transfigured future. LSD was McKenna's first psychedelic. At Berkeley in 1966 he lived across the hall from Barry Melton of Country Joe and the Fish, who supplied him with Sandoz acid. "For about an hour I just

ricocheted between tears of awe and tears of hilarity," he told Richard Gehr in 1992. He took LSD frequently thereafter, but eventually he decided that mushrooms and DMT made better evolutionary agents. "I hope this doesn't insult current LSD fans, but the last time I did it, it seemed like a Sopwith Camel or something.... What *I* had become used to was the cockpit of the Space Shuttle." McKenna died in 2000, twelve years before the apocalyptic event he predicted that would end history and vault humanity into hyperspace.

"Mellow Yellow." This Donovan song was mistakenly interpreted as referring to the supposed psychedelic properties of bananas. See *Bananas; Donovan.*

Merry Pranksters. "The Merry Pranksters" was the nickname of a group of LSD adventurers who had a major influence on psychedelic culture and the emergence of the hippie movement. At the same time that Timothy Leary and friends were experimenting with LSD at his estate in Millbrook, New York, the Merry Pranksters formed their own psychedelic community on the other side of the country. The California Pranksters had a very different style from the New York Learyites. Leary emphasized safety, expert guidance, and links with traditional spiritual wisdom; the Pranksters prized spontaneity, took playful risks, and provoked confrontations with mainstream society. As the Western counterpart to Leary's Eastern avant garde, the Pranksters had an equal and complementary influence on the development of psychedelic culture. Tom Wolfe's bestselling account of the Pranksters helped spread their reputation to the broader public (see *Electric Kool-Aid Acid Test*).

The Pranksters formed around novelist Ken Kesey and a few friends who shared his enthusiasm for LSD and related social experimentation. Kesey first tried LSD when he volunteered as a subject in the Menlo Park clinical trials sponsored by the CIA and the military. He spread news of the drug's extraordinary effects and generated interest among his artistic friends in Palo Alto and the Bay Area. Because Kesey had earned acclaim and money for his first novel, *One Flew over the Cuckoo's Nest,* he was able to purchase a house in La Honda, California suitable for communal living. One person who joined him there already had a considerable reputation from the Beat scene: Neal Cassady, the model for the character Dean Moriarty in Jack Kerouac's *On the Road.*

In the spring of 1964, the Pranksters decided to take a road trip of their own. They bought an old school bus, covered it with day-glo paint, and outfitted it with audio equipment, so that they could both amplify ambient noises and broadcast music and messages to the world outside the bus. They painted a mock warning sign on the back—"CAUTION: WEIRD LOAD" —and posted their destination as "FURTHUR." Cassady did much of the driving. He was famously adept as a driver, even in altered states; he was also an imaginative if rambling talker and finessed his way out of several awkward situations with authorities. Wolfe described an early example: when a police officer stopped them and noticed the broken hand brake, Cassady explained, "Well, yes sir, this is a Hammond bi-valve serrated brake, you understand, sir, had it put on in a truck ro-de-o in Springfield, Oregon, had to back through a slalom course of baby's bottles and yellow nappies, in the existential culmination of Oregon," and so forth. The officer listened for a while and decided not to pursue his inquiry.

The nominal goal of the bus trip was to reach the World's Fair in New York, but the real point was to foist their psychedelic antics on mainstream America. In Phoenix, for example, they paraded up and down the streets with a mock campaign sign for Goldwater: "A Vote for Barry Is a Vote for Fun!" Another time, they parked the bus at a Louisiana beach reserved for African-Americans and improvised a noisy psychedelic party until police broke it up. All across the country, they took acid and filmed their adventures. Some of the acid trips had unpleasant effects: one woman left the bus after she became delusional about her lost son, and another Prankster turned paranoid after a bad trip. Some of the Pranksters began to quarrel about Kesey's efforts to control the trip. Still, the communal spirit endured, and their favorite slogan amounted to a test of Prankster loyalty: "You're either on the bus, or you're off the bus." They made it to New York, where they visited Leary at Millbrook. The meeting of Western and Eastern LSD colonies did not go well. Leary was indisposed and stayed away from his visitors, and other Millbrook residents found the Pranksters annoying. The Pranksters soon tired of what they viewed as an uptight Millbrook scene: as Wolfe noted, Prankster Ken Babbs referred to their meditation rooms as "crypt trips."

When the bus finally made it back to La Honda, the Pranksters experimented with larger psychedelic parties—despite the fact that police had begun to take an interest in their doings. The Pranksters became interested in mixing with groups that seemed unlikely psychedelic partners. Once they all attended a conference of Unitarians, where their playful behavior upset the older members but intrigued some of the younger ones. Another time, Kesey invited the notorious Hell's Angels to a party at La Honda. According to Hunter S. Thompson, who joined the party as part of his Hell's Angels research, "Contrary to all expectations, most of the Angels became oddly peaceful on acid." Thompson described the La Honda mix of Pranksters and Angels as his favorite psychedelic experience, "complete with all the mad lighting, cops on the road, a Ron Boise sculpture looming out of the woods, and all the big speakers vibrating with Bob Dylan's 'Mr. Tambourine Man'" (*Hell's Angels;* see *Thompson, Hunter S.*).

Eventually Kesey came up with the idea of holding public parties where anyone could come share the psychedelic spirit of the Pranksters. These "Acid Tests" were held on approximately a dozen occasions in various locations (see *Acid Test*). The Pranksters advertised them with cryptic posters that asked, "Can You Pass the Acid Test?" Those who came found themselves in the middle of a chaotic event, more or less a combination of concert and carnival. Usually the Grateful Dead played as the unofficial house band for the Acid Tests (see *Grateful Dead*), surrounded by light shows and movies. Attendees were encouraged to wear costumes, dance, and express themselves by means of any available sound equipment. LSD was in plentiful supply. Wolfe described one Acid Test where the drug was mixed into a big vat of Kool-Aid: some who drank the Kool-Aid did not know its special ingredient. In January, 1966, Prankster Stewart Brand orchestrated an Acid Test on a much larger scale, called "The Trips Festival," which launched the broader hippie movement that culminated in the Summer of Love (see *Trips Festival*).

After Kesey was arrested on marijuana charges (and fled to Mexico), the Pranksters held together under Ken Babbs and Wavy Gravy. When Kesey returned, he told the Pranksters it was time to go beyond acid: psychedelic evolution should now be achievable without the drug. He organized one last event, the Acid Test Graduation, to mark the new era. Only some of the Pranksters attended, however—many of them, including Owsley, did not agree with his stance on LSD—and it was widely considered a flop. Not long afterward, Neal Cassady died in Mexico from an apparent drug overdose. Kesey served his prison sentence and then moved back to Oregon to resume his writing career.

Other Pranksters went on to interesting careers that reflected their youthful adventures. Stewart Brand created the *Whole Earth Catalog* and had a major influence on the environmental movement. Wavy Gravy founded the Hog Farm commune that, among other things, provided security for Woodstock and started a camp for underprivileged children. The Grateful Dead carried psychedelic music into the latter decades of the twentieth century, and as their concerts attracted both old and new hippies, they became more popular than ever. One of the Dead's early songs, "That's It for the Other One," pays tribute to the Pranksters—particularly to Neal Cassady, close friend and inspiration to the fledgling band. See *Babbs, Ken; Brand, Stewart; Cassady, Neal; Garcia, Carolyn; Garcia, Jerry; Grateful Dead; Kesey, Ken; Krassner, Paul; Owsley; Wavy Gravy*.

Metzner, Ralph. Metzner is a psychotherapist who worked on experiments with LSD and other hallucinogens as part of the group organized by Timothy Leary at Harvard University in the early 1960s. All three men were dismissed from Harvard but continued their work on LSD as independent researchers. Along with Harvard colleague Richard Alpert, Metzner helped Leary write *The Psychedelic Experience*, a manual for trippers based on *The Tibetan Book of the Dead*. Metzner has more recently blended his interests in altered consciousness and mysticism with new theories of the environment and ecology. He started the Green Earth Foundation, "an educational and research organization dedicated to the healing and harmonizing of the relationships between humanity and the Earth" (*GreenEarthFound.org*). See *Leary, Timothy; Alpert, Richard; Psychedelic Experience*.

Microdots. This version of LSD delivered the drug in tiny tablets. The most famous microdots came from the Welsh lab of chemist Richard Kemp, who was arrested in Operation Julie. See *Kemp, Richard; Operation Julie*.

Miles, Barry. Miles was a prominent figure in London's psychedelic scene of the 1960s. He co-owned the Indica Gallery, a popular gathering place for countercultural celebrities, and helped found the underground publication *International Times*. In 2003 he published *Hippie,* a detailed remembrance of people and events from the psychedelic era. At the 2006 Basel symposium to mark Albert Hofmann's 100th birthday, Miles gave a talk on "LSD and Its Impact on Art, Design, and Music."

Military Testing. Because they strongly suspected that the Soviet Union—with a plentiful natural supply of ergot—was working on LSD as a potential weapon, the American military launched a testing program of their own. Beginning in the early 1950s and continuing for approximately twenty years, the U.S. Army Chemical Corps tested LSD and other drugs on military personnel at the Edgewood Arsenal in Maryland. The point was to judge the effectiveness of the drug as a potential weapon for the battlefield: to observe how severely an acid trip might impair soldiers' ability to fight. These tests occurred during the same period that the CIA was conducting its own experiments with LSD (see *MK-Ultra*). The Army, unlike the CIA, used only subjects who had volunteered for the testing. Nevertheless, controversies arose after details of the program became public in the 1970s. Some military volunteers claimed that they had been inadequately informed about LSD and had suffered damages to their mental health. One ex-volunteer who sued for damages was James Stanley, who maintained that the LSD tests had impaired his ability to function normally in marriage or career; his case went all the way to the Supreme Court, which ruled against him in 1987 by a 5–4 vote (see *Supreme Court*). After the controversial testing program became known to the public, the Army undertook a follow-up study of nearly 700 soldiers who had participated in the experiments. The study concluded that "the majority of subjects evaluated did not appear to have sustained any significant damage from their participation in the LSD experiments." However, the study also found irregularities in the process for soliciting and informing volunteers.

The British military also conducted LSD tests on their own personnel. At the Porton Down base in the 1950s and 1960s, the military ran a program called "Operation Moneybags." The codename came from a pun on initials: "l.s.d." was also the notation for "pounds, shillings, pence." The alternative video source "Undercurrents" found newsreel footage from 1964 that shows a squad of soldiers attempting to carry out a battle exercise after they had taken acid. One member of the squad had a bad reaction and required medical attention, but the others "began to relax and giggle," according to the voiceover narration. The camera shows a radio crew laughing as their wires get hopelessly tangled, a rocket launcher team with "very impaired efficiency," and an attack group that lost not only its orientation but "all sense of urgency." Finally, "with one man climbing a tree to feed the birds, the troop commander gave up, admitting he could no longer control himself or his men. He himself then relapsed into laughter."

Despite these promising results, LSD was never deployed by the British or the Americans as a military weapon. In addition to ethical issues related to the use of chemical agents in warfare, military authorities saw practical problems with dissemination and dosage. As for the threat that sparked the testing, it remains unclear how much LSD testing was actually carried out by the Soviets. Little documentation has surfaced, although a video shown recently on Czech television shows Soviet testing of LSD on Czech soldiers.

Millbrook. After Timothy Leary was dismissed from Harvard, he set up a colony of psychedelic enthusiasts at a mansion in Millbrook, New York, near Poughkeepsie (see *Leary, Timothy*). The property had been loaned to him by Billy Hitchcock of the Mellon family, who found LSD intriguing and wanted to support Leary's experiments (see *Hitchcock, William Mellon*). With 64 rooms and 4,000 forested acres, Millbrook offered an ideal situation for Leary and dozens of psychedelic utopians, mainly poets, artists, psychologists, and philosophers. They took acid frequently, frolicked in the woods, meditated in candlelit rooms, and helped each other negotiate bad trips. While at Millbrook, Leary formed the League for Spiritual Discovery and co-authored *The Psychedelic Experience* (see *League for Spiritual Discovery; Psychedelic Experience*). As Leary described it in *Flashbacks,* Millbrook was an attempt to assemble "a social molecule, what Kurt Vonnegut calls a 'karass,' a structure of people whose neural characteristics fit together. We hoped that by living and re-imprinting via LSD with different kinds of people we could develop a hive consciousness, each person contributing a specific function, playing a definite role in the completed family." Poet Diane DiPrima's role, for example, was chief cook: she found herself assigned to fix all meals for 50 people during her stay at Millbrook (see *DiPrima, Diane*).

Hitchcock's neighbors did not appreciate the exotic intruders, and Millbrook increasingly came under scrutiny by law enforcement agents. Chief Leary tormentor was G. Gordon Liddy, then assistant district attorney. Liddy and Leary sparred over searches and surveillance; eventually Liddy arrested Leary for possession of marijuana. As his legal troubles mounted, Leary left Millbrook in 1967, and Hitchcock soon evicted the stragglers.

Mindbenders. Many years after they were originally distributed, four LSD documentaries from the late 1960s were packaged by "Something Weird Video" in a tape called *Mindbenders*. Something Weird marketed the product as campy hilarity for savvy veterans of the 1960s, but only one of the documentaries is dominated by caricature and misinformation. Although their bottom line messages are all monitory, the other three make concessions to the aesthetic, spiritual, and therapeutic claims of LSD enthusiasts.

The first documentary was produced in cooperation with the Inglewood Police Department for use in schools. "LSD: Trip or Trap?" presents anti–LSD propaganda embedded within a fictional narrative. Chuck and Bob are high school friends whose paths diverge when someone offers them LSD: Chuck takes an acid trip while Bob takes notes at the library. Bob learns that LSD induces listlessness, alienation, and sometimes derangement and self-mutilation. "Trip or Trap" does not mention therapeutic or religious uses of the drug, and the film refers incongruously to pushers, kids getting hooked, LSD addicts breaking into cars to steal money, and so on—all of which apply more to drugs like heroin and cocaine. "Trip or Trap" ends with warnings about chromosome damage (images of a thalidomide baby) and flashbacks (leading to Chuck's fictional death).

The other three documentaries attempt no narrative and present information about LSD in a more complex way. The Navy film "LSD" offers a lecture for sailors of the psychedelic era. Although the medical officer exaggerates some of the psychological dangers, he treats LSD's spiritual nexus with a measure of respect. People on LSD, he says, experience altered perceptions of space and time, and they interpret these sensations as "religious and beautiful and godlike—perhaps because they expect them to be." He notes the practical dangers of mysticism for a sailor on a warship. "It becomes hard to know where you stop and the chair starts: hard to know if you're thinking something or if, say, the bulkhead is thinking something." The Navy doctor minimizes LSD's aesthetic and spiritual claims in the name of common sense: "I have no intention of risking my career, my judgment, my ambition, my kids, and my sanity so I can sit for twelve hours and watch pretty colored lights behind my eyeballs."

The third documentary, "The Mind-Benders: LSD and the Hallucinogens," came from the Food and Drug Administration. "The Mind-Benders" covers both benefits and dangers, and although it concludes with a mild warning—"the facts of the matter suggest caution"—the film is surprisingly generous in acknowledging helpful effects. "Mind-Benders" mainly focuses on three implied questions: Does LSD do more good than harm in its effects on health? Does it promote or inhibit normal social interaction? Does it enhance creativity, and if so, at what cost? The documentary slaloms back and forth between the good and the bad, and lets various witnesses speak for themselves.

The last documentary, an ABC television special produced and narrated by Tim Knight, offers a curious mixture of messages about LSD. There are stories of psychotic violence, and the segment about chromosome damage includes images of deformity and mental retardation. But "Trip to Where" acknowledges the successes of LSD psychotherapy, presents a sympathetic interview with Timothy Leary, and ends with Tim Knight admitting that he took his own acid trip as part of his research: "During the course of filming this documentary I took my own acid trip. I was lucky—I came out undamaged. In fact, I had a good trip: that's what I tried to reproduce in the dream sequence earlier. But I believe that the danger of LSD far outweigh the benefits. And scientists agree. It's just not worth it." The ABC documentary ambiguously confirms both countercultural and mainstream messages about LSD.

Mirage. After losing its famous "Siegfried and Roy" show, this Las Vegas hotel contracted with Cirque du Soleil to produce a new signature attraction—this time featuring Beatles instead of tigers. The show "Love" offers a spectacular performance of psychedelic music and images (see *Cirque du Soleil*). The Mirage also installed the Beatle-themed REVOLUTION lounge as a further attraction for nostalgic Baby Boomers.

MK-Ultra. "MK-Ultra" was the code name given to a secret CIA program begun in the early 1950s to test LSD and other drugs as potential mind-control agents. MK-Ultra evolved from the earlier "Project Artichoke," also supervised by the CIA. The American government had become interested in European psychiatric experiments with the powerful drug derived from the ergot fungus; because the Soviet Union had an abundant supply of natural ergot, the CIA feared that the Soviets could gain the upper hand in the development of an LSD superweapon. From 1951 until the mid–1960s, Artichoke and MK-Ultra designed and funded elaborate experiments with LSD. Details about the two programs only became public two decades later as journalists and scholars gained access to confidential records. The history of MK-Ultra reveals fascinating but disturbing details about Cold War paranoia and attendant ethical lapses.

CIA researchers first thought that LSD might make an effective truth serum. Early psychiatric use of the drug suggested that it might facilitate access to unconscious materials, and a few tests on military and CIA personnel looked promising. However, LSD proved too mind-blowing and unpredictable to serve as a truth serum. The CIA soon shifted its focus to a second application, essentially the opposite of the first one: instead of getting an enemy prisoner to reveal secrets, LSD might allow a captured CIA agent to avoid telling the enemy anything useful. Under this second theory, an agent might carry around a dose of acid as an alternative to a suicide pill. Once the agent started tripping, his or her behavior would become so bizarre that captors would abandon any attempt at interrogation. Ultimately, neither the truth serum theory nor the anti-truth serum theory proved practical. MK-Ultra examined a third potential use of LSD, this time as a tool for brainwashing. They funded the experiments of a Canadian psychiatrist, Ewen Cameron, who subjected over fifty mental patients to frequent LSD dosing in combination with electroshock and sleep manipulation. The idea was to recondition defective or damaged minds, but the CIA was interested in the technique as a means of reprogramming a normal mind. The use of LSD in brainwashing also turned out to be impractical. The CIA conceived of one final application for LSD, which looked to be the most sensible of the four theories. Covert agents might be able to slip LSD into the food or drink of a political leader who was considered a threat to American security. Disoriented by the surprise acid trip, the leader would act in ways that caused self-doubt and public embarrassment, perhaps leading to his downfall. Fidel Castro was one of the leaders specified by MK-Ultra as a potential target for LSD attack. Before approving such a tactic, agency scientists wanted to test the drug on subjects who received it unawares in a public situation. Led by Dr. Sidney Gottlieb see *Gottlieb, Sidney*), the CIA began giving surprise acid to CIA and military personnel, in order to observe their behavior. Such testing on subjects without their consent violated the ethical standards set out at Nuremberg following World War II, but MK-Ultra's work remained secret and went unchallenged through the duration of the program. One CIA employee who received LSD from Gottlieb was Dr. Frank Olson, a biochemist who worked for the drug testing program. Not long after his unexpected acid trip, Olson apparently committed suicide by jumping from a hotel window. Twenty years later, the U.S. government officially acknowledged the secret drug tests and issued an apology to the Olson family. The death of Frank Olson remains a matter of controversy, however: his son has developed a theory that Olson was murdered by CIA agents who feared that he was about to disclose Artichoke and MK-Ultra secrets (see *Olson, Frank*). Olson's death did not discourage MK-Ultra from pursuing its testing of LSD on unwitting subjects. In one of the boldest plans, someone was going to spike the punch at the CIA Christmas party. An official nixed the idea just before the party; psychedelic punch would have to wait an-

other decade or so for the Merry Pranksters' electric kool-aid (see *Merry Pranksters*). Another outrageous testing scheme did receive the green light. In "Operation Midnight Climax," CIA agents hired prostitutes in San Francisco to lure men to an apartment. After a prostitute slipped some LSD into her client's drink, an agent watched and took notes behind a two-way mirror to gauge the effects of the drug.

The LSD experiments of MK-Ultra finally came to an end sometime in the mid–1960s. Ironically, it was this secret, in many ways sinister government operation that prepared the way for recreational and spiritual uses of LSD by the hippie counterculture. CIA funding brought significant amounts of LSD into the U.S., improved methods for manufacturing the drug, and supported clinical tests in hospitals. Among the subjects were eventual acid evangelists and celebrities, including Allen Ginsberg and Ken Kesey.

Moby Grape. Moby Grape was a prominent psychedelic rock band during the prime years of the San Francisco music scene. They headlined several concerts and had some measure of critical and commercial success; their success was short-lived, however, and their work was overshadowed by a few San Francisco bands that had more lasting impact, such as the Grateful Dead and Jefferson Airplane. Moby Grape was formed in 1966 by two members of the original Jefferson Airplane, Skip Spence and Matthew Katz. They assembled a group that featured three guitarists—Spence, Jerry Miller, and Peter Lewis—who all contributed "lead" elements. This unusual arrangement gave Moby Grape its distinctive sound, and in their best work, such as the song "Omaha," the three guitars compete and combine artfully.

Moby Grape declined quickly as a result of poor management and the LSD-related collapse of Skip Spence. Spence developed psychotic symptoms during a period of heavy use of the drug. After spending several months in Bellevue Hospital, Spence recovered sufficiently to record a solo album, but he never rejoined Moby Grape. Spence's collapse has sometimes been compared with that of Pink Floyd's Syd Barrett (see *Pink Floyd; Barrett, Syd*).

Monkees. This rock band was assembled for an American television show in the wake of the Beatles' success. Producers of the show modeled *The Monkees* on the first Beatles' movie, *A Hard Day's Night*. When the Beatles moved into their psychedelic phase (see *Beatles*), the Monkees answered with a psychedelic movie of their own, *Head* (1968). *Head* was directed by Bob Rafelson, one of the creators of the television show, and co-written by Rafelson, the four Monkees, and Jack Nicholson. Nicholson's interest in psychedelic film grew out of his own use of LSD, both for therapy and recreation (see *Nicholson, Jack*); at roughly the same time he worked on *Head*, he also wrote *The Trip* and acted in *Easy Rider* (see *Trip; Easy Rider*). Unlike those two LSD-related movies, *Head* satirized the serious elements of Beatles-style psychedelia.

Head flopped in 1968 but gained a cult following in later decades. It has no real plot—just a series of scenes that make fun of movie artifice and psychedelic culture. Three aspects of psychedelic culture receive satirical treatment. The first target of satire is the psychedelic experience itself. In one scene, Davy Jones is whistling "Strawberry Fields Forever" as he enters a bathroom; when he opens the medicine cabinet, he sees a giant eye and recoils in terror. When a second Monkee opens the cabinet, it's just a cabinet. *Head* also satirizes the Beatles' interest in transcendental meditation and Eastern spirituality. At one point, Peter Tork listens to a robed guru's vacuous lecture, in the midst of what looks like sacramental incense. Eventually the guru giggles, says "But why should anyone listen to me? I know nothing," and the camera pulls back to reveal a steam-filled sauna. A third target from

psychedelic culture is the commercialism of the music industry. The movie opens with the Monkees singing a parody of their television theme song, which ends with a bitter chorus about music and money. In sounding this note, *Head* brings to mind Frank Zappa's parody of *Sergeant Pepper*, his album entitled *We're Only in It for the Money* (see *Zappa, Frank*). Appropriately, Zappa performs a cameo role in *Head*. He meets Davy Jones and criticizes him for spending too little time on his music: "You should spend more time on it, because the youth of America depends on you to show the way." Zappa's absurd figure (he is wearing a suit and tie, and for no apparent reason, leading a cow), along with his deadpan delivery, undercut the solemnity of his remarks. Zappa thereby helps the Monkees satirize the industry that gave them life as pseudo–Beatles.

Monterey Pop. The first large-scale rock festival was held in Monterey, California over three days in June of 1967, attracting a total attendance of 200,000. John Phillips of the Mamas and the Papas wrote a hit song to promote the festival, "San Francisco (Be Sure to Wear Some Flowers in Your Hair)." Monterey Pop helped to popularize psychedelic music and usher in the Summer of Love; D.A. Pennebaker's documentary film of the concert broadened its impact. The major San Francisco bands all played there, but the most stirring performances came from Janis Joplin and Jimi Hendrix, who electrified the crowd and burst into prominence (see *Joplin, Janis; Hendrix, Jimi*). Joplin sang a memorable version of "Ball and Chain," and after the concert, Columbia signed her band to a recording contract (see *Big Brother and the Holding Company*). Hendrix's performance was even more striking. He had taken some of the "Monterey Purple" LSD that Owsley had made specifically to supply the event (see *Owsley*). At the end of his set, the tripping Hendrix poured lighter fluid on his Stratocaster, lit it on fire, smashed it to pieces, and then threw the fragments into the crowd—a good number of whom had also taken Monterey Purple.

Moody Blues. The English band Moody Blues developed a distinctive style of psychedelic rock that blended elements of classical music with more traditional rock forms. Their 1967 album *Days of Future Passed* used the London Festival Orchestra to produce a song cycle representing the course of a single day. Two of these songs, "Tuesday Afternoon" and "Nights in White Satin," became popular hits. The Moody Blues' orchestral style to some degree reflected the Beatles' experiments on *Sergeant Pepper,* but Moody Blues' songs were smoother in musical texture and less disorienting.

Their most psychedelic music came on the following album, *In Search of the Lost Chord* (1968). The album cover art aims for psychedelic sublimity, with fluid lettering and images of an embryo on one side and a skull on the other. The songs contain various psychedelic themes. "Legend of a Mind," flautist Ray Thomas' tribute to Timothy Leary, raises the topic of LSD most prominently. He begins by announcing Leary's figurative death, by which he means that Leary has transcended the limitations of ordinary mortal consciousness. This song salutes Leary as the ultimate trip guide. The song features an Indian sitar sound appropriate to the subject, along with ethereal flute solos. The more conventional hit song "Ride My See-Saw" touches on a few common themes in psychedelic lyrics: a setting of child-like innocence, sensory alteration, and criticism of mainstream social values. Unlike many of their contemporaries, the Moody Blues survived psychedelic celebrity with little difficulty and continued to record and perform for decades.

Moore, Alan. Graphic novelist Moore ran into trouble as a teenager because of his adventures with LSD. Moore not only used the drug but sold it to classmates in the English city of Northampton. When authorities caught on, they expelled the 17-year-old Moore from school. He later described himself as "one of the world's most inept LSD dealers": "The problem with being an LSD dealer, if you're sampling your own products, is your view of reality will probably become horribly distorted. And you may believe you have supernatural powers and you are completely immune to any form of retaliation and prosecution, which is not the case."

Moore eventually sorted things out and found his calling. His graphic novels have been highly successful critically and commercially, both when he offered new takes on inherited characters (including Superman and Swamp Thing) and when he composed entirely original narratives, such as *Watchmen, From Hell,* and *V for Vendetta.* In *V for Vendetta,* Moore returned to the subject of LSD. Despite his comments quoted above about LSD inducing a "horribly distorted" view of reality, Moore gave the drug a starring role in *Vendetta* as a tool for discovering deep truth. One of the main characters, Eric Finch, takes LSD to help him solve a mystery; he ends up not only with a solution to the mystery but a crucial insight about his own life. Finch works as police chief in a London ruled by fascists who came to power after a nuclear war. He has been struggling to capture a terrorist who calls himself V. When Finch finds out that V had earlier been held in a government concentration camp, he goes to the site of the abandoned camp to learn what he might about his antagonist's identity. He takes four hits of LSD to loosen up his mind. In the pages that follow, Finch hallucinates images of imprisonment and torture. These visions help him intuit V's hiding place, but more climactically, they lead to self-recognition: the acid trip prompts Finch to understand that he has imprisoned himself in a life he finds repugnant and dishonest. He asks himself, "Who imprisoned me here," and "Who can release me? Who's controlling and constraining my life, except me?" As soon as he reaches this epiphany, the frightening visions disappear (as do his clothes: he's naked for the last few panels). He ends up carrying out his mission against V, but at the end of the novel, Finch walks away from London and his job.

Moore's depiction of Finch's acid trip suggests one theory of how LSD can be dangerous and two theories of how it can be useful. In giving Finch terrifying hallucinations, Moore acknowledges the panic that sometimes accompanies an intense psychedelic experience and might prove psychologically damaging. But the LSD also triggers two positive results: it enhances Finch's creative ability as an investigator, and it facilitates a compressed, self-service dose of existential psychoanalysis. The movie version of *V for Vendetta*—which Moore did not like—preserved Finch's epiphany but deleted the LSD.

Morning Glory. Many species of this flower contain ergot alkaloids, the natural chemical from which LSD was derived. Morning Glory seeds make an impractical psychedelic, however: their potency is much lower than LSD, and commercial seeds have been treated with preservatives or other chemicals that make consumption dangerous. See *Flower Power*.

Moscoso, Victor. Moscoso was a prominent poster artist in San Francisco during the peak psychedelic years (see *Psychedelic Posters*). He had more formal training in art than any of his peers in psychedelic poster design: Moscoso studied under painter Josef Albers at Yale, where he learned about color theory. Moscoso has said that when he began making psychedelic posters, he applied this theory in an unusual way: "Everything I learned in school, I reversed." In order to produce eye-jarring effects suggestive of psychedelic perception, Moscoso juxtaposed bright colors so that the edges of his designs seemed to vibrate. Moscoso began his psychedelic career by making posters for concerts at the Avalon Ballroom (see *Avalon Ballroom*); soon he developed his

own imprint, Neon Rose, and produced designs for a variety of events and underground publications. Later he contributed graphic art to Zap Comix (see *Zap Comix*).

Moss, Thelma. American screenwriter Moss read Aldous Huxley and decided to try psychedelic psychotherapy for symptoms of depression and frigidity (see *Huxley, Aldous; Psychiatry*). After several sessions with a Beverly Hills psychiatrist, she found herself transformed. She wrote about her LSD therapy in the bestselling *Myself and I* (1962), published under the pseudonym Constance Newland. Moss explained that she discovered alarming underlying aspects of her psyche—including sadistic and masochistic impulses—but she emphasized the positive effects of her therapy: "I lost my fear of dentists, the clicking in my neck and throat, arm tensions, and my dislike of clocks ticking in the bedroom. I also achieved transcendental sexual fulfillment." Her account of these psychedelic revelations was graphic enough that some libraries classified *Myself and I* as pornography.

Moss devoted the rest of the decade to studying at UCLA's Neuropsychiatric Institute, where she earned a Ph.D. and an academic position. She developed a keen interest in parapsychology and became a consultant on matters of telekinesis, e.s.p., and ghosts.

Mouse, Stanley. Mouse (born Stanley Miller) teamed with Alton Kelley to produce some of the most memorable posters from the psychedelic years in San Francisco. Mouse grew up in Detroit, where he began designing t-shirts and other items related to "hot rod" culture. He moved to San Francisco in 1965 and met Kelley, a member of the hippie group "Family Dog" that sponsored dance concerts at the Avalon Ballroom (see *Avalon Ballroom; Family Dog; Kelley, Alton*). Mouse and Kelley collaborated on many posters for Avalon shows. Ordinarily, Kelley would conceive of ideas for designs and Mouse would do most of the drawing and coloring. They moved into an old firehouse that served as a studio; during the height of the Haight-Ashbury scene, they invited fellow artists to "jam" as they worked on posters side-by-side.

Mouse and Kelley posters interpreted psychedelia with a strong influence from Art Nouveau. Their lettering, while psychedelic in style, was typically more legible than the lettering of some of their peers, especially Wes Wilson and Rick Griffin (see *Wilson, Wes; Griffin, Rick*). Frequently Mouse and Kelley borrowed images from old books, magazines, and advertisements. One of their first notable posters reproduced the image of the "Zig-Zag" man from the brand of cigarette rolling papers. For their single best known work, the "Skeleton and Roses" poster for a Grateful Dead concert, they found the perfect image in a nineteenth-century edition of the *Rubaiyat of Omar Khayyam.* "So we used it on that poster that became the famous icon," said Mouse many years later. "I'm most famous for something I didn't even do! All I did to it was color it in" (*Washington Post,* April, 2009). The Skeleton and Roses poster has hung in museums and fetches high prices in the collectibles market. See *Psychedelic Posters.*

Mullis, Kary. Mullis, a Nobel Prize winning chemist, told Albert Hofmann that LSD helped him conceptualize the polymerase chain reaction that won him the Nobel in 1993. In a 1994 interview with *California Monthly,* Mullis said, "Back in the 1960s and early 1970s I took plenty of LSD. A lot of people were doing it in Berkeley back then. And I found it to be a mind-opening experience. It was certainly much more important than any courses I ever took." In his autobiography, Mullis went even further: "I think I might have been stupid in some respects, if it weren't for my psychedelic experiences."

Murray, Henry. Murray was a prominent psychological researcher at Harvard when Timothy Leary arrived (see *Harvard; Leary, Timothy*). Formerly an officer in military intelligence, he worked on subjects related to mind control and brainwashing as well as more conventional psychological topics. Murray took an interest in Leary's research and did his own experiments with LSD and other psychedelic drugs. Murray himself took LSD in 1961, out of "curiosity and the envisaged possibility that I might revel in a little efficacious lunacy." Decades later when the case against Unabomber Ted Kaczynski emerged, Murray's name surface again: Kaczynski had been a volunteer subject in one of Murray's Harvard studies testing effects of various stressful conditions. Although some who wrote about the case speculated that Kaczynski might have been given LSD as part of Murray's experiments, Kaczynski did not recall taking the drug, and there is no evidence that acid played a part in his mental deterioration.

Murray, John Courtney. An American Jesuit priest who advised JFK and had considerable influence on the 1960s modernization of Catholicism, Murray experimented with LSD between sessions of the Second Vatican Council. See *Jesuits.*

Museums. Although Ken Kesey refused the Smithsonian when they tried to acquire his Prankster bus (see *Merry Pranksters*), three museums have staged major exhibits of psychedelic materials. The first came in 1997 at the Rock and Roll Hall of Fame and Museum in Cleveland: "I Want to Take You Higher: The Psychedelic Era, 1965–1969" was the inaugural show mounted by the new museum. In 2005, Tate Liverpool presented "Summer of Love: Art of the Psychedelic Era" (which later traveled to New York's Whitney Museum), and in 2009, the Denver Art Museum organized its collection of psychedelic posters into an exhibit called "The Psychedelic Experience." All three exhibits represent the period in faithful detail, with an impressive array of artifacts and surrounding commentary. As accurate as they are in their re-creation of psychedelic culture, these exhibits cannot overcome an inherent incongruity between the world of museums and the world of psychedelia: the psychedelic experience privileged spontaneity and the ineffable uniqueness of the present moment, whereas museums place art and artists in historical context. The blurb from the Cleveland show, for example, adjusts Leary's slogan to mark the difference between a countercultural past and a mainstream present. Instead of "Turn on, tune in, drop out," it reads, "Turn on, tune in, and take a spectacular trip from 1965 to 1969 with the Rock and Roll Hall of Fame and Museum." Essays from the Liverpool exhibit historicized and demystified elements of psychedelic culture, such as free love, which "did rather little to alleviate the socialized sexism of the period" (Austin). At the Denver show, amid quotations from artists who flouted legibility in the name of psychedelic hipness, docents with laser pointers matter-of-factly decoded the posters.

Navy. At a time when the American military was beginning to research LSD as a mind-control weapon (see *Military Testing*), one naval doctor wanted to explore its potential in therapy for sailors suffering from depression. In 1952, Lieutenant Charles Savage of the U.S. Navy Medical Corps received a supply of LSD from Sandoz to run a trial at the Bethesda naval hospital. Savage concluded that results with LSD were about the same as with traditional methods, but he noted that the drug produced effects useful for psychoanalysis: "Improvement obtained during the course of LSD therapy was not greater than that obtained without its use in comparable cases. However, LSD affords therapeutically valuable insights into unconscious processes by the medium of the hallucinations it produces."

Another naval connection to LSD surfaced in 1966 in a *Life* magazine cover story about the drug (see *Life).* The story included a note about John Busby, a retired Navy captain who "used LSD just once and solved an elusive problem in pattern recognition while developing intelligence equipment for a

Navy research project" (see *Busby, John).* Captain Busby said that LSD helped him circumvent "the normal limiting mechanisms of the brain."

Captain Busby's good experience notwithstanding, the Navy soon felt compelled to warn sailors of the psychedelic era about the dangers of LSD. In the 1968 documentary "LSD," a naval doctor explains the effects of the drug and concludes that its risks greatly outweigh any benefits: "I have no intention of risking my career, my judgment, my ambition, my kids, and my sanity so I can sit for twelve hours and watch pretty colored lights behind my eyeballs" (see *Mindbenders).*

Neo-American Church. In 1965, Arthur Kleps founded the Neo-American Church, a religion based on the use of LSD. Kleps declared that "psychedelic substances are the true host of the Church," and defined the "religious duty of all members to partake of the sacrament on regular occasions." Kleps' writings about his church strongly suggest that his intentions were satirical, and a court eventually ruled that the Neo-American Church was not entitled to the protections granted to valid religious groups. See *Religion; Kleps, Arthur; Chief Boo-Hoo.*

Newland, Constance. Thelma Moss published her bestselling LSD memoir *Myself and I* under this pseudonym. See *Moss, Thelma.*

Nichols, Charles. A pharmacology professor at LSU, Nichols received a substantial grant from NIH in 2009 to test LSD on rats and fruit flies in an effort to improve understanding of the neurochemistry underlying psychosis and schizophrenia. According to the university press release, "Genes and proteins that are abnormally turned on or off by LSD in the rat brain, and found to participate in causing relevant behaviors in the fruit fly, may represent novel therapeutic targets for neuropsychiatric disorders." See *Schizophrenia; Nichols, David.*

Nichols, David. A professor of pharmacology at Purdue, Nichols was one of the few scientists in the decades following the 1960s to pursue serious LSD research. He synthesized and tested on rats a number of chemical variants on the LSD compound, some of which had even stronger effects; several of these compounds are described in Shulgin's *TiHKAL* (see *Shulgin, Alexander; TiHKAL*). Nichols' son Charles has taken up his father's research interests (see *Nichols, Charles*).

Nicholson, Jack. Nicholson first took LSD in the early 1960s, when he was struggling to build a career and having troubles in his marriage. A therapist who was counseling Nicholson and his wife (Sandra Knight) recommended that they try LSD therapy, which was getting good publicity in Hollywood circles, especially through the work of psychiatrist Oscar Janiger (see *Janiger, Oscar*). The therapist gave LSD to Sandra first, and as Nicholson told biographer Peter Thompson, it was not a pleasant experience. "At one point, she looked at me and saw a demon, a totally demonic figure. For whatever reason, either because it's true about me, or because of her own grasping at something, it was pretty bad." Nicholson's own LSD experience was intense and productive. As Thompson reports, "At one point, he was screaming at the top of his voice; he also relived his own birth, met his fears of homosexuality, and had the most terrifying fright. He said it was all highly graphic visually, especially the part when he was inside his mother's womb." Nicholson continued to use LSD, although his wife did not, and eventually they divorced.

Nicholson later wrote the screenplay for *The Trip* (1967), the Roger Corman movie about a man's first acid trip, which starred Peter Fonda and Dennis Hopper (see *Trip; Fonda, Peter; Hopper, Dennis*). Like Nicholson's own first trip, this fictional one was taken for therapeutic purposes in the context of a failing marriage. In 1968 he starred in the psychedelic B-movie *Psych Out* (see

Psych Out). A year later, he joined Fonda and Hopper in the cast of *Easy Rider,* another film that depicts an LSD trip (see *Easy Rider*); his performance in that film was widely praised and launched his career.

Nin, Anaïs. Nin took LSD in 1955 under the supervision of psychiatrist Oscar Janiger (see *Janiger, Oscar*). She wrote about the experience in an entry that was eventually published as part of her collected diaries. Nin had been reading *The Doors of Perception* (see *Huxley, Aldous*), and one of her friends encouraged her to volunteer for Janiger's LSD studies. She took LSD in Janiger's office, with a guide attending her. The resulting diary entry is much shorter than *The Doors of Perception*, but Nin's account, vivid and though-provoking, stands as one of the earliest prose poems about LSD visions.

As the drug took effect, Nin felt "as if I had been plunged to the bottom of the sea, and everything had become undulatory and wavering." Later on, she returned to this ocean theme. She had started to weep, and after first reprimanding herself—"What a ridiculous thing to spoil a voyage through space by weeping"—she told her guide emphatically why women weep: "IT IS THE QUICKEST WAY TO REJOIN THE OCEAN." In general, when her visions involved planets and space, she tended to feel lonely and shrunken. She was much happier with visions of oceans, temples, and jewels. In her worst moment, she had trouble breathing and sought comfort from her guide and Dr. Janiger; in her best moment, she saw the world turn golden, "the most pleasurable sensation I had ever known, like an orgasm. It was the secret of life, the alchemist's secret of life."

Nin later reflected that most of the images in her LSD visions had been suggested by literary sources. From Saint-Exupery's *The Little Prince*, she took the image of a lonely self standing at the edge of a planet; from *Alice's Adventures in Wonderland*, the feeling of sudden shrinking. She also recognized that the underwater, undulating imagery resembled passages from her own first novel, *House of Incest*. Although she enjoyed the LSD experience, she later told Huxley that people should not depend on drugs to gain access to unconscious materials and reawaken their sensory powers. Huxley became "irritable" when she said so, according to Nin. Huxley told her, "You're fortunate enough to have a natural access to your subconscious life, but other people need drugs, and should have them."

No-Hitter. Dock Ellis of the Pittsburgh Pirates threw a no-hitter in 1971 when he was high on LSD. See *Ellis, Dock*.

"Okie from Muskogee." This number one country hit explicitly rejected LSD and its surrounding culture. See *Haggard, Merle*.

Olson, Frank. Olson was a biochemist employed by the CIA in the years following World War II. He worked in secret programs for the development and testing of drugs, including LSD, that might be deployed as weapons or as tools for interrogation and mind control. Olson died on November 28, 1953 under mysterious circumstances. According to the official account of his death, Olson committed suicide by jumping from a hotel window in New York City. He had been sent there under supervision, because colleagues at the CIA had noticed symptoms of mental instability; they attributed these symptoms to the LSD that Olson had been given on November 18 as part of a CIA experiment.

Olson was given the drug without his consent. As Ed Regis explains, CIA scientists gathered at Deep Creek Lake for what was described as a retreat. In fact, head researcher Sidney Gottlieb intended to carry out "an impromptu mind-control experiment" to gauge the effects of LSD on people who did not know they had taken it (see *Gottlieb, Sidney*). After dinner, Gottlieb dissolved some LSD in a bottle of Cointreau and offered the liqueur to his guests, including Frank Olson. Ten days later, Olson was dead. The story of a CIA researcher's suicide eventually entered the public record as a cautionary tale about the dangers of LSD for mental health, especially with people who take it unknowingly or without proper preparation. This account of the Olson death did not come out until over twenty years after the event. In 1953, the public report simply referred to an "accident" involving an "Army scientist"; the Olson family was told that he had either fallen or jumped from the hotel window. No mention was made of the CIA or the drug testing programs on which Olson was working. On June 11, 1975, a story in the *Washington Post* revealed the secret LSD connection:

> A civilian employee of the Department of the Army unwittingly took LSD as part of a CIA test, then jumped 10 floors to his death less than a week later, according to the Rockefeller commission report released yesterday. The man was given the drug while attending a meeting with CIA personnel working on a test project that involved the administration of mind-bending drugs to unsuspecting Americans. 'This individual was not made aware he had been given LSD until about 20 minutes after it had been administered,' the commission said. 'He developed serious side effects and was sent to New York with a CIA escort for psychiatric treatment. Several days later, he jumped from a tenth-floor window of his room and died as a result.'

Once these details came out, President Ford formally apologized to the Olson family, and Congress passed a bill authorizing compensation for their loss.

Despite these revelations and apologies, members of Frank Olson's family remain skeptical about the circumstances of their father's death. His son Eric pursued the case and developed a new theory. Eric Olson gathered information from previously classified materials, from conversations with a few of his father's colleagues, and from an exhumation of Frank Olson's body in 1994. The new information led him to theorize that his father's death was a case of murder, not suicide. According to Eric Olson, "Frank

Olson did not die because he was an experimental guinea pig who experienced a 'bad trip.' He died because of concern that he would divulge information concerning a highly classified CIA interrogation program called 'ARTICHOKE' in the early 1950s, and concerning the use of biological weapons by the United States in the Korean War." Eric Olson's new information was compelling enough for Manhattan District Attorney Robert Morgenthau to reopen the case in 1996. Cold case specialists worked on the investigation over the next few years, but did not turn up sufficient evidence to bring a murder charge. The death of Frank Olson lingers as the most intriguing mystery from the earliest period of America's LSD history.

One Fearful Yellow Eye. John D. MacDonald's 1966 detective novel features LSD in an important and ambiguous role: MacDonald presents the drug at its best and at its worst. Early in the plot, a dying doctor and his young wife take LSD to ease their psychological pain, and the drug delivers the promised therapy (see *Dying*). Near the end of the book, the chief villain—who suspects that the wife has discovered an extortion scheme—gives her a massive surprise dose. The panicking wife is easily persuaded that her body is on fire, and she runs off to drown herself; hero Travis McGee rescues her and arranges for psychiatric rehabilitation. At one point, McGee recalls his own ambiguous history with LSD, apparently involving a reckless testing program: "It could still give me the night sweats to remember one Doctor Varn and the Toll Valley Hospital where they had varied the basic compound and boosted the dosage to where they could not only guarantee you a bad trip, they could pop you permanently loose from reality if you had any potential fracture line anywhere in your psyche. As a part of mending the damage they did to me, a bright doctor gave me some good trips and had given me in that special way the ability to comprehend what had happened in my head during the bad ones."

Operation Julie. This was the codename for the police operation that resulted in the most important LSD arrests in British history. In the mid 1970s, police received tips that two labs were producing millions of doses: one in London, and an even bigger facility in rural Wales. The Welsh lab was run by chemist Richard Kemp and his girlfriend Christine Bott, who produced acid in "microdots" of legendary purity (see *Kemp, Richard; Bott, Christine*). Kemp had begun his work after receiving a big batch of ergotamine tartrate from American Ronald Stark, a leader of the Brotherhood of Eternal Love (see *Stark, Ronald; Brotherhood of Eternal Love*). Several police officers went undercover disguised as hippies; one of these officers, Sergeant Julie Thompson, lent her name to the operation. After many months of surveillance, the police raided both labs in 1977. Although prosecutors had little physical evidence, their case was strong enough to persuade seventeen defendants to plead guilty. Kemp received a thirteen-year jail sentence, four years longer than Bott's. American writer and editor David Solomon was among those convicted and jailed (see *Solomon, David*).

Operation Julie greatly diminished the supply of LSD in the U.K.: prices more than doubled in the year following. Although rumors abounded that Kemp and Bott had managed to stash millions of doses somewhere, no such horde of Welsh microdots has ever turned up. In 1978, punk group the Clash released a musical commentary on Operation Julie: "Julie's Been Working for the Drug Squad" (see *Clash; Strummer, Joe*).

Operation Moneybags. The program for LSD testing in the British military was given this codename as an inside joke: the abbreviation for pre-decimal British currency was "l.s.d.," which stood for pounds, shillings, pence (from Latin *librae, solidi, denarii*). See *Military Testing*.

Oracle. The *San Francisco Oracle* was the most widely-read and influential underground newspaper published during the psychedelic era. It lasted through twelve tabloid editions from September, 1966 through February, 1968. The *Oracle* was founded by Allen Cohen, editor, and Michael Bowen, art director. Cohen and Bowen set out to produce a newspaper that would disseminate countercultural ideas accompanied by graphic art in high psychedelic style. Themes engaged by the *Oracle* included the mystical implications of LSD experience, anti-war activism, sexual revolution, and ecological awareness. Despite limited funds, the staff found ways to print colorful, intricate designs that made the newspaper lavishly psychedelic. According to Cohen, the *Oracle* aimed to represent "the evocative states unveiled by marijuana and LSD," and their artists usually undertook the task while in altered states themselves. "To achieve the oracular effects we wanted, we would give the text, whether prose or poetry, to artists and ask them to design a page for it, not merely to illustrate it, but to make an organic unity of the word and the image. Most of the artists would conceive and manifest their designs in a state of expanded awareness" (notes for *Oracle* on CD, 2005). *Oracle* contributors included prominent poster artists Rick Griffin, Stanley Mouse, and Alton Kelley, whose designs accompanied writings by Timothy Leary, Ken Kesey, Allen Ginsberg, and many other notables from the psychedelic world.

The *Oracle* eventually expanded its print run to 125,000 copies, and Cohen estimated that each copy was shared by at least five people. From its home base in Haight-Ashbury, the newspaper made its way all over the country. The staff used a simple distribution system: they would give a few copies for free to anyone interested in selling them on the street, and they allowed individuals to purchase more copies if they wanted to expand their informal sales job. This arrangement proved beneficial both for the *Oracle* and the network of hippie vendors. At the peak of Haight-Asbury psychedelia, the *Oracle* employed more locals than any other business in the district. The newspaper's office also stayed open nights to provide free food and social services. Cohen referred to this operation as a "transcendental Red Cross," which "fed the hungry out of a giant pot of rice and beans, eased down and straightened out the bad trippers, and gave impromptu seminars in cosmic consciousness for the heads, the FBI, and the undercover cops who wandered through."

Oracle no. 5 celebrated the first Human Be-In, an event initiated by Bowen that is often considered the high point of Haight-Ashbury counterculture (see *Human Be-In*). Only a year later, however, amid all the problems associated with the Summer of Love—widespread use of speed and heroin, increasing crime, the sense that hippie values had been commercialized and distorted—the *Oracle* ceased publication.

Orange Sunshine. After Owsley's arrest in 1967 ended his prime years of LSD production (see *Owsley*), the job fell to his apprentice Tim Scully along with partner Nick Sand (see *Scully, Tim; Sand, Nick*). Scully and Sand manufactured acid in the form of small, barrel-shaped orange tablets that they named "Orange Sunshine." The Brotherhood of Eternal Love took over distribution (see *Brotherhood of Eternal Love*). At a 1969 concert in Anaheim, the Brotherhood gave away thousands of free barrels, and Orange Sunshine was on its way to becoming the most widely used brand of acid in the U.S. and the world (including Vietnam, where American soldiers took it: see *Vietnam*). Later versions of Orange Sunshine manufactured by Ronald Stark were thought by some acid veterans to be of inferior quality. Michael Hollingshead, for example, wrote that the latter-day Sunshine was "too 'electric,' too 'speedy,' and too 'mind-shattering.'"

Os Mutantes. Os Mutantes (Portuguese for "The Mutants") was an influential psychedelic rock band in Brazil from the mid 1960s through the early 1970s. Os Mutantes originally consisted of three members: brothers Arnaldo and Sergio Baptista, who played guitars, bass, and keyboards, and lead singer Rita Lee. They performed regularly on Brazilian television as well as in concerts. Brazil at the time was ruled by a repressive military government that did its best to discourage the popularity of American and British popular music. Prominent musicians Caetano Veloso and Gilberto Gil, who encouraged and collaborated with Os Mutantes, were eventually arrested and exiled. Os Mutantes faced repeated government censure but not exile.

Os Mutantes' music shared several characteristics with American and British psychedelic rock. Like the Beatles, they sang in pretty harmonies, and their lyrics ranged from playful pop romance through surreal, allusive poetry. Their guitarists made liberal use of wah-wah pedal and distortion. In concert, they indulged in longer pieces full of psychedelic improvisation. Os Mutantes also showed a distinctively Brazilian flavor, especially in the rhythms of their songs. The band sometimes dressed as typical psychedelic musicians—beads, dark glasses, hippie hats—but other times they wore carnival-like costumes.

All of the members of Os Mutantes took LSD, but one of the founding brothers, Arnaldo, used it so frequently that his friends became concerned. In 1973 Arnaldo spent time in a mental institution, where he jumped out a window and suffered serious injury. His troubles have sometimes been compared to those of Pink Floyd's Syd Barrett and the Beach Boys' Brian Wilson, two of his contemporaries whose mental illnesses may have been triggered or aggravated by LSD use (see *Pink Floyd; Beach Boys*). Baptista, like Brian Wilson, eventually recovered and went on to perform again.Os Mutantes had a significant influence on American musicians of the 1980s and beyond. Beck confessed to an almost obsessive attachment:

"When you first hear their music, it attacks your immune system until you are completely at their mercy. For years it was pretty much the only thing I listened to." David Byrne of Talking Heads used his influence to promote their music, and Nirvana's Kurt Cobain tried to persuade them to reunite and tour.

Osmond, Humphry. Osmond trained as a psychiatrist in England before taking a position in a mental hospital in Saskatchewan. He and colleague John Smythies had moved there in 1951 in hopes of finding a more supportive environment for their unorthodox theories. Osmond and Smythies proposed that LSD and similar drugs altered consciousness in ways that resembled the effects of schizophrenia; they speculated that schizophrenic brains may be producing a hallucinogenic chemical that causes psychotic symptoms. Among their eventual conclusions, they identified niacin as an effective treatment for schizophrenic episodes, and they recommended that psychiatrists themselves take hallucinogens in order to understand more profoundly the mental world of their patients. Although his theories never gained the support of mainstream psychiatry, Osmond had a significant influence on the practice of LSD-assisted psychotherapy in the later 1950s and early 1960s (see *Psychiatry*).

Writer Aldous Huxley heard about Osmond's work, and in 1953 Huxley asked him to supervise a mescaline trip. Huxley's experience inspired *The Doors of Perception*, one of the most important books in psychedelic literature (see *Huxley, Aldous*). As Osmond and Huxley continued their conversations about the drugs known as hallucinogens or psychotomimetics, they agreed that a new name was needed. One of Osmond's suggestions pleased both men: "psychedelic," from Greek roots meaning "mind-manifesting" (see *Psychedelic*).

Osmond continued his research into psychiatric applications for LSD and other psychedelics. Of particular note was his work with LSD as a tool for helping to cure alcoholism. He and colleague Abram Hoffer conducted a series of clinical trials using LSD in the context of psychotherapeutic care. Their success rate of 50 percent was unprecedented; Alcoholics Anonymous founder Bill Wilson tried LSD himself and saw great potential in Osmond's method (see *Wilson, Bill*). Skeptics from mainstream psychiatry disputed the results, however, and soon legal complications put an end to the experiments (see *Alcoholism*).

Owsley. The man best known as "Owsley" or by his nickname "Bear" was born Augustus Owsley Stanley. He came upon LSD in the early 1960s when he was a student at Berkeley. Up to that point in his life, he had shown a considerable aptitude for science, but had never applied himself in any focused way to studies or work. He decided to focus on manufacturing high quality LSD for the countercultural community gathering around the Bay Area. Owsley found the recipe for LSD in a chemistry journal; soon he was producing the drug in very pure form and distributing it liberally. It is estimated that Owsley made more than 1.25 million doses of LSD between 1965 and 1967.

Owsley supplied acid to the Merry Pranksters and joined in their adventures (see *Merry Pranksters*). Although Owsley experienced at least one LSD trip that brought on frightening visions (at an Acid Test held on Muir Beach), he remained a champion of the drug. As Tom Wolfe recorded in *The Electric Kool-Aid Acid Test*, Owsley sharply disagreed with Ken Kesey's plan to move the Pranksters "beyond acid": "Bullshit, Kesey! It's the *drugs* that do it. It's all the drugs, man. None of it would have happened without the drugs." During his time with the Pranksters, Owsley developed a close relationship with the Grateful Dead (see *Grateful Dead*). He supplied the Dead not only with acid but with sound equipment he devised for their concerts. Although the

technical results were mixed—the new equipment had definite advantages, but was vulnerable to glitches—Owsley made important recordings of Dead concerts in the band's psychedelic prime. Owsley also designed one of the Dead's most enduring logos, the "Steal Your Face" lightning bolt skull, to mark their equipment. Owsley supplied LSD to many other musicians, including Jimi Hendrix at the Monterey Pop Festival of 1967 (see *Hendrix, Jimi*).

Owsley's LSD came in pill form with a standard dosage of 250 micrograms. He dyed each major batch a different color. As Lee and Shlain note, "Although there was no difference between the tablets, street folklore ascribed specific qualities to every color: red was said to be exceptionally mellow, green was edgy, and blue was the perfect compromise." Other well known Owsley acids included "White Lightning" and "Monterey Purple." Owsley said that his mission was to provide LSD that was reliably pure for all who wanted it. His name has officially become synonymous with good acid: in the *Oxford English Dictionary*, the noun "owsley" means "an extraordinarily potent, high quality type of LSD; a tablet of this."

Owsley was eventually arrested and served jail time in California. Later he moved to Australia to live in seclusion. In a 2007 interview (*SFGate*.com, July 12), he expressed no regrets about what he had done. "I wound up doing time for something I should have been rewarded for," he said. "What I did was a community service, the way I look at it." Owsley even hinted that his acid days were not over: "Anytime the music on the radio starts to sound like rubbish, it's time to take some LSD."

Oz. The underground magazine *Oz* began in Australia and moved to London in early 1967. *Oz* was more satirical than the San Francisco *Oracle* (see *Oracle*), but both underground publications featured colorful psychedelic graphics and became popular among young readers with countercultural inclinations. The first issue of London *Oz* (February 1967) parodied Leary's slogan—"Turn on, Tune in, Drop Dead"—and subsequent issues included a number of features related to LSD. *Oz* 3, for example, contained articles about both Leary and the Merry Pranksters (see *Leary, Timothy; Merry Pranksters*); Martin Sharp's cover collage depicted Mona Lisa smoking and framed by bananas (an allusion to the rumor about psychedelic bananas: see *Bananas*). In early 1970, *Oz* devoted a whole issue to LSD. "Acid Oz" had a cover by R. Crumb (a face with detached eyeballs hanging from springs), a Martin Sharp graphic tltled "Acid Is Good for You," an article about Charles Manson, and reviews of recent records by the Grateful Dead and Jefferson Airplane. *Oz* faced obscenity trials first in Australia and then in England. The English trial, which stirred much controversy and inspired a song by John Lennon and Yoko Ono, resulted in convictions that were overturned on appeal. The prosecutor emphasized sex but included drugs in his complaint: *Oz* intended "to debauch and corrupt the morals of children" with materials related to "homosexuality, lesbianism, sadism, perverted sexual practices, and drug taking."

Pahnke, Walter. With degrees in both divinity and psychiatry, Pahnke combined his areas of expertise by studying LSD and other psychedelics. He constructed the famous "Good Friday Experiment" while a graduate student at Harvard in 1962. Under the supervision of Timothy Leary, he gave psilocybin to ten theology students and an active placebo to ten others; nine of ten who took psilocybin reported a profound religious experience, compared to only one from the control group (see *Religion*). Pahnke went on to work with LSD psychotherapy at the Maryland Psychiatric Research Center, where he studied LSD in treatment for alcoholics and people dying of cancer. Before his accidental death in 1971, he wrote several

essays about psychedelics, including "LSD and Religious Experience" from 1967. There he distinguished five types of psychedelic experiences: psychotic (bad trips), psychodynamic (release of unconscious materials), cognitive (unusual clarity and complexity of thought), aesthetic (fascinating expansion of sensory experience), and transcendental or mystical. Pahnke's greatest interest lay in this fifth type, which he analyzed carefully to judge its impact on traditional religious thinking. He concluded that LSD can catalyze spiritual experiences with profound and lifelong consequences, although it is not "the magic answer to anything." Psychedelic insights must be validated and sustained within broader religious contexts.

Panton, Verner. Panton was a Danish designer who produced striking psychedelic furniture during the 1960s. Panton liked bright colors and undulating shapes for chairs and other interior pieces, which he would enhance with psychedelic pillows and lighting effects.

Perry, Charles. Perry worked at *Rolling Stone* from its founding and eventually wrote *The Haight-Ashbury: A History* (1984). He was introduced to LSD as a student at Berkeley in the early 1960s. During his last term there he roomed with Owsley, and the two remained friends; after Owsley started making LSD in 1965, recalled Perry, "I never bought LSD again. All I had to do was stick out my hand and maintain eye contact, and he'd keep pouring " (see *Owsley*). In a 2007 interview, Perry evaluated the importance of LSD for the Bay Area counterculture. "It loosened everybody up," he recalled. "At the time it all seemed to come from LSD." He also said that the drug's psychotropic power led to a "delusion" of common purpose: "LSD speaks in accents of great seriousness like secrets are being revealed right now. You almost think that it's the universe itself talking to you, and you think that inevitably everybody must be feeling the same things you do." Perry added,

"After the first couple of trips, you really don't learn anything new, and it actually just turns into a hall of mirrors, but nobody knew that at the time" (Mezz).

Phish. Concert tours of this latter-day psychedelic band shared several features with those of the Grateful Dead, including a loyal fan base with many LSD enthusiasts (see *Grateful Dead*). Members of the band also used LSD, and on at least one occasion, psychedelic excess spoiled their act. According to the Mockingbird Foundation's *Phish Companion,* before a concert at Goddard College in Vermont, they drank too much LSD-spiked Vermont apple cider and were unable to play. By 2000, acid had been largely replaced by ecstasy at Phish concerts (see *Ecstasy*): Preston Peet noted that at their Big Cyprus New Year's festival, "For the first time, ecstasy had flooded the market, while acid was difficult to find. Since Big Cyprus, shows at which acid once seemed to be given away at the door have become centers for the sale of ecstasy."

Pickard, William. In November of 2000, DEA agents and Kansas police arrested William Pickard, 56, and seized equipment and raw materials associated with the production of LSD. The DEA estimated that 16 million doses of acid could have been manufactured from the seized materials. Pickard and a colleague (Clyde Apperson) were both convicted of conspiracy and possession with intent to distribute over 10 grams. Because Pickard had prior convictions, he received a sentence of life without parole. The DEA announced that this was the biggest LSD seizure the agency had ever made. Studies have shown that the supply of LSD significantly dwindled in the first decade of the new century, and the Pickard arrest is often cited as one of the primary reasons.

The Pickard case is notable not only for its effect on LSD supply, but for thought-provoking ironies surrounding the man and his lab. The lab was located in a decommis-sioned Atlas missile silo in Kansas: an acquaintance had purchased the Cold War relic and renovated it. Pickard and his associate were convicted of retooling the old site of nuclear war to make the drug associated with hippie peace and love. The remote, underground location suited Pickard for the same reasons it suited the military. Pickard even managed to escape for a day into the rural countryside after officers stopped his car near the silo. The other ironies have to do with Pickard himself. He had at least minor connections with several of the country's most prestigious universities, including Princeton, Berkeley, Stanford, Harvard, and UCLA. He learned enough organic chemistry to become an expert technician, but his academic interests also lay in public drug policy. At Harvard in the mid 1990s, he enrolled in the Kennedy School of Government and co-wrote papers about drug abuse in the U.S. and the former Soviet Union. At UCLA he held the position of assistant director of the Drug Policy Analysis Program, where he focused on their "Future and Emerging Drugs Study." He held that position until his arrest in 2000.

Pickard was also known for a healthy lifestyle. According to journalist Seth Rosenfeld *SFGate.com,* June 10, 2001), Pickard was a vegetarian and a marathon runner, and he viewed "addictive drugs as a blight: 'I agree with (hippie leader) Wavy Gravy. There's blood on heroin and cocaine.'" But as Rosenfeld noted, he "seemed to see psychedelic drugs as beneficial." His connections to LSD go all the way back to the Summer of Love. He went to San Francisco in 1967 and found the scene very attractive: "No one had quite seen anything like it," he told Rosenfeld. "So many people stepping out of line: discussing theology and philosophy, seeking explanations, exploring their place in life." He made the acquaintance of Tim Scully, apprentice to the famous Owsley (see *Owsley*), at Scully's LSD trial in 1974. Scully told Rosenfeld that Pickard "was trying to express some brotherhood of underground chemists," all of whom felt "we were doing a public service." Pickard was arrested on LSD charges for the first time in 1988 and served a few years in prison. When he got out, his philosophical and spiritual aspirations led him to the San Francisco Zen Center. While living there, he attended gatherings of so-called "psychonauts"—prominent figures who had interests in altered consciousness, including MDMA pioneer Alexander Shulgin, psychotherapist John Weir Perry, and former astronaut Buzz Aldrin. Amid all these conversations about mental evolution, Pickard evidently took up his chemicals again to provide fuel for the cause. The DEA put an end to his plans when they decommissioned the Atlas silo for good.

Pinchbeck, Daniel. The author of *Breaking Open the Head: A Psychedelic Journey into the Heart of Contemporary Shamanism* (2003), Pinchbeck advocates the use of LSD and other psychedelic drugs to correct humanity's destructive loss of mystical insight and psychological harmony. Vanessa Grigoriadis' cover article in *Rolling Stone* dubbed him the leader of a "New Psychedelic Elite." In *Breaking Open the Head*, Pinchbeck discusses the fortuitous timing of Albert Hofmann's discovery of LSD as something more than coincidence (see *Hofmann, Albert*). He notes that LSD appeared at roughly the same time as many terrible events of twentieth-century history, including the Holocaust and the use of nuclear weapons. "If I could suspend disbelief, even for a moment, of the possibility that there were extradimensional beings involved in human affairs, then it seemed sensible to understand the timely appearance of LSD as an interpolation into our realm. The chemical catalyst was a connective cord or something like a dial-up connection to a higher dimensional entity of enormous intelligence, somewhat cold but essentially empathic, dispensing foresight and catalyzing knowledge. The 'other' had used Hofmann as a means of getting into our world."

Pink Floyd. At the same time the Beatles were producing *Sergeant Pepper's Lonely Hearts Club Band* (see *Beatles, The; Sergeant Pepper*), Pink Floyd wrote and performed songs that put them in the avant garde of London psychedelic music. Syd Barrett led Pink Floyd during their first and most emphatically psychedelic period of 1966–1967. Barrett took an astonishing number of LSD trips during those two years—trips that inspired his music and may also have triggered the psychotic behavior that ended his career prematurely. According to John Marsh, who directed light shows for Pink Floyd concerts, "Everyone know that if you went round to see Syd, never have a cup of tea, because everything was spiked with acid." Pink Floyd manager Peter Jenner believed that LSD caused both his creativity and his madness: "He was extraordinarily creative and what happened was catastrophic: a total burnt-out case. All his talent just came out in a flood in two years and then it was burnt out. Syd got burnt out from the acid in his coffee every morning."

Psychiatric experts usually analyze more cautiously the relationship between LSD and psychosis. Evidence suggests that the drug does not "cause" psychosis in any simple sense, but it may sometimes lead to the activation of an underlying mental illness hitherto dormant (see *Health Risks*). In Syd Barrett's case, the mental illness soon prevented him from functioning in public, and he lived the rest of his life as a recluse in the basement of his mother's house. Barrett has sometimes been compared with Brian Wilson of the Beach Boys: both men took LSD, flourished as musical innovators, and suffered mental breakdowns at the peak of their careers. However, Barrett took much more LSD than Wilson did, and Wilson eventually regained sufficient mental composure to write and perform music again (see *Wilson, Brian*).

Before he became dysfunctional, Syd Barrett led Pink Floyd's innovative performances that highlighted the London psychedelic scene. They played at the most popular clubs, including the UFO Club (see *UFO Club*), where they projected liquid light shows and experimented with lasers and pyrotechnics. They recorded their first album, *The Piper at the Gates of Dawn,* in the same studios and at the same time the Beatles were working on *Sergeant Pepper.* Pink Floyd's version of psychedelic music differed from the Beatles' most dramatically in its emphasis on spacy instrumental improvisations. Barrett's guitar joined with Rick Wright's organ, Roger Waters' bass, and Nick Mason's drums to create extended psychedelic jams. "Interstellar Overdrive" is the longest such piece on *Piper,* with a loose musical structure, and instruments and amplifiers producing otherworldly sounds. The first track on *Piper,* "Astronomy Domine," adds spacy lyrics to spacy sounds. Barrett sketches a psychedelic landscape located out among the planets and moons, with equal parts paradise and underworld, and conflicting emotions of wonder and fear. An echo machine and unusual chord combinations contribute to a feeling of psychedelic disorientation.

Syd Barrett bowed out of Pink Floyd following a series of incidents in which he behaved very strangely at concerts—aimlessly strumming a detuned guitar, refusing to sing, staring off into space. The last song that he recorded with Pink Floyd, "Jugband Blues," offers a glimpse into his increasingly psychotic depersonalization: he announces that he simply is not here anymore. Pink Floyd went on to great success without the tormented genius who shaped their early psychedelic music, but they honored him in some of their later songs. In "Shine On You Crazy Diamond," they recall him as their visionary leader; and in "Wish You Were Here," they provide an elegiac reply to the loss recorded in "Jugband Blues."

Pregnancy. LSD has been implicated in two risks for women who are pregnant. In the late 1960s some studies suggested that the drug may cause birth defects, but these results were later corrected, and LSD is no longer considered a teratogen (see *Chromosomes*). However, early testing by Sandoz indicated that LSD may stimulate uterine contractions, and for this reason it poses a legitimate risk for pregnant women. See *Health Risks.*

President's Analyst. This 1967 film starred James Coburn as a presidential psychoanalyst who flees to avoid political danger and ends up tripping with a psychedelic band. See *Coburn, James.*

Previn, Andre. In the late 1950s, noted pianist-composer-conductor Previn took part in LSD trials supervised by psychiatrist Oscar Janiger (see *Janiger, Oscar*). Previn listened to classical music on his first trip and reported impressive results: "I have never before or since been so strongly affected by music. I listened to recordings of some Brahms, Mozart, and Walton, and was moved to tears almost immediately. I then played the piano for approximately 40 minutes. I felt that I played extremely well and possibly with more musical insight than before."

Psych Out. This 1968 B-movie starred Jack Nicholson as the leader of an up-and-coming psychedelic band and Susan Strasberg as a deaf runaway who hooks up with him in Haight-Ashbury. The young woman is looking for her brother, an artist now known as "The Seeker," who left her this note: "God is alive and well and living in a Sugar Cube." See *Nicholson, Jack.*

Psychedelic. The family of drugs to which LSD belongs was given the clinical name "psychotomimetic" under the assumption that these drugs induce mental effects similar to psychosis. The name was appropriate for the use of LSD and similar drugs in psychiatric contexts, although its evocation of mental derangement did not sit well with enthusiasts of the 1950s and 1960s. A narrower and similarly negative name was "hallucinogenic," which named the drugs for one of the psychotic symptoms they seemed to induce. Both "psychotomimetic" and "hallucinogenic" remain in use as classifying adjectives for LSD and related drugs.

In the mid-1950s, Aldous Huxley and Humphry Osmond (the psychiatrist who supervised Huxley's trip that inspired *The Doors of Perception*) set out to give these drugs a new name, untainted by the premise of psychological dysfunction (see *Huxley, Aldous; Osmond, Humphry*). Osmond was the one who eventually coined the term "psychedelic," derived from the Greek words for mind and to manifest or reveal. (Huxley had a similar idea, but with different Greek roots: "phanerothyme," from words meaning spirit made visible.) Osmond originally spelled his neologism "psychodelic," which was formally correct, but he wisely tweaked a vowel to get rid of the connotations of "psycho." "Psychedelic" won out over several alternatives with the same prefix. "Psyche" was the easy part; it was more difficult to choose a suffix that best described what the drugs did to someone's mind. Osmond considered "psychephoric" (mind moving), "psychehormic" (mind rousing), "psycheplastic" (mind molding), "psychezynic" (mind fermenting), "psycherhexic" (mind bursting forth), and "psychelytic" (mind releasing), before settling on "psychedelic" (mind manifesting). "Psychedelic" has now become so commonplace that the choice seems inevitable, but "psycherhexic," for example, would have had similar implications. Both "psychedelic" and "psycherhexic" emphasize the mind's inherent power rather than the drugs' manipulative influence (as in "psychephoric" or "psycheplastic"). A "Psycherhexic Era" would have invoked the mind bursting forth instead of just showing through, but "psychedelic" is more euphonious and avoids the taint of "hex." Later still, some users of psychedelics wanted a name that would convey their most serious spiritual aspirations. They coined the term "entheogenic," again from Greek roots, to foreground the role played by these drugs in helping humans generate an awareness of God. "Entheogenic" remains in usage, but it is a rarer and more specialized term than "psychedelic." The older names also remain current, with "hallucinogenic" more common than "psychotomimetic" except in scientific contexts. "Psychedelic" has become the most common term: it occupies a middle ground semantically between psychiatric symptoms and religious sublimity. The *Oxford English Dictionary* finishes its entry on "psychedelic" by noting its broad cultural connections with music, art, and fashion—areas of reference not shared by its competitors for the naming rights. See *Hallucinogen; Entheogen; Psychotomimetic.*

Psychedelic Art. LSD strongly influenced visual art of the 1960s and early 1970s. Psychedelic artists worked in traditional media of elite art, but also in any number of vehicles for popular art: concert posters, album covers, light shows, movies and videos, advertisements, t-shirts, comic books, lunch boxes, even hits of blotter acid itself. In *Psychedelic Art,* Masters and Houston defined a psychedelic artist as someone "whose work has been significantly influenced by psychedelic experience and who acknowledges the impact of the experience on his work. Most of the artists whose works are included in this book have used one or more psychochemicals.... LSD was the substance used most often." Some artists surveyed for *Psychedelic Art* reported that they liked to work while tripping, while others tripped first and did the art later. Because a few prominent artists associated with psychedelia did not acknowledge the influence of LSD on their work—Peter Max, for example, or Stanley Kubrick (see *Max, Peter; Kubrick, Stanley*)—an inclusive definition of psychedelic art must attend to stylistic features, not simply artists' personal history with drugs.

Psychedelic style refers first of all to vivid coloring. Psychedelic artists use color promiscuously, often in unusual or eye-jarring combinations. Poster artist Victor Moscoso, who studied color theory in graduate school at Yale, found his psychedelic niche by deliberately violating the rules he had learned for combining colors (see *Moscoso, Victor*). From the most ordinary tie-dye t-shirts to museum quality paintings, psychedelic art attempts to convey the tripper's heightened sensitivity to color. Many works of psychedelic art also present intricate geometrical forms—mandalas, spirals, fractals, radiant lines—of the sort often seen by acid trippers with their eyes closed. Several artists told psychiatrist Stanley Krippner that LSD had enriched their supply of images: in addition to the interior shapes made visible by the drug, they reported a refreshed capacity to perceive ordinary objects. One sculptor wrote that his psychedelic experiences "have offered me a limitless amount of subject matter. I have been reintroduced to a sense of wonder" (quoted in *Psychedelic Art*). Masters and Houston pointed to a "kinetic" quality of psychedelic art, embedded in designs that suggest cosmic connections: "The initial response to much psychedelic art might be its aliveness, its crackling and leaping energies.... Mandalas irradiate and writhe. Buddha has a flashing light in his middle. Microcosmic-macrocosmic interaction: protozoan explodes and is a planet."

Just as psychedelic rock drew from traditional forms of music like blues and folk (see *Psychedelic Rock*), psychedelic art adopted elements of earlier artistic movements. Psychedelic art has stylistic affiliations with Dada and Surrealism, Art Nouveau, Fauvism, and Pop Art. Sometimes artists mined images not from their psychedelic experiences but from older works of art. For their famous "Skeleton and Roses" Grateful Dead poster, Mouse and Kelley took the central image straight from a Victorian edition of the *Rubaiyat of Omar Khayyam* (see *Mouse, Stanley; Kelley, Alton*). Masters and Houston included in their book several paintings by artists from earlier centuries who seemed psychedelic *avant la lettre*. They suggested that William Blake "manifests psychedelic sensibility," and even further back, Hieronymous Bosch: "Of all the artists of the past, none is more evocative of multiple aspects of the psychedelic experience."

As more and more artists of the 1960s acknowledged LSD as a muse, an important question needed to be addressed: does LSD infuse a person with artistic genius? Masters and Houston backed away from any such claim: "The artists (and the authors of this book) are under no illusion that alteration of consciousness confers the ability to create works of art. The artist, not the chemical, has to provide the intelligence, feeling, imagination, and talent." They hedged a little, however, when they noted that "extraordinary experience has always been a factor of importance in shaping artists' work," and taking LSD is an extraordinary experience—a voyage to "what Aldous Huxley called the antipodes of the mind." Psychiatrist Oscar Janiger conducted trials with LSD and artists to try to evaluate the drug's effects on creativity (see *Janiger, Oscar*). In his primary experiment, he had 70 artists draw a Hopi Kachina Doll on two occasions: once before they took acid, and once while they were tripping. Janiger showed the resulting works to an art historian. While he declined to compare the aesthetic value of the two sets of images, he noted that the psychedelic Kachina Dolls were more colorful and more abstract than their non-psychedelic counterparts, and that the tripping artists usually filled up more of the canvas. Janiger later reflected, "It is of special interest to note that many of those elements that are universally reported under the influence of LSD are those features traditionally associated with heightened artistic creativity."

See *Advertising; Blotter Art; Crumb, Robert; Grey, Alex; Griffin, Rick; Kelley, Alton; Light Shows; MacLean, Bonnie; Max, Peter; Moore, Alan; Moscoso, Victor; Mouse, Stanley; Psychedelic Fashion; Psychedelic Posters; Sharp, Martin; Tie-Dye; Wilson, Wes.*

Psychedelic Experience. In 1964, Timothy Leary and two colleagues from his Harvard days, Ralph Metzner and Richard Alpert, wrote a manual for people taking LSD or other hallucinogenic drugs. They based *The Psychedelic Experience* on a composite Buddhist funerary text known to English readers as *The Tibetan Book of the Dead,* which offers a set of rituals, meditations, prayers, and instructions for the use of a dying person. The presiding lama's goal is to help that person navigate the transitional stages between life and death. For each of these intervals, called "bardos," the sacred instructions are meant help the person break free from illusory attachments and find enlightenment.

Leary, Metzner, and Alpert saw parallels between the Tibetan experience of dying and their own experience during LSD trips. In both experiences, a person makes the transition from normal consciousness to an altered state filled with uncertainty and risk but promising spiritual evolution. They based *The Psychedelic Experience* on the basic structure of *The Tibetan Book of the Dead,* which distinguished three bardos. The first bardo is called "Moment of Death," when the subject has access to "the clear light of reality." Leary's psychedelic equivalent of the first bardo is "The Period of Ego-Loss or Non-Game Ecstasy." The second bardo, "Experiencing of Reality," becomes "The Period of Hallucinations" in psychedelic translation; the third bardo, "Rebirth," becomes "The Period of Re-Entry." For each bardo, *The Psychedelic Experience* adapts materials from its Tibetan model for use by a guide as he or she counsels a tripper. In Leary's view, a psychedelic guide—the equivalent of a Buddhist lama—performs "the most exciting and inspiring role in society. He is literally a liberator, one who provides illumination."

The Psychedelic Experience places considerable emphasis on reassurance and safety. Many times the guide reminds a tripper that there is no danger, and that all fearful moments are merely mental constructions: "All interpretations are the products of your own mind. Dispel them. Have no fear." The manual suggests that care be taken to arrange a comfortable setting for a trip. "Natural settings such as gardens, beaches, forests, and open country have specific influences which one may or may not wish to incur. The essential thing is to feel as comfortable as possible.... If the session is held indoors, one must consider the arrangement of the room and the specific objects one may wish to see and hear during the experience." The manual even recommends which snacks to have around ("simple, ancient foods like bread, cheese, wine, and fresh fruit"). Leary's cautious approach to planning a trip put him at odds with his West Coast counterparts, the Merry Pranksters, who prized spontaneity and daring. But his version of the psychedelic experience was fundamentally one of spiritual advancement, and he belittled the lesser motives of Prankster-like trippers: "Rebellion against convention may be the motive of some people who take the drug. The idea of doing something 'far out' or vaguely naughty is a naïve set which can color the experience." Of the four goals that he sets out for trippers to choose from—"accelerated learning," "help of others," "aesthetic pleasure," and "attainment of mystical union"—Leary's manual emphasizes the fourth, which he considers the most valuable.

The Psychedelic Experience is the bestselling of Leary's books and has gone through several editions. See *Leary, Timothy; Alpert, Richard; Metzner, Ralph; Religion; Zen Buddhism.*

Psychedelic Fashion. During the mid–1960s, hippie clothing had considerable influence on the world of fashion, despite the fact that psychedelia and high fashion made an awkward pairing. In many ways, the culture surrounding hippies and LSD was antithetical to the traditional culture of fashion. As Cally Blackman has observed, the hippie style in clothing "cannot be called 'fashion'; rather, anti-fashion, in that it constituted an oppositional statement visibly mediated through clothing that challenged sartorial norms and rejected established consumer values." Traditional fashion was founded on the concept of "design," Blackman notes, while "the essence of the [hippie] look depended on it being created by the wearer from a ragbag of sources and inspiration."

Nevertheless, elements of the hippie look made their way into the mainstream fashion world after their germination in psychedelic counterculture. Hippie-inflected fashion included several features that implied the influence of psychedelic perception. Colors were brighter and deployed in eccentric combinations. Dresses and shirts were decorated with flowers and geometric patterns, sometimes in a refined tie-dye style see *Tie-Dye*). The psychedelic mindset emphasized improvisation and flouted decorum; accordingly, the fashionable hippie look encouraged whimsical accessories, such as floppy hats, feather boas, and untraditional jewelry. The main articles of clothing drew from more "primitive" cultures untainted by Western modernity—loose cotton dresses from India, leather and beads from Native American dress. To indicate an affiliation with working class rather than managerial-professional class values, designers adapted blue jeans for all occasions. The defining elements of the hippie look flourished first in the Haight-Ashbury district of San Francisco, where thrift shops and free stories supplied the psychedelic crowd with colorful castoffs. Even in the Haight, however, the improvisational, Goodwill approach to clothing was appropriated by high fashion. Designer Linda Gravenites specialized in hippie wear for notables including Janis Joplin. Blackman describes Gravenites' work as "custom-made clothing incorporating hand embroidery in floral motifs and glass beads, worked on satins, velvets, chiffon, and lace." In the southern capital of California psychedelia, Los Angeles, fashion's appropriation of hippie style was even more aggressive. As Blackman summarizes, "LA was quick to commercialize the hippie style and

transform it into a marketable commodity— in typically lavish fashion Michelle Phillips, singer of the Mamas and Papas, invited 900 guests to a party at her Bel Air mansion, where they gathered on the lawns in feathers and silks, Indian paisleys, beads, saris, Nehru suits, very long hair, sequins, and all the semi-precious stones that were so popular with young hippies."

At the same time in London, hippie styles were displacing the more restrained "Mod" look of designers like Mary Quant (of mini-skirt fame). Singer Marianne Faithfull described the new London scene as "essentially an extension of Mary Quant's London, only with drugs." As in Los Angeles, commercial fashion assimilated hippie clothing trends. Affluent, trendy young Londoners, including members of the Beatles and Rolling Stones, became psychedelic dandies. Blackman notes that they "tended to shun the circus that by now Carnaby Street had become, preferring to buy their clothes at more outré boutiques like Hung on You.... Hung on You sold coloured and velvet suits, extravagantly printed shirts, buckled belts and knee-high boots." In 1967 the Beatles themselves started a fashion enterprise, Apple Boutique, that offered clothing designed by psychedelic artists.

1967 marked the high point of psychedelic influence on fashion, but elements of hippie style reappear on the runway from time to time. Dolce and Gabbana has shown a particular fondness for hippie motifs in their collections. In 2009, Macy's created a "Summer of Love" theme to promote hippie styles for women, including the "Aquarius-inspired maxi dress, long, cool, and flowing," with colors sufficiently muted to suit latter-day psychedelic tastes.

Psychedelic Posters. From 1965 through the early 1970s, concerts that featured psychedelic bands were advertised with posters designed in a distinctive artistic style. The artists who created these posters took their cues from certain features of the psychedelic experience: heightened sensitivity to color, recognition of complex patterns, and a fluid, undulating quality of visual perception. A number of psychedelic poster artists flourished during the heyday of Haight-Ashbury. Their designs survive not only as posters but as handbills, album covers, and t-shirts.

The first psychedelic poster advertised a concert by the Charlatans at the Red Dog Saloon in Virginia City, Nevada see *Charlatans*). Two members of the Charlatans, George Hunter and Mike Ferguson, designed a poster to distribute around the Bay Area. "The Seed," as this poster has been nicknamed, pioneered essential features of what became the psychedelic style: wavy lines and a gentle subversion of linear organization; hippie-themed images of flowers, vines, and stars; and letters with "melting" look. The lettering in The Seed presented only a mild challenge to those accustomed to more straightforward posters, but soon psychedelic poster artists pushed the limits of legibility. In the ordinary world of advertising, a graphic design aims for clarity of message and an immediate recognition of the event or product in question. But psychedelic poster artists made their messages legible only to an in-crowd of initiates. As their letters curved, undulated, and merged with other elements of the design, they informed and entertained those who knew the visual codes; all others would either have to adapt to a new visual complexity or remain on the outside. As psychedelic dance concerts came to San Francisco, a handful of graphic artists were called upon to provide appropriately mind-bending posters. Chet Helms, head of the group called "Family Dog" that organized concerts at the Avalon Ballroom, turned to his friend Alton Kelley. Kelley teamed up with fellow hot-rod-enthusiast-turned-acidhead Stanley Mouse, and these two produced several memorable posters, including "Zig-Zag Man" and "Skeleton and Roses" (see *Kelley, Alton; Mouse, Stanley*). At the same time, Bill Graham hired Wes Wilson as house poster artist for the Fillmore

Auditorium. Wilson's elaborate lettering and crowded imagery made his work fascinating but difficult to read (see *Wilson, Wes*). When Wilson quit, Bonnie MacLean took over and designed elegant posters that often featured somber looking human figures (see *MacLean, Bonnie*). Other prominent poster artists included Victor Moscoso, who studied painting at Yale and decided to disobey the rules he had learned for combining colors (see *Moscoso, Victor*), and Rick Griffin, a perfectionist who made intricate, surreal designs (see *Griffin, Rick*).

In 2009, the Denver Art Museum mounted a major exhibit of psychedelic poster art (see *Museums*). The museum received a gift from a collector in Boulder who had gathered and preserved hundreds of posters. Reproductions of psychedelic posters are readily available in art books and online galleries; designs by the major artists fetch high prices as collectibles.

Psychedelic Rock. The use of LSD and other psychedelic drugs profoundly influenced rock music in the middle and later 1960s, led by artists in America and England. American psychedelic bands flourished in San Francisco at the same time the Beatles helped to spark a psychedelic scene in London. In sound and lyrical content, as well as in the light shows that accompanied concerts, psychedelic rock attempted to represent the alterations in consciousness induced by these drugs. Psychedelic rock dominated popular music only for a short time—the peak period was 1967–1969—but these bands and their music have remained influential.

The body of popular music labeled psychedelic ranges through a variety of musical styles. The gentlest psychedelic mode derived from a folk paradigm. Bob Dylan's "Mr. Tambourine Man," for example, uses a traditional acoustic guitar and simple folk chords, even as the lyrics set a new standard for surreal complexity in popular music. Other bands aimed for improvisation and experimental strangeness, as in the early work of Grateful Dead in San Francisco and Pink Floyd in London. For all their avant garde aspirations, many psychedelic musicians—including the Charlatans, pioneers of the genre—took a good portion of their repertoire from traditional blues and other folk materials. A few African-American musicians, including the Temptations and Sly Stone, fused psychedelia with R & B in a distinctive subgenre that became known as "Psychedelic Soul." Psychedelic bands that emphasized the raw intensity of the beat and the punch and volume of amplified instruments, like Iron Butterfly and Steppenwolf, have often been cited as the forerunners of heavy metal music. Psychedelic songs often featured extended instrumental jams in their recordings and live performances. The Grateful Dead developed an extreme version of improvisational style when they played as the unofficial house band at the Acid Tests organized by the Merry Pranksters in 1965 (see *Acid Test; Merry Pranksters*). In regular concert venues, the Dead's performances took on more structure, but they often linked successive songs with long instrumental segues, and drew out some individual songs over 30 minutes in length. In London, Pink Floyd had a psychedelic style that similarly emphasized instrumental experimentation and long periods of freeform jamming. Most psychedelic bands did not use extended improvisation to the degree that Grateful Dead and Pink Floyd did, but longish instrumental breaks became common for at least a few tracks on psychedelic albums. Sometimes a hit song like the Doors' "Light My Fire" or Iron Butterfly's "In-A-Gadda-Da-Vida" would be shortened for radio play but appear on the album in much longer form.

Although psychedelic bands deployed the usual array of rock instruments—electric guitar, bass, drums, keyboard—some groups followed the Beatles' lead and introduced Indian elements of sitar and tabla. The Beatles used these Indian instruments on songs produced during the period when their interests in LSD and Eastern spirituality converged. One prominent example is "Tomorrow Never Knows" from *Revolver,* which contains lyrics that John Lennon borrowed from Timothy Leary's tripping manual based on the Tibetan Book of the Dead (see *Psychedelic Experience*). Psychedelic bands also found ways to give traditional rock instruments untraditional sounds. Guitarists often used heavy distortion to thicken or "fuzz" the notes and chords. They made liberal use of reverberation and wah-wah pedal to produce an undulating sound—the sonic equivalent of stroboscopic lighting. Psychedelic musicians also experimented with using the jarring effects of feedback deliberately, as if to challenge normal expectations for musical beauty. The Grateful Dead actually recorded a whole track that consisted solely of feedback sounds ("Feedback" from *Live Dead*). In collaboration with record producers and studio engineers, psychedelic bands pioneered exotic sound effects. They were attempting to offer listeners an experience that mimicked the disorienting sublimity of LSD tripping. The Beatles' *Sergeant Pepper* was particularly notable for such devices, including filters that altered instruments and voices, tape tricks that produced backwards instrumental sounds, and synthesized bits of non-musical background sounds.

Lyrics to psychedelic songs reveal several recurring themes. The most obviously psychedelic topic has to do with the subversion of normal identity and perception. Many songs have lyrics that complement strange sound effects with comparably surreal imagery. These surreal gestures sometimes amount to simple inversions of common sense, but some important psychedelic songs create alternate worlds by means of metaphorical invention. Bob Dylan led the way with songs like "Mr. Tambourine Man," which created a psychedelic landscape from poetic tropes in the style of French Symbolism. Psychedelic musicians' affection for surreal imagery often prompted them to name their bands accordingly. A number of bands fashioned their names from an apparently incongruous adjective-noun combination. Some of the most important bands had such a name, like Grateful Dead and Pink Floyd, establishing a convention that lesser bands followed—e.g., Ultimate Spinach, Strawberry Alarm Clock, Chocolate Watchband.

A different sort of subversion can also be found in many psychedelic songs: a subversion of mainstream political and social values. Sometimes the political commentary focuses explicitly on Vietnam, as in Country Joe and the Fish's "Feel Like I'm Fixin' to Die Rag." Other songs imagined a broader apocalyptic ruin. Jefferson Airplane's "Wooden Ships" describes a post-nuclear landscape, and their even darker "House at Pooneil Corners" foretells cosmic destruction. Elsewhere Jefferson Airplane optimistically predicts revolutionary change led by psychedelic youngsters ("Volunteers"). The elegiac tone of the Beatles' "A Day in the Life" suggests a quieter complaint about the emptiness of modern life, more an existential lament than any specific political or social criticism.

Lyricists not only criticized the existing world but offered utopian alternatives. Often they imagined a version of paradise accessible only to those whose minds had been freed by psychedelic powers. Joni Mitchell's "Woodstock" calls for a return to the garden, with bombers transforming into butterflies above the heads of enlightened youngsters. Jimi Hendrix named his paradise "Electric Ladyland," where an improved version of love could be found in abundance; "Electric" in the title refers both to his musical tools and to the LSD that inspired him. A few Beatles' songs from the *Sergeant Pepper* era suggest a version of paradise connected with child-like innocence, including "Lucy in the Sky with Diamonds" and "Strawberry Fields Forever"; both of these songs, however, suggest an undercurrent of loneliness and alienation. Like many psychedelic songs, "Strawberry Fields Forever" announces a journey to an alternate world that is not "real" in any simple sense.

Happier journeys might come in the form of "magic carpet rides" (a trope used by both Hendrix and Steppenwolf), airplanes, or various modes of travel on and under the ocean. Some songs describe a journey from this world to an ambiguous, indefinite other world. In the Doors' "Break on Through," for example, we are urged to cross a threshold to another side, but the nature of the destination remains vague. For all their investment in alternate worlds and altered consciousness, psychedelic lyrics share one theme with popular songs from every era: finding "Somebody to Love" (Jefferson Airplane). A romantic plot underlies several hit songs from psychedelic rock. The singer of Tommy James' "Crimson and Clover," impressed with his psychedelic aura but a little lonely, waits for a girl to come over. "In-A-Gadda-Da-Vida" has a similarly basic message: psychedelic boy meets girl and invites her to join the trip. Other songs imagine a more complex romantic plot. David Crosby's "Triad," for example, describes a mentally liberated threesome. Because LSD inspired the "Summer of Love" and was used psychiatrically to help people develop their capacity for relationships, it is not surprising to find so many love songs coming from the altered imaginations of psychedelic songwriters.

"Psychedelic rock" and "acid rock" are often used synonymously, although some critics prefer to reserve "acid rock" for the intense, beat-driven version of psychedelic rock that led to heavy metal music in the 1970s (see *Acid Rock*). See *Beach Boys; Beatles; Big Brother and the Holding Company; Blue Cheer; Byrds; Charlatans; Clash; Country Joe and the Fish; Cream; Donovan; Doors; Dylan, Bob; Gamblers; Grateful Dead; Hendrix, Jimi; Holy Modal Rounders; Iron Butterfly; James, Tommy; Jefferson Airplane; Joplin, Janis; Moby Grape; Monkees; Moody Blues; Os Mutantes; Phish; Pink Floyd; Quicksilver Messenger Service; Rolling Stones; Santana; Sly and the Family Stone; Steppenwolf; Strawberry Alarm Clock; Talking Heads; Temptations; Ultimate Spinach; Who; Zappa, Frank.*

Psychedelic Shop. In January of 1966, brothers Ron and Jay Thelin opened The Psychedelic Shop on Haight St. near the intersection with Ashbury. Their father had managed the Woolworth's across the street, but his sons' store suited the contemporary neighborhood better. Their market was the growing hippie community, to whom they sold books about Eastern religion, records, concert tickets, posters, Indian fabrics, incense, pipes, and rolling papers. They helped to fund the *Oracle* (see *Oracle*), and despite the fact that they sold things rather than giving them away, they got along well with the Diggers (see *Diggers*). Like the Diggers, the Thelins became increasingly concerned about the migration of young people into Haight-Ashbury; they turned a big portion of their shop into a "Calm Center," where people could rest and meditate. When the Diggers staged their mock funeral for "Hippie," they removed the sign from The Psychedelic Shop and ritually buried it in Buena Vista Park. The Thelin brothers closed their shop soon afterwards.

Psychiatry. Shortly after Albert Hofmann reported the mind-altering effects of the chemical he had synthesized (see *Hofmann, Albert*), Swiss psychiatrist Werner A. Stoll conducted the first experiments to test LSD's potential value as a psychotherapeutic agent (see *Stoll, Werner A.*). Stoll began by taking LSD himself. In careful notes he recorded powerful sensory changes and moments of both despair and euphoria. Stoll published the first scientific paper on LSD in 1947. He did not conclusively affirm or deny LSD's effectiveness for psychiatry, but he noted that its extraordinarily intense effects on the brain might provide clues about biochemical conditions associated with mental disorders. The pharmaceutical company Sandoz followed Hofmann's and Stoll's recommendations and made LSD available to psychiatrists under the trade name "Delysid" (see *Sandoz; Delysid*). Sandoz suggested two uses for Delysid: "to elicit release of repressed material and provide mental relaxation, particularly in anxiety states and obsessional neuroses"; and to allow psychiatrists, by experimenting with the drug themselves, "to gain an insight into the world of ideas and sensations of mental patients."

Psychiatrists in several countries applied for Delysid to test its therapeutic effectiveness. By 1951, LSD therapy had made enough progress to be the subject of a presentation at the American Psychological Association. During the 1950s and early 1960s, psychiatrists in Canada, the U.S., England, Germany, and Czechoslovakia used LSD in clinical trials. Several psychiatrists published studies of their work, including Humphry Osmond in Canada, Ronald Sandison in England, Stanislav Grof in Czechoslovakia, and Americans Sidney Cohen and Oscar Janiger (see separate entries for each). They developed two different methods for LSD therapy. In the method referred to as "psycholytic" therapy, patients received a series of small doses of the drug—usually 25 micrograms to start—as psychiatrists guided them through weeks or months of psychotherapy. "Psycholytic" comes from Greek roots meaning a relaxation of the mind: the idea was to help patients overcome resistance to therapy and gradually gain access to repressed materials. In the other method, "psychedelic" therapy, a patient would take LSD only once, but in a much bigger dose (as much as 500 micrograms). After weeks of preparation, patients took a single intense trip, which in theory could inspire a fundamental reshaping of their mental world. In follow-up sessions, patients would talk and write about what they had felt during their experience.

Psychiatrists took care to screen patients for underlying mental disorders that the drug might trigger or aggravate, such as schizophrenia or suicidal tendencies. LSD therapy seemed to work well with alcoholics (see *Alcoholism*) and showed promise with other common psychiatric problems, including depression, anxiety, and obsessive-compulsive disorders. LSD was also used in trials to alleviate the distress of patients who had been diagnosed with terminal cancer (see *Dying*). In a 1960 study of side-effects and complications, Sidney Cohen concluded that LSD therapy was fundamentally safe if carried out with appropriate safeguards and clinical expertise. The treatment began to receive publicity in the late 1950s and early 1960s when it became something of a fad among Hollywood celebrities. Both *Look* and *Good Housekeeping* published cover stories about Cary Grant, who described a dramatic transformation of his life resulting from LSD sessions with his psychiatrist (see *Grant, Cary; Hartman, Mortimer A.*).

Although LSD therapists were reporting generally successful results, the broader scientific community began to question the validity of their work. Historian Erika Dyck has analyzed how psychedelic psychiatry came into conflict with new standards for clinical experimentation. Skeptical scientists pointed out that LSD studies lacked proper controls for environmental variables, and they suspected that psychiatrists' enthusiasm was skewing results. Researchers in Toronto who had read of Osmond's success in treating alcoholism tried to duplicate his results in a more rigorously controlled trial. In order to minimize the influence of environmental factors, they conducted LSD sessions in an austere setting and used blindfolds and physical restraints. Their results did not show the rate of cure that Osmond had reported, and they concluded that whatever real success he had achieved was not caused directly by the drug.

Dyck and others have discussed how political pressures played at least as large a role as scientific skepticism in bringing down psychedelic psychiatry. When LSD started to gain notoriety in the 1960s as a recreational drug and became associated with countercultural values, even former supporters of LSD therapy began to issue warnings. Sidney Cohen worried that unsupervised use of the drug could lead to major problems for young people who were taking it recklessly, cheered on by acid evangelists like Timothy Leary. By the late 1960s, LSD was made illegal, and scientists faced so many restrictions on its clinical use that research all but stopped. In 1970, LSD was classified as a Schedule I controlled substance, which officially put an end to therapeutic claims: the Schedule I label indicates that a drug has no legitimate medical use (see *Laws*).More recently, with political pressures somewhat diminished, a few scientists have resumed experiments in LSD psychiatry. Groups in Switzerland, Israel, Spain, and the U.S. tested LSD and other hallucinogens in therapy for the terminally ill and in treatment for various medical and psychiatric disorders. The non-profit organization MAPS (Multidisciplinary Association for Psychedelic Studies) promotes and tracks such work (see *MAPS*). British psychiatrist Ben Sessa recommended to his colleagues that they endorse the resumption of psychedelic psychiatry: "I don't see why either ethically or technically or professionally it shouldn't be used in the future. But anything done now has to be very different from what we did. All the expertise developed in those years by a large number of people has been lost, so we have to start again" (*Guardian*, 11 January 2006).

Psycholytic. English psychotherapist Ronald Sandison coined this term to describe his preferred method of administering LSD (see *Sandison, Ronald; Psychiatry*). Psycholytic therapy differed from psychedelic therapy in the strength of dosage: psycholytic patients were given low doses over the course of many sessions, whereas psychedelic patients received one or a few large doses. "Psycholytic" comes from Greek roots meaning "mind-relaxing": the drug was supposed to facilitate access to unconscious materials by relaxing conscious defenses. Psycholytic therapy was generally favored in Europe, while American psychiatrists often used psychedelic therapy.

Psychotomimetic. LSD was first classified as a drug that mimics symptoms of psychosis. Humphry Osmond and Aldous Huxley later proposed replacing "psychotomimetic" with "psychedelic." See *Psychedelic*.

Punk. The punk subculture that developed in 1970s Britain defined itself in opposition to hippies. Punk styles sharply reversed hippie styles in fashion, music, drugs, and attitude. Hippies wore colorful, flowing clothes and costumey accessories (see *Fashion*), whereas punks preferred black t-shirts and rough piercings. Punk music eschewed the long instrumental passages and vocal harmonies central to psychedelic rock (see *Psychedelic Rock*); Johnny Rotten of the Sex Pistols wore a t-shirt that read, "I Hate Pink Floyd" (see *Pink Floyd*). The punk drugs of choice were amphetamines and alcohol rather than LSD. Punks tended to regard hippies as indolent hedonists from a more comfortable and complacent era. In contrast with hippie idealism, punk ethos was founded on economic resentment and a political edginess that verged on anarchy.

For all these differences, punks shared with hippies a fundamental rejection of mainstream culture and an emphasis on unfettered self-expression. The history of Joe Strummer and The Clash illustrates the overlap between hippie psychedelia and the world of punk: Strummer liked to trip on LSD, and he started and ended his exemplary punk career with an appreciation for psychedelic themes. See *The Clash*.

"Purple Haze." This 1967 hit single by Jimi Hendrix was associated with "Monterey Purple" acid. See *Hendrix, Jimi; Owsley*.

Pynchon, Thomas. Pynchon's second novel, *The Crying of Lot 49* (1966), featured LSD as an important element of the plot. See *Crying of Lot 49*.

Quicksilver Messenger Service. Quicksilver was one of the more prominent psychedelic rock bands during the height of the San Francisco music scene. They played many concerts at the Avalon and Fillmore venues, either as the headline act or as one of two or three top acts. Like the Grateful Dead, Quicksilver did its best work in instrumental jams, and their most highly regarded recordings came from live performances. Their second album, *Happy Trails*, consists mainly of live Fillmore performances. Quicksilver guitarists John Cipollina and Gary Duncan played in a style that reflected jazz influences, and their sound depended less on special effects (distortion, reverberation, wah-wah) than was the case with many psychedelic bands.

Rave. A latter-day version of the Acid Tests from the 1960s, raves were musical parties where attendees commonly took the hallucinogen MDMA (see *Ecstasy*), although some used LSD. See *Acid Test; Ecstasy; Acid House*.

Red Dog Saloon. This old saloon in Virginia City, Nevada was the site of the earliest psychedelic concerts. A group of proto-hippies who had been experimenting with LSD booked a band called the Charlatans for an extended gig (see *Charlatans; Seed*), and the concerts attracted the psychedelic avant garde that had been gathering around the Bay Area. The Red Dog Saloon pioneered key features of later psychedelic concerts, including light shows, dancing, and tripping by musicians as well as members of the audience.

Religion. Several scholars who experimented with LSD and similar drugs have argued that the psychedelic experience has important religious implications. Some have even proposed renaming these drugs "entheogens," meaning that they generate within the mind a sense of God. Aldous Huxley concluded that psychedelic drugs gave him temporary access to the world of mystics like St. John of the Cross and Jakob Boehme (see *Huxley, Aldous*). Other psychedelic researchers studied religious rituals that made use of organic hallucinogens; a group of researchers, including Albert Hofmann, developed a theory that a hallucinogenic drink lay at the heart of the Eleusinian Mysteries in ancient Greece (see *Eleusinian Mysteries*). Timothy Leary, Richard Alpert, and Ralph Metzner saw similarities between Hindu and Buddhist philosophies and psychedelic consciousness. The three of them collaborated on a manual for tripping based on the Tibetan Book of the Dead (see *Psychedelic Experience*). A few years earlier, a Catholic priest in Vancouver, Monsignor J.E. Brown, had taken LSD supplied by Al Hubbard; deeply moved by the experience, he recommended it to parishioners in a letter that ended with the following prayer: "We humbly ask Our Heavenly Mother the Virgin Mary, help of all who call upon Her, to aid us to know and understand the true qualities of these psychedelics, the full capacities of man's noblest faculties and according to God's laws use them for the benefit of mankind here and in eternity." In the early 1960s, several Jesuit priests, including influential theologian John Courtney Murray, had experimented with LSD as a way to intensify their spiritual lives (see *Jesuits; Murray, John Courtney; Johnson, Don Hanlon*).

Religion scholar Huston Smith wrote a number of essays in which he reflected on how a psychedelic experience might provide an occasion for deep religious insight. Many of these essays have been reprinted in the retrospective collection *Cleansing the Doors of Perception*. Smith had been a participant in the Good Friday experiment conducted in the 1960s by Walter Pahnke, then a graduate student at Harvard. Smith was one of several divinity students who was given psilocybin and ended up reporting a profound spiritual experience. Pahnke wrote up the results in his doctoral dissertation. Pahnke later reflected at length on the connections between LSD and religion (see *Pahnke, Walter*). Drawing on his own research at Harvard, Pahnke listed nine characteristics of "spontaneous mystical experiences," all of which "also precisely describe experimental psychedelic ones." He was careful to say that LSD "is only a trigger, a catalyst" for mystical experience, and he warned potential users of the drug that "psychotic reactions are the easiest to produce; mystical experiences are the hardest, certainly not automatic, even under optional conditions."

Pahnke also briefly described a handful of religious communities that used psychedelics in sacramental ritual. Two of these groups specifically named LSD as the key to their religious practice. One had been founded in 1966 by Timothy Leary: the League for Spiritual Discovery. Leary quickly recruited a few hundred members and registered the L.S.D. as a religion with the state of New York. He went on publicity tours where he spread his psychedelic gospel and encouraged others to start their own groups; he distributed a pamphlet called "Start Your Own Religion." Pahnke treated Leary's League respectfully in his paper, summarizing its core mission as "a withdrawal from the meaningless games in which we are involved, to allow full-time commitment to spiritual exploration." Although Pahnke recognized the L.S.D. as a serious religious community, the courts did not: they saw it as a ruse engineered by Leary to beat a drug arrest. In *Leary v. United States* (1967), a circuit court ruled that Leary's use of illegal drugs was not legitimated by the religious structure he had created. The court sharply distinguished the "bona fide [peyote-based] religious ceremonies of the Native American Church" from "the private and personal use" of illegal drugs "by any person who claims he is using it as a religious practice" (see *Leary, Timothy; League for Spiritual Discovery; Laws*).

The other LSD-based religion was Arthur Kleps' Neo-American Church, incorporated in California in 1965. Pahnke mentioned this church only briefly, as a group that seemed not to take itself very seriously. Indeed, Kleps seemed more interested in satirizing the very idea of institutionalized religion than in setting up a serious structure of beliefs and rituals. Kleps referred to himself as "Chief Boo Hoo, Patriarch of the East," declared that "the psychedelic substances, such as LSD, are the true Host of the Church," and defined the "religious duty of all members to partake of the sacrament on regular occasions." Each disciple carried a membership card that left room for a "Martyrdom Record" in case of arrest ("Persecuting Officer Please Sign: 1. ___ Hero; 2. ___ Master; 3. ___ Saint."). Card-carrying Neo-American Judith Kuch, who was arrested on LSD charges, ended up suing the government on the basis of religious freedom. In *United States v. Judith H. Kuch* (1968), Judge Gerhard Gesell acknowledged that "the dividing line between what is, and what is not, a religion, is difficult to draw," and that "courts must be ever careful not to permit their own moral and ethical standards to determine the religious implications of beliefs and practices of others." Nevertheless, he dismissed the notion that Kleps' church was a serious religious entity:

> Reading the so-called 'Catechism and Handbook' of the Church containing the pronouncements of the Chief Boo Hoo, one gains the inescapable impression that the membership is mocking established institutions, playing with words and totally irreverent in any sense of the term.... The official songs are 'Puff, the Magic Dragon' and 'Row, Row, Row Your Boat.' In short, the 'Catechism and Handbook' is full of goofy nonsense, contradictions, and irreverent expressions. There is a conscious effort to assert in passing the attributes of religion but obviously only for tactical purposes.

Kuch's conviction—and her "martyrdom"—were upheld (see *Kleps, Arthur; Neo-American Church*).

Revolver. This 1966 Beatles' album was the first to show clear psychedelic influence. See *Beatles.*

Rich Kids on LSD. Despite its name, this California punk band of the 1980s and 1990s had no significant connection with psychedelic culture. According to lead singer Jason Sears, the name "was kind of like a joke, it happened that some guy said, 'Ha, those kids will never be anything, they're just a bunch of rich kids on LSD.' The first party we played we didn't have a name for the band, so we put that one on the flyer and it just stuck" (*Thrasher* magazine, March 2010). Sears speculated that putting LSD in their name hurt the band's chances for product endorsements.

Rinkel, Max. Boston psychiatrist Rinkel was the first person to bring LSD into the U.S. After hearing about the new drug from Austrian colleague Otto Kauders, Rinkel applied to Sandoz for a research supply. He first tested it on colleague Robert Hyde, whose reactions lent credence to the theory that LSD induced temporary psychosis (see *Hyde, Robert*). In another early experiment, Rinkel gave LSD to artist Hyman Bloom (see *Bloom, Hyman*). Rinkel was one of many American scientists involved in CIA-funded research on LSD in the early 1950s (see *MK-Ultra*).

Rolling Stone. Jann Wenner and Ralph Gleason founded the iconic magazine in 1967 at the peak of the psychedelic era. Their early content was dominated by music and culture of the San Francisco psychedelic scene. According to copy editor Charles Perry, Wenner once told him how to choose among the hundreds of records sent by labels for review: "Just keep the acid rock" (see *Perry, Charles*). *Rolling Stone* published not only music reviews and interviews but ambitious essays, including Hunter S. Thompson's hallucinogenic narrative *Fear and Loathing in Las Vegas* (see *Thompson, Hunter S.*). The magazine has successfully carried on through the post-psychedelic decades, with Wenner still in charge; some have complained that *Rolling Stone* gives disproportionate emphasis to the hippie music and politics of its founding years. In 2006, they published a cover story on "Daniel Pinchbeck and the New Psychedelic Elite" (see *Pinchbeck, Daniel*).

Rolling Stones. In 1967 the Stones released *Their Satanic Majesties Request,* their answer to the Beatles' *Sergeant Pepper's Lonely Hearts Club Band* and the only Stones album done in high psychedelic style (see *Beatles*). Members of the band have acknowledged that they were taking LSD throughout the making of the record. Critical opinion was not particularly favorable, even from the Stones themselves. Mick Jagger said in a 1995 interview, "There's two good songs on it: 'She's a Rainbow' and '2000 Light Years from Home.' The rest of them are nonsense. I think we were just taking too much acid. We were just getting carried away, just thinking anything you did was fun and everyone should listen to it. The whole thing we were on acid."

As Keith Richards recalled, the Stones even took acid for the cover photograph. "We built the set on acid, went all around New York getting the flowers and the rest of the props; we were painting it, spraying it. We were just loony, and after the Beatles had done *Sergeant Pepper,* it was like, let's get even more ridiculous." The cover for *Satanic Majesties* imitates the costume-and-collage effect of *Sergeant Pepper.* The Stones pose in fairy-tale garb, with Jagger wearing a conical wizard's cap. Jagger said at the time that the cover was "not meant to be a nice picture at all. Look at the expressions on our faces. It's a Grimm's fairy tale—one of those stories that used to frighten as a young child." The Stones thereby preserved their trademark sinister edge, but there was no denying the atypical hippie trappings: flowers, beads, cute hats, bright colors.

Of the two songs cited by Jagger as worthwhile, the first one reflects the hippie landscape not typical of the Stones. "She's a Rainbow" is filled with colors and sunny romance. The other song, "2000 Light Years from Home," has a darker tone: a traveler in space finds desolation and unrelenting loneliness. Both songs can be called psychedelic, but "2000 Light Years" belongs to a gothic or sublime psychedelic style—like the Grateful Dead's "Dark Star" (see *Grateful Dead*)—as opposed to the hippie pastoral mode of "She's a Rainbow."

Ruck, Carl A.P. A professor of Classical Studies at Boston University, Ruck collaborated with Albert Hofmann and Gordon Wasson on *The Road to Eleusis: Unveiling the Secrets of the Mysteries* (1978). The three men proposed that the ancient Greeks consumed an ergot alkaloid—the organic foundation of LSD—during their sacred rituals (see *Eleusinian Mysteries; Hofmann, Albert; Wasson, R. Gordon*). Ruck was one of the first to promote a new term for the class of drug to which LSD belongs: "entheogen." See *Entheogen; Psychedelic*.

San Francisco Mime Troupe. This acting troupe stirred up trouble with obscenity charges in the mid 1960s and became increasingly active in politically subversive street theatre. The Mime Troupe had important connections with San Francisco's psychedelic counterculture. Bill Graham became their business manager and organized his first Fillmore concert as a benefit for the Troupe (see *Graham, Bill*). Several members of the group, including Peter Berg, Peter Coyote, and Emmett Grogan, went on to found the Diggers (see *Diggers; Berg, Peter; Coyote, Peter; Grogan, Emmett*).

San Francisco Sound. "The San Francisco Sound" was a label applied to rock music that flourished in the city during the psychedelic era. The San Francisco Sound amounts to a regional but broadly influential subgenre of psychedelic rock (see *Psychedelic Rock*). Although there were significant differences among San Francisco bands, most of them shared a few essential characteristics. Most San Francisco rock musicians used LSD and embraced psychedelic challenges to social and musical conventions. Nurtured in the Acid Tests and the dance concerts of the Avalon and Fillmore (see *Acid Test; Avalon; Fillmore*), they relied on traditional rock beats but added instrumental improvisations. Many San Francisco bands believed that their best and most representative work came in live performances. Lyricists often aimed for poetic complexity, in the manner of the Beats and Bob Dylan, both important influences on the San Francisco Sound. Musical influences included blues, folk, jug band, early rock and roll, and jazz.

The Charlatans are usually cited as the first San Francisco psychedelic band, but Jefferson Airplane had the greatest early success, and the Grateful Dead had the longest and most influential career. See *Big Brother and the Holding Company; Charlatans; Country Joe and the Fish; Grateful Dead; Jefferson Airplane; Moby Grape; Quicksilver Messenger Service; Santana.*

Sand, Nick. After spending time with Timothy Leary at Millbrook (see *Leary, Timothy; Millbrook*), Sand began manufacturing LSD with partner Tim Scully (see *Scully, Tim*). Sand and Scully were responsible for making the famous brand of acid called Orange Sunshine, distributed by the Brotherhood of Eternal Love (see *Orange Sunshine; Brotherhood of Eternal Love*). In 1973 both Sand and Scully were convicted on drug charges, but during the appeal process Sand escaped to Canada. Two decades later, when authorities moved against a huge LSD manufacturing operation in Canada, one of the leaders turned out to be Sand; he was again convicted and this time served his sentence.

Sandison, Ronald. Sandison was the first English psychotherapist to use LSD in clinical practice. He began trials in 1952 at Powick Hospital in Worcestershire, where for twelve years he administered LSD to hundreds of patients. Sandison coined the term "psycholytic therapy" to describe his preferred method: he liked to give patients low doses of LSD over the course of several sessions, in contrast with "psychedelic therapy," which uses a single large dose (see *Psychiatry*). "Psycholytic" comes from Greek roots meaning to relax or loosen the mind.

Sandoz. Albert Hofmann worked for Sandoz Laboratories, a Swiss pharmaceutical company, when he first made LSD in 1938 (see *Hofmann, Albert*). Sandoz and Hofmann were interesting in researching ergot alkaloids for potential medical uses. In his 25th compound based on lysergic acid (key constituent of the ergot alkaloids), Hofmann was aiming for a drug to improve circulation and respiration. He tried LSD-25 on animals, but when nothing notable happened, he set it aside. Five years later, he dosed himself—first accidentally, then intentionally—and discovered his drug's extraordinary psychotropic powers.

Sandoz patented LSD under the commercial name of "Delysid" (see *Delysid*) and conducted research to gauge its applications for psychotherapy. In 1947, Werner Stoll, Hofmann's colleague and son of the Sandoz president, published the first scientific article about LSD's effects on perception and consciousness (see *Stoll, Werner*). Through the 1950s and into the 1960s, Sandoz provided Delysid free of charge to medical and psychiatric researchers, with the stipulation that their results would be shared with Sandoz. At the same time, LSD was being tested in the U.S. and elsewhere for its value as a Cold War weapon. Eventually the American company Eli Lilly, supported by the CIA, developed a cheaper and more efficient method for manufacturing LSD (see *Lilly*). As a result, Sandoz no longer held full control of LSD production and distribution.

As the psychedelic counterculture gained momentum, Sandoz faced increasing political pressure to cut its ties with LSD. Dr. A. Cerletti, pharmaceutical director of the company, finally declared in August, 1965 that they would no longer make or distribute the drug: "In spite of all our precautions, cases of LSD abuse have occurred from time in varying circumstances completely beyond the control of Sandoz. Very recently this danger has increased considerably and in some parts of the world has reached the scale of a serious threat to public health.... A worldwide spread of misconceptions of LSD has been caused by an increasing amount of publicity aimed at provoking an active interest in lay people by means of sensational stories and statements."

Ironically, some of these "sensational stories" related to the unmatchable quality of authentic Sandoz LSD. Acidheads of the 1960s spoke reverentially of Sandoz LSD as the purest, most potent version of the drug ever made; legends grew about the superiority of Sandoz to all street varieties. In 2006, Erowid gathered a group of acid veterans to do a psychedelic Pepsi challenge. They compared doses taken from a vial of Delysid made in 1951 with contemporary blotters. Results indicated that the Sandoz acid was no stronger or purer than ordinary acid (*Erowid.com,* June 2006).

Santa Cruz. This city on Monterey Bay in California, once known mainly as a beach resort, developed important connections with LSD. In November of 1965, the Merry Pranksters held the first Acid Test at a ranch near Santa Cruz (see *Acid Test; Merry Pranksters*). That same fall, the newest branch of the University of California opened in the redwoods above the city; the campus quickly became known for countercultural innovation, and psychedelic culture flourished there. Faculty at UCSC included LSD pioneer Frank Barron, a former colleague of Leary's at Harvard (see *Barron, Frank*); mathematician Ralph Abraham, who drew on his psychedelic experiences to forge Chaos Theory (see *Abraham, Ralph*); and anthropologist Gregory Bateson, who had run early clinical experiments with LSD (see *Bateson, Gregory*). In 1977, the campus hosted a conference called "LSD: A Generation Later," which was attended by the most impressive roster of LSD luminaries ever assembled, including Albert Hofmann, Timothy Leary, Allen Ginsberg, and Oscar Janiger. UCSC also hosted a fiftieth anniversary celebration of Bicycle Day in 1993 (see *Bicycle Day*). In 2008, the Grateful Dead announced that they would deposit their archives in the campus library (see *Grateful Dead*). Chancellor George Blumenthal noted on the occasion that "the Grateful Dead and UC Santa Cruz are both highly innovative

institutions—born the same year—that continue to make a major, positive impact on the world." Santa Cruz is also home to the Multidisciplinary Association for Psychedelic Studies (see *MAPS*).

Santana. Carlos Santana founded the band that bears his name in 1966 to play in the hippie dance halls of San Francisco. The band Santana featured distinctive Afro-Latin percussive rhythms in combination with Carlos Santana's expressive lead guitar. At first Santana played as an opening act for the better known San Francisco bands, but when concert promoter Bill Graham took over as manager for Santana (see *Graham, Bill*), the band received greater exposure and became a headliner. The defining moment for Santana came at Woodstock in 1969: their set was widely considered among the most impressive of the whole event, and their performance of "Soul Sacrifice" was a highlight of the Woodstock album and the movie. Carlos Santana later admitted that he performed at Woodstock while in the middle of an unnerving acid trip. In a 2008 interview (*Allaboutjazz.com*), he said his Woodstock experience was "beyond scary, because I was at the peak of acid. I said, 'God, please help me stay in tune. Please help me stay in time. I promise I'll never touch this stuff again.' Of course I lied." His guitar, he said, looked like an "electric snake" writhing around: "So that's why you see my face, like making all these ugly faces, like 'Stand still,' you know."

Saturday Night Live. In the show's early years, not far removed from the psychedelic era, two episodes contained memorable routines about LSD. The first was improvised by guest host Richard Pryor in his opening monologue (December 13, 1975). Pryor mentions that he doesn't like acid, but "White dudes take acid. They take acid and see *The Exorcist.* They crazy. White dude gave me some acid at a party." For the rest of the monologue, Pryor acts out his bad trip: he stares at his hands, starts moving and speaking in slow motion, panics that he can't remember how to breathe, and says "I'm gonna die." In the midst of his distress, a nerdy "white" voice comes from the person who gave him the LSD: "Told ya it was far out!" The second piece came from their second season, early in Jimmy Carter's presidency (Marcy 12, 1977). The president is taking questions from random callers. A young man tells Carter (Dan Aykroyd), "I took some acid. I'm afraid to leave my apartment, and I can't wear any clothes—and the ceiling is dripping—and ..." Walter Cronkite (Bill Murray) wants to cut him off, but Carter steps in like a veteran psychedelic guide:

> PRESIDENT: Peter, what did the acid look like?
> PETER: They were these little orange pills.
> PRESIDENT: Were they barrel shaped?
> PETER: Uh—yes.
> PRESIDENT: OK, right, you did some Orange Sunshine, Peter. Everything is going to be fine. Try taking some vitamin B complex, vitamin C complex. If you have a beer, go ahead and drink it. Just remember you're a living organism on this planet, and you're very safe. Relax, stay inside and listen to some music.

Saturday Review. One of the earliest accounts of LSD appeared as a *Saturday Review* cover story in 1963: "Experiment with LSD: They Split My Personality." See *Asher, Harry.*

Schizophrenia. In the earliest years of psychiatric experimentation with LSD, the drug was connected to schizophrenia by two theories. One theory proposed that LSD produced temporary schizophrenia in normal subjects; if this premise proved valid, scientists could study the neurochemistry of people on LSD and use their observations to improve drug-based therapy for schizophrenics. The so-called psychotomimetic theory of LSD was never clearly proven or disproven, but as time went on, some experts questioned the equation of psychedelic states with naturally occurring psychoses. In recent years, as controls on LSD research has eased

somewhat, a few scientists have resumed animal experiments to look for chemical links between LSD and schizophrenia (see *Nichols, Charles*).

A second theory suggested that LSD might be used not to induce temporary schizophrenia but to stimulate long-term psychotherapeutic benefits. If schizophrenics were given LSD in psychiatric trials, they might benefit from such therapy in the way that, for example, alcoholics had seemed to do in several studies. A number of psychiatrist ran LSD experiments in the 1950s to determine its effect on schizophrenic patients. In general, the drug seemed much more likely to aggravate than to relieve psychotic symptoms. A 1957 report by Paul Hoch concluded, "The majority of schizophrenics displayed intensification of their pre-existing symptomatology on administration of mescaline or LSD-25. The reactions of schizophrenic patients to mescaline and LSD-25 are usually marked with severe anxiety and other emotional patterns, while disorganization of thought and behavior patterns may be profound" (Second International Conference of Psychiatry, Zurich; see *Hoch, Paul*). Some psychiatrists acknowledged these results but suggested that the intensified symptoms and mental disorganization might constitute an intermediate stage on the way to improvement. See *Psychiatry; Alcoholism; Autism.*

Scully, Tim. Scully was one of the most prolific manufacturers of high-quality LSD in the late 1960s and early 1970s. He apprenticed under the legendary Owsley (see *Owsley*), with whom he collaborated on the brand of acid called "White Lightning" (as well as sound equipment for the Grateful Dead). After Owsley was arrested in 1967, Scully teamed up with Nick Sand to make another famous brand of acid, "Orange Sunshine," which was distributed by the Brotherhood of Eternal Love (see *Sand, Nick; Brotherhood of Eternal Love*). Both Scully and Sand were convicted on drug charges in 1974 and served prison sentences. Scully was released from prison in 1980 and began working on topics in biofeedback and computer technology.

Seed. "The Seed" is the nickname given to the first example of a psychedelic poster. The poster advertised a 1965 concert by the Charlatans at the Red Dog Saloon in Virginia City, Nevada; it was designed by two members of the Charlatans, George Hunter and Mike Ferguson. Although it was more legible than many subsequent psychedelic posters, "The Seed" did contain essential features of the genre: hippie-themed images of flowers, vines, and stars; wavy lines and a gentle subversion of linear organization; and a few letters with the "melting" look that would become a staple of psychedelic design. See *Charlatans; Psychedelic Posters*.

Sergeant Pepper's Lonely Hearts Club Band. This 1967 Beatles' album earned critical acclaim and had a huge influence on psychedelic music. It was the first rock album to win the Grammy award for album of the year; decades later, when *Rolling Stone* listed the top 500 rock albums of all time, *Sergeant Pepper* came in as #1. See *Beatles*.

Set and Setting. Timothy Leary popularized these terms to describe pre-conditions that influence the LSD experience (see *Leary, Timothy*). "Set" refers to a person's physical and psychological makeup at the time of the trip: genetic predispositions, current state of physical and emotional health, degree of experience with psychotropic drugs, and expectations about the drug's effects. "Setting" refers to the context in which the drug is taken, and includes variables related to location, time, music, food, social relations, and absence or presence of a guide. Leary preferred trips that were supervised in a carefully planned setting, and psychiatrists who used LSD always screened for potential problems with a given subject's set. Others, like the Merry Pranksters, deemphasized planning and control, and traded the risk of bad trips for the benefits of spontaneity and surprise. Psychiatrist Norman Zinberg's *Drug, Set, and Setting* presents a thorough analysis of how set and setting influence the effects of many common drugs.

Sex. In *Myself and I* (1962), Thelma Moss wrote that LSD therapy had helped her overcome frigidity and achieve "transcendent sexual fulfillment" (see *Moss, Thelma*). A few years later, Timothy Leary claimed that enhanced sexual pleasure was one of the great benefits of LSD use. Leary told *Playboy* that LSD was an aphrodisiac, and not only in the mundane way of promoting erection and orgasm: it renovated the whole body for a more deeply satisfying, spiritually uplifting sexual experience.

> There is no question that LSD is the most powerful aphrodisiac ever discovered by man. Sex under LSD becomes miraculously enhanced and intensified. I don't mean that it simply generates genital energy. It doesn't automatically produce a longer erection. Rather, it increases your sensitivity a thousand percent. Let me put it this way: compared with sex under LSD, the way you've been making love, no matter how ecstatic the pleasure you think you get from it, is like making love to a department-store dummy [September, 1966].

Robert Masters, co-author of *The Varieties of Psychedelic Experience*, sharply disagreed with Leary's depiction of LSD as the ultimate aphrodisiac (see *Masters, Robert*). "Such claims about LSD are not only false, they are dangerous. By suggesting that this drug is a powerful sex stimulant, desperate people will fail again, but this time in a state of heightened suggestibility that can do them grave harm. Leary's claims are causing much distress" (quoted in Bryan). Masters' studies of LSD users showed a wide variety of responses in matters of body image, mood, and other factors that affect sexual behavior.

Careful evaluation of evidence supports Masters' caution more than Leary's enthusiasm. The relationship between LSD and sexual experience is complex and ambiguous. Ernest Abel has sorted through the available studies in *Psychoactive Drugs and Sex* (1985). Some of the most useful reports were compiled by George Gay and Charles Sheppard of the Haight-Ashbury Free Clinics. Gay and Sheppard studied responses from several young people who came their way during the peak years of San Francisco psychedelia. Most of the people said that LSD did not stimulate their desire for sex; but most also said that if they ended up having sex while on LSD, the drug did enhance their sexual pleasure. Some of their responses brought to mind Leary's cosmic euphoria: according to one person, "To make love on acid is to make perfect love and gain protoplasmic unity." A later study by Gay showed that drug users rated LSD third for its effectiveness in improving the sexual experience, behind marijuana and cocaine. Gay found that subjects gave high ratings for LSD in certain aspects of sexual performance, and low ratings in others. LSD's best ratings came in "ability to have sexual fantasies" and "affecting pleasure associated with touching and being touched." The worst ratings related to more routine matters of male erectile quality.

Studies cited by Abel also include anecdotal evidence of LSD acting more like an anaphrodisiac, inhibiting sexual desire. Sometimes the problem stemmed from a troublesome hallucination. In a case reported by Dahlberg (1971), for example, "One mature man of undoubted virility became impotent with his newly married wife following one horrendous LSD trip. Under the influence of the drug, he hallucinated her as a shark and thereafter this image was repeated whenever he attempted intercourse with her." Even when no vivid hallucinations occur, LSD users often report perceptual alterations that can have the effect of diminishing sexual attraction: features of bodies may appear grotesque and distorted. A tripper might also withdraw into a solipsistic world where the drug experience preempts sexual interaction. A study by Freedman (1976) referred to a man who "claimed phenomenal sexual powers while under the in-

fluence," but "was observed during his whole trip crouched in a corner."

Available evidence suggests that LSD is inherently neither an aphrodisiac nor an anaphrodisiac. Depending on variables of set and setting, trippers may find themselves indifferent to sex, repelled by it, or intensely engaged in it. See *Homosexuality*.

Sexual Paradise of LSD. Marsha Alexander wrote this 1967 paperback in order to "discover, once and for all, if this unpredictable drug is a poisonous threat to mental and physical health or a potential for sexual salvation." She says that her book presents "case studies" based on "long and exhaustive interviews" with people who have had sex on LSD. Although she cites psychiatric research and refers to writings by Timothy Leary and Thelma Moss (see *Sex; Leary, Timothy; Moss, Thelma*), mainly the book offers erotic confessions of tripping lovers. The prose is pulpy and pornographic throughout, mixed with routine psychedelic tropes: "Hours, maybe years thudded past, my body bubbling more each second. I had at least four orgasms during that time alone." Alexander's case studies do not yield a definitive answer to her question about LSD as poison or remedy: "The sexual act in the uncertain world of LSD can be horrendously monstrous," she concludes, "but it can just as frequently be a utopia of euphoric splendors."

Sharp, Martin. Australian artist Sharp was a primary artistic contributor to the underground magazine *Oz*, which moved to London in 1967 (see *Oz*). Sharp produced psychedelic covers, posters, and other graphic designs for *Oz*, several of which became collectors' items. He also designed the cover for two *Cream* albums, *Disraeli Gears* and *Wheels of Fire* (see *Cream*).

Shulgin, Alexander. Russian-American chemist Shulgin synthesized, studied, and wrote about dozens of psychedelic drugs. Shulgin is best known for his work with MDMA (see *Ecstasy*), which he manufactured for use by psychologists in treatment of depression and post-traumatic stress disorder. He synthesized variations of many chemicals in the two main psychedelic families, phenethylamines and tryptamines, and co-wrote with his wife two controversial books that gave detailed chemical instructions for making all of these compounds: *PiHKAL* (*Phenethylamines i Have Known And Loved*) and *TiKHAL* (*Tryptamines i Have Known And Loved*). Shulgin's formula for LSD appears in *TiHKAL,* along with the following apology for only the briefest of "Qualitative Comments": "In the case of LSD, it seems presumptuous to attempt to select typical comments for quotation" from "innumerable anecdotal tales of pleasure and pain." The Shulgins also invented the "Shulgin Scale" for measuring the intensity of a psychedelic experience, ranging from "plus one" to "plus four." A "plus four" experience, the strongest and rarest, is "a religious experience, divine transformation ... a state of bliss, a connectedness with both the interior and exterior universes." They add, "If a drug were ever to be discovered which would consistently produce a plus four experience in all human beings, it is conceivable that it would signal the ultimate evolution, and perhaps the end of the human experiment." See *Shulgin, Ann.*

Shulgin, Ann. With her husband Alexander (see *Shulgin, Alexander*), Shulgin experimented with LSD and other psychedelic drugs to evaluate their potential for therapeutic and spiritual benefits. She worked as a psychologist using a Jungian paradigm, and co-wrote with Alexander two books of essays and chemical information about psychedelic drugs: *PiHKAL* (*Phenethylamines i Have Known And Loved*) and *TiHKAL* (*Tryptamines i Have Known And Loved*).

Simpsons. One measure of the importance of a person, movie, or theme in recent American culture is the number of times it has been satirically treated on *The Simpsons.* Psychedelic drugs fare quite well on the *Simpsons* scale. In the single most striking psychedelic episode, Homer's vision quest dominates the plot. After he eats "Guatemalan insanity peppers" at a chili cook-off, Homer ventures out on a desert journey reminiscent of Carlos Castaneda; he meets an animal guide, hears bits of wisdom, and at the end of the trip realizes that he has been crawling around the sand trap of a local golf course.

Although only one episode explicitly mentions LSD, several others refer implicitly to LSD and psychedelic culture of the 1960s. The direct reference comes after Marge has been falsely accused of using crack. Reunited with her children, she assures authorities, "The only thing I'm high on is Love for my Son and Daughters. Yes, a little LSD is all I need." Marge has an actual psychedelic trip in another episode when a rival town spikes Springfield's water supply. "Ooh, the walls are melting," she says, before hallucinating a flying turkey. (The LSD poisoning of a city's water supply was often raised as a danger during the psychedelic era: see *Water Supply.*) In a different episode, Lisa Simpson drinks contaminated water on an amusement park ride; she starts tripping ("I can see the music") and delivers a little allusion to Jim Morrison: "I am the lizard queen." Even straight-laced Milhouse has a psychedelic moment as he observes the new school uniforms turning tie-dye in the rain ("I'm freaking out!")

Homer has a few other psychedelic incidents besides the insanity peppers. One takes the form of the famous "Stargate" sequence from Kubrick's *2001* (see *2001*)—although Homer's trip was triggered by an expensive massage chair, not acid or aliens. Elsewhere Homer starts tripping after licking toads in the South Pacific. Ironically, it is "bad boy" Bart who chides his father for this behavior ("Dad, have you been licking toads?"), and only Bart among the major characters has no psychedelic adventure. In the real world of psychedelic drugs, however, a popular issue of blotter acid featured the smiling face of Bart Simpson.

Skidoo. Groucho Marx took LSD to prepare for his role as God in this unsuccessful 1968 movie (see *Marx, Groucho*). God consorts with hippies in *Skidoo* but does not take acid, although acid provides the plot's *deus ex machina:* a jailed mobster doses the prison population to manage his escape.

Slick, Grace. Slick joined Jefferson Airplane for their second and most popular album, *Surrealistic Pillow* (1967). *Surrealistic Pillow* included her song "White Rabbit," which became a top ten hit and psychedelic anthem during the Summer of Love (see *"White Rabbit"*). Slick and her Jefferson Airplane colleagues were enthusiastic acidheads during this period, and later albums contained songs that were more obvious examples of psychedelic rock (see *Jefferson Airplane; Psychedelic Rock*). Slick once plotted to sneak LSD into Richard Nixon's teacup. Because she and Tricia Nixon had been classmates in private school, Slick was invited to a 1970 White House reception. She and date Abbie Hoffmann filled their pockets with powdered LSD, but the secret service turned her away as a security risk. As Slick later wrote, "I hadn't done anything subversive that I knew of—it must have been some of my lyrics."

Decades later, Slick disavowed the subversively drug-friendly lyrics to "White Rabbit." In her 1998 memoir *Somebody to Love?*, she said that she "missed the mark with the lyrics." Her intended message was not to encourage psychedelic adventure but to criticize hypocrisy: "What I'd intended was to remind our parents (who were sipping highballs while they badgered us about the new drugs) that *they* were the ones who read all these 'fun with chemical' children's books to us when we were small. Contrary to popular belief, the 'adults' were the original experimenters with the ups, downs, and sideways manufactured by the 'legal' drug dealers—Roche, Johnson and Johnson, Merck, Rorer, Eli Lilly, Yuban, Smirnoff, American Tobacco Company, and the list

goes on. Fun with alcohol and cigarettes. Fun and deadly." In the same book, Slick also admitted that her plot to slip Nixon LSD was "irresponsible and dangerous."

Sly and the Family Stone. This psychedelic group founded in San Francisco by Sly Stone was notable not only for its distinctive fusion of psychedelia and funk, but for its interracial membership, which included both men and women. In hit songs such as "Everyday People," they articulated themes of integration and tolerance. Stone (born Sylvester Stewart) got his start as a dj and record producer in the early days of the San Francisco Sound (see *San Francisco Sound*). He produced the earliest version of Grace Slick's "Somebody to Love" by the Great Society; when that band declined his offer to join them, he gathered his own group. Their first hit was "Dance to the Music" (1968), and several others followed, including "I Want to Take You Higher." Sly and the Family Stone played at Woodstock and influenced groups such as the Temptations and Funkadelic (see *Temptations; Funkadelic*).

Smith, David. Physician Smith founded the Haight-Ashbury Free Clinic in June of 1967, at the start of the Summer of Love (see *Summer of Love*). Smith had done research on LSD and other drugs when he was studying medicine at the University of California, San Francisco. As he observed the hippie scene developing in the city, Smith recognized that the young people coming into Haight-Ashbury would have a difficult time getting medical care through the established institutions. He tried to get public funding for a clinic, but when his efforts failed, he used his own money to buy an apartment that became the Haight-Ashbury Free Clinic. Smith managed to keep the clinic afloat with help from two sources: students and doctors from UCSF who volunteered their services, and members of San Francisco psychedelic bands who played benefit concerts. Promoter Bill Graham was particularly active in organizing these concerts (see *Graham, Bill*). Smith later acknowledged that his clinic "was built on rock and roll."

Smith's clinic fit well with the anti-capitalist philosophy espoused by the Diggers: "Everything is free, do your own thing" (see *Diggers*). Just as the Diggers provided free food and clothing, he provided free medical care. He also assured young people that at his clinic they would be free from moral judgments about drug use and sexual behavior. The Haight-Ashbury Free Clinic survived the difficult conditions of the Summer of Love and has remained open ever since. Smith went on to become a prominent authority on psychoactive drugs and treatments for drug addiction.

Smith, Huston. An authority on world religions then teaching at MIT, Smith took LSD with Harvard's Timothy Leary in the early 1960s (see *Leary, Timothy; Harvard*). Smith developed a keen interest in psychedelic drugs as catalysts for profound spiritual experiences, although he always cautioned that a drug does not "cause" religious enlightenment in the simple sense of the word (see *Religion*). He warned Leary that LSD was too powerful and complex to be publicized recklessly. Smith later criticized Leary and other acid evangelists for creating a "wild, chaotic, irresponsible" culture of recreational use (interview in *Salon*, 2000). He told an LSD conference in 1966 that socio-political controversies made serious LSD research impossible: "There is no hope of telling the truth about [LSD] at this point" (Stafford). Smith wrote a number of essays about the relationship between religion and psychedelic drugs—or as he preferred to call them, entheogens (see *Entheogen*)—most of which were collected in *Cleansing the Doors of Perception* (2000). Although in the 1960s he often warned about careless drug use and specious religious claims, in later essays he emphasized the value of entheogenic epiphanies. Smith told *Salon* in 2000 that he now felt obliged to

argue for LSD on the grounds of religious freedom: "I was extremely fortunate in having some entheogenic experiences while the substances were not only legal, but respectable. It seemed like only fair play, since I value those experiences immensely, to do anything I could to enable a new generation to also have such experiences without the threat of going to jail."

Smythies, John. With colleague Humphry Osmond, British psychiatrist Smythies moved to Saskatchewan and conducted successful LSD therapy for alcoholics. See *Osmond, Humphrey; Alcoholism*.

Spiders. In the mid 1960s, scientists Peter N. Witt and Charles F. Reed tested various psychotropic drugs on spiders to see how each drug affected their production of webs. Witt and Reed reported the results in "Spider-Web Building," a 1965 paper that appeared in *Science*. In general, the druggy spiders didn't fare so well. With most of the drugs, including nitrous oxide, phenobarbitol, and even caffeine, the webs were defective in important categories of web competence. However, given very low doses of LSD, the tripping spiders delivered a surprising result: they wove webs of greater regularity than those woven by their non-psychedelic counterparts. See *Elephant; Dolphins*.

Spontaneous Underground. In early 1966, American Steve Stollman organized the first of several London events that came to be known as "Spontaneous Underground." Prominent figures from the English counterculture soon took a leading role, including John Hopkin and Barry Miles (see *Hopkin, John; Miles, Barry*). These gatherings shared several features with American Acid Tests (see *Acid Test*). Attendees took LSD, wore exotic costumes, danced to psychedelic music (often by Pink Floyd: see *Pink Floyd*), watched light shows, and improvised revels. The first such events took place at the Marquee Club, but the most notable gatherings happened at the Roundhouse, an old industrial building with charm but few amenities. The first Roundhouse party in October of 1966 launched the underground newspaper *International Times*. Guests included Paul McCartney (see *McCartney, Paul*) and film director Michelangelo Antonioni, who was filming *Blow-Up* in the city. According to John Platt, "Some 2,000 people turned up and were greeted by Miles handing out sugar cubes (which turned out not to be of the LSD-coated variety, despite legend to the contrary)." Pink Floyd played in front of a liquid light show: "Few people had seen one before and the audience was transfixed," noted Platt. "Musically the Floyd played one of their best sets, even though the power short-circuited in the middle of 'Interstellar Overdrive.'" The Sunday *Times* ran a story on the Roundhouse party and gave Spontaneous Underground its first national publicity. Before long, the center of London psychedelia shifted to the UFO Club, where it flourished through the summer of 1967 (see *UFO Club*).

Stafford, Peter. Stafford, who first experimented with psychedelics at Reed College in 1961, co-wrote with Bonnie Golightly one of the first comprehensive books about LSD (see *Golightly, Bonnie*). Their *LSD: The Problem-Solving Psychedelic* (1967) described the effects of the drug, gave advice on how to trip safely, and examined evidence for potential benefits. The problems they suggested LSD might solve included creative blocks, sexual dysfunction, and alcoholism. Stafford also wrote the *Psychedelics Encyclopedia*, which gave technical, psychological, and cultural information about all the known psychedelic drugs.

Star Trek. The original *Star Trek* television series, which ran during the peak years of the psychedelic era, featured three episodes that revolved around hippie and psychedelic themes. In "Shore Leave" from late 1966, the Enterprise crew finds itself on a planet that gives corporeal form to unconscious fantasies. The first such moment occurs when Dr. McCoy sees Alice chasing the White Rabbit. The planet's philosopher king eventually reassures Captain Kirk that these visions are recreational and benign; all members of the crew happily partake in their psychedelic shore leave, except Mr. Spock, who declines and returns to the ship.

The other two episodes contrarily depict Spock as the crew member most sympathetic to hippie values. "This Side of Paradise" (1967) takes the Enterprise to a planet where flower power literally transforms the inhabitants: a native flower shoots spores that induce euphoria. After Spock inhales the spores, he turns giddy, falls in love, and ignores his captain's call to duty. Kirk finally rouses Spock from this version of the land of the lotos-eaters, but Spock looks back wistfully to the time he spent high on spores: "For the first time in my life, I was happy." A similar invitation to paradise confronts Spock in "The Way to Eden" (1969). This time the story presents an obvious allegory of hippie culture. The Enterprise rescues a colorful band of antinomians that includes a charismatic "doctor" (as in Leary). They mock authority and seek out a planet named Eden. Only Spock among the Enterprise crew respects their aspirations: he exchanges a peace sign with them and calls for oneness and harmony. When the hippie musician stages a concert, Spock joins in. Even after a messy fight with the Edenites (and the discovery that their "paradise" contains poisonous plants), Spock encourages the space hippies to keep searching for Eden.

Stark, Ronald. In 1969 Stark took over operations for the Brotherhood of Eternal Love, the largest producer and distributer of LSD (see *Brotherhood of Eternal Love*). A mysterious figure in LSD history, he was thought to have connections with international financiers, political activists in America and Europe, organized crime, and the intelligence community. After arrests shut down the Brotherhood in 1972, Stark fled to Europe, where he provided raw materials for LSD manufacture to the English chemist Richard Kemp (see *Kemp, Richard; Operation Julie*). Stark eventually faced drug charges in Europe. By the time he returned to the United States in the early 1980s, authorities were unable to assemble a case against him on the decade-old LSD charges. The most vivid accounts of Stark's career as an acid entrepreneur appear in Tendler and May's *The Brotherhood of Eternal Love* and Black's *Acid: The Secret History of LSD*.

Starr, Ringo. Starr took LSD after his colleagues John Lennon and George Harrison reported that the drug had significantly altered their perceptions (see *Lennon, John; Harrison, George*). Starr's experience with LSD was mixed, however, and he never became an acid enthusiast like Lennon and Harrison. Starr's first trip took place in Los Angeles with Lennon, Harrison, and a few friends. Starr recalls "swimming in jelly in the pool" and having "a fabulous day," but "the night wasn't so great, because it felt like it was never going to wear off. Twelve hours later and it was, 'Give us a break now, Lord.'" Starr later sang "Yellow Submarine," a song from *Revolver* that took on psychedelic associations with the making of the animated film of the same name (see *Yellow Submarine*).

Steadman, Ralph. Steadman is the Welsh artist whose drawings provided a suitably psychedelic accompaniment to Hunter S. Thompson's *Fear and Loathing in Las Vegas* (see *Thompson, Hunter S.*). Steadman and Thompson first bonded on an earlier assignment to cover the America's Cup in Newport, Rhode Island. Because Steadman was an uneasy sailor, he borrowed pills from Thompson that he assumed the writer was taking for seasickness. It turned out the pills were not Dramamine but LSD. The two men proceeded to cavort wildly amidst the yachting crowd; eventually Steadman flew to New York, where a doctor gave him a shot of Librium. According to Steadman's memoir, this memorable acid trip "established a pattern of journalism, if that is what it was, that cemented my friendship with Hunter and laid the groundwork for future assignments. It remains a defining moment in the evolution of gonzo and, without doubt, a dress rehearsal for *Fear and Loathing in Las Vegas*."

Steppenwolf. Originally named "Sparrow," this Canadian-American rock band rechristened itself after the title of a novel by Herman Hesse, a writer whose work had become popular in countercultural circles. As Sparrow, the band played at the Matrix in San Francisco during the Summer of Love (see *Matrix; Summer of Love*); as Steppenwolf, they had the hit singles "Born to Be Wild"—the first song on the soundtrack of *Easy Rider* (see *Easy Rider*)—and "Magic Carpet Ride." Some critics point to Steppenwolf as one of the precursors to heavy metal, a phrase that comes from "Born to Be Wild." See *Acid Rock; Psychedelic Rock*.

Stoll, Werner A. Stoll was the first psychiatrist to take LSD, and the first to conduct a clinical trial of the drug. Stoll was a professor at the University of Zurich and the son of Arthur Stoll, president of Sandoz, where Albert Hofmann discovered LSD (see *Sandoz; Hofmann, Albert*). Because of his connections to Sandoz and Hofmann, Werner Stoll heard about the new drug's unusual effects shortly after Hofmann reported them. He decided to organize a series of experiments. After testing LSD on selected mental patients as well as a group of healthy volunteers, he published the first scientific paper on LSD in 1947. He did not make any definitive claim abut the drug's usefulness to psychiatry, but he noted its extraordinary mind-altering effects and suggested that it might help scientists understand the biochemistry of mental disorders.

Before he gave LSD to anyone else, Stoll tried it on himself. He took a fairly small dose—60 micrograms, or roughly one-quarter the dose Hofmann had taken on his first intentional trip in 1943. Still, the results were dramatic. Stoll wrote a detailed report of the experience that he included in his paper. He characterized his sensory alteration as "an unprecedented experience of unimaginable intensity"; he saw an "unbelievable profusion of optical hallucinations.... At first, the hallucinations were elementary: rays, bundles of rays, rain, rings, vortices, loops, sprays, clouds, etc. Then more highly organized visions also appeared: arches, rows of arches, a sea of roofs, desert landscapes, terraces, flickering fire, starry skies of unbelievable splendor." Stoll also described his emotional states at different moments of the trip. He swung from euphoria to depression and back again. At one point the depression gripped him so firmly that he "thought with interest of the possibility of suicide." That feeling passed, however, and "in the evening I was again euphoric.... It seemed to me that a great epoch of my life had been crowded into a few hours."

Based in part on Stoll's clinical study and self-experimentation, Sandoz decided to make LSD available to psychiatric researchers (see *Delysid*). They suggested that psychiatrists might benefit from taking the drug themselves, because it could improve their understanding of the inner world of their patients.

Stonehenge. Beginning in the 1970s, British hippies took to gathering at Stonehenge for a month-long festival culminating in the summer solstice. LSD was one of the drugs most commonly used at Stonehenge: one survey concluded that approximately half of the attendees took acid. As the popularity of the festival grew, tens of thousands of young revelers came to the Druid stones for music, drugs, and neo-pagan fellowship. As attendance swelled, authorities began to restrict access to the monument: fences were erected in 1977, and by 1985 the regulatory body called English Heritage banned the use of Stonehenge for these occasions. Despite the ban, a group of regulars showed up for the usual festival, and the subsequent confrontation with the police became known as "The Battle of the Beanfield."

Strawberry Alarm Clock. This psychedelic band had one notable hit: "Incense and Peppermints" became one of the most popular rock songs of the psychedelic era, although the band had reservations about the quality of the lyrics. Record executives had given the job of writing lyrics for "Incense and Peppermints" to a songwriter who was not a member of the band (John Carter). Strawberry Alarm Clock's lead singer, Lee Freeman, found Carter's lyrics so uninspiring that he was unable to record an acceptable vocal track. According to band member George Bunnell, "Lee didn't like it. So, he wasn't putting forth his best effort" (interview with Gary James, *classicbands.com*). Since none of the other band members could sing lead, the producer found a young musician who happened to be in the studio (Greg Munford), handed him the lyrics, and recorded his performance. Thus Strawberry Alarm Clock's only memorable song reached the airwaves with an outsider singing lyrics that had been written by another outsider. The lyrics feature some common psychedelic elements, including two Timothy Leary slogans and a touch of synaesthesia. These conventional elements may have embarrassed the lead singer, but they contributed to the popularity of a song that came out shortly after hippie culture crested during the Summer of Love.

"Strawberry Fields Forever." Intended for inclusion on *Sergeant Pepper's Lonely Hearts Club Band* but released instead as a single, this John Lennon song contained pioneering psychedelic musical effects. See *Beatles*.

Strummer, Joe. The co-founder of The Clash had affiliations with psychedelic culture. See *The Clash; Punk*.

Strychnine. Persistent but misleading rumors connect LSD with the poison strychnine. Two versions of the story have been passed along since the late 1960s. In one account, strychnine is said to be a common by-product of LSD when the drug is imperfectly manufactured. No rigorous chemical argument supports this hypothesis, and as chemist Alexander Shulgin explains, strychnine and LSD are based on "totally unrelated plants; there has never been a report of strychnine and an ergot alkaloid co-existing in a single species" (*TiHKAL*). A second strychnine rumor developed around blotter acid (see *Blotter Art*): it was said that manufacturers needed strychnine to bond LSD to the paper. Again, no chemical argument validated such a claim, and tests of blotters have not turned up strychnine. The strychnine rumors received a boost from LSD discoverer Albert Hofmann when he published *LSD: My Problem Child* (see *Hofmann, Albert*). Hofmann reported an incident in which two people took what they thought was powdered LSD but turned out to be strychnine. Hofmann's story, however, does not validate the rumors: this is a case of someone substituting strychnine for LSD, not an accidental by-product of manufacture.

Sugar Cubes. Before tablets, gels, and blotters dominated LSD production, liquid doses of the drug were commonly dropped onto sugar cubes and distributed in that form. Early acidheads thus ingested their first LSD through the same delivery system that had given them Sabin Oral Polio Vaccine. Despite its aesthetic attractions, LSD in sugar cubes has two disadvantages: sugar makes the drug degrade more quickly, and federal sentencing guidelines use "carrier weight" to measure the severity of a drug crime. Under these guidelines, someone caught with as few as five doses of LSD on sugar cubes would receive a ten-year mandatory sentence, while someone else holding 19,999 doses in pure form would not even qualify for a mandatory five-year sentence (see *Laws; Supreme Court*).

Suicide. Although LSD has been linked with two cases of suicide by public figures — CIA scientist Frank Olson, and Diane Linkletter, daughter of television personality Art Linkletter — psychiatric studies have shown no correlation between LSD use and an increased risk of suicide. See *Health Risks; Olson, Frank; Linkletter, Diane.*

Sullivan, Ed. Sullivan adapted to the psychedelic era by inviting rock musicians to appear on his television show and staging appropriate lighting and video effects. Although he had an angry run-in with Jim Morrison of The Doors (see *Doors*), who broke his promise not to sing the word "higher" in "Light My Fire," Sullivan hosted several other psychedelic bands without incident. Jefferson Airplane opened the 1968 season by singing "Crown of Creation" with a passable imitation of a light show as backdrop. Other guests on Sullivan's psychedelic stage included the Beach Boys ("Good Vibrations"), Janis Joplin ("Maybe"), Tommy James and the Shondells ("Crimson and Clover") and Steppenwolf ("Magic Carpet Ride").

Summer of Love. By the middle of 1967, news had spread widely about a San Francisco counterculture dedicated to psychedelic drugs and music, free love, political dissent, and utopian social experiments. National media first paid attention in January of 1966 at the Trips Festival, a larger scale version of the Acid Tests (see *Trips Festival; Acid Test*). A year later, an even larger event, the Human Be-In, attracted tens of thousands to a celebration of the psychedelic lifestyle (see *Human Be-In*). Between these two landmark moments, the American public had become sufficiently alarmed about LSD and surrounding culture that the drug was made illegal. However, a significant number of young people reacted with enthusiasm instead of alarm. A hit song "San Francisco" invited them to come to the city with flowers in their hair. When schools let out in 1967, a multitude of teenagers and young adults from all over the country poured into Haight-

Ashbury to join in the psychedelic happenings they had been warned about. The Thelin brothers, who owned the well-known Psychedelic Shop on Haight Street, gave this moment the name that stuck: the Summer of Love.

The utopian name soon proved misleading. Haight-Ashbury could not support the influx of 100,000 young people, most of whom arrived without means of support. The network of social services that had worked well beforehand—most notably the Diggers' distribution of free food, clothing, and medical care (see *Diggers*)—was overtaxed. Many young people lived on the streets in unsanitary conditions; sexually transmitted diseases proliferated. LSD and marijuana remained popular among the new inhabitants, but other, addictive drugs became increasingly prevalent, especially speed. Crime increased substantially. According to Bob Weir of the Grateful Dead, the new scene was very different from the early years of Haight-Ashbury:

> We started getting break-ins and stuff like that. There were a lot of people on the street. Whereas before everybody had a place to go, everybody had something to do. We were in a band. The guys who were running the coffee shops were running the coffee shops, or the clothing shops or the head shops. The Diggers were doing their thing. The poets were writing and poster artists were making posters.... But starting around June, the creativity of the scene was starting to be piled over by just having to batten down the hatches, bar your doors and windows 'cause there were speed freaks on the street. I had the front room at 710 Ashbury, and people were coming through my front window with fair regularity. They dressed the part— they were dressed like hippies. But I don't think that they really got it [*SFGate*, May 20, 2007].

Amid these difficult conditions, many of the original hippies left Haight-Ashbury, but media and tourists abounded. Tour buses ran along Haight Street to give visitors a look at the exotic subculture. Hippies started holding up mirrors in front of the buses, so that tourists would be taking pictures of themselves: if you are curious about freaks, they implied, just look in the mirror.

By October, the Diggers had seen enough. They organized a mock funeral procession to mark their disgust and disillusionment. They called the event "The Death of Hippie": Diggers carried through the streets a coffin inscribed, "Hippie—Son of Media." Hippie counterculture would continue to flourish nationally for another two years, culminating in the Woodstock Festival (see *Woodstock*); but the Haight-Ashbury psychedelic community that started things going went into decline just as it appeared to be peaking, during the Summer of Love.

Supreme Court. The United States Supreme Court has handed down two decisions in cases directly connected with the use of LSD. The first case, *United States v. Stanley* (1987), involved an Army sergeant who was given LSD in the Cold War military experiments with the drug (see *Military Testing*). James B. Stanley had volunteered to take part in what was characterized as a chemical warfare testing program. Experimenters gave him LSD to observe how he could perform normal tasks under the influence of the drug. Stanley claimed that the acid trips had induced personality changes that cost him both his military career and his marriage. Justices disagreed sharply over the fundamental principles of the case. In the end, they voted 5–4 that Stanley should not receive compensation for the harm done. Writing for the majority, Justice Antonin Scalia argued that courts must not interfere with the proper exercise of military discipline: "A test for liability that depends on the extent to which particular suits would call into question military discipline and decision making would itself require judicial inquiry into, and hence intrusion upon, military matters." Dissenting justices led by William Brennan invoked the Nuremberg Code that emerged from postwar trials of Nazi scientists: "The medical trials at Nuremberg in 1947 deeply impressed upon the world that experimentation with unknowing human subjects is morally and legally unacceptable.... In defiance of this principle, military intelligence officials began surreptitiously testing chemical and biological materials, including LSD." The second case had to do with sentencing guidelines and the method for calculating the weight of LSD seized in an arrest. In *Neal v. United States* (1995), Meril Gilbert Neal sought to overturn his ten-year sentence for possession of LSD. Neal had received the long sentence based on the weight of the drugs seized. The judge had applied the law that spelled out minimum sentences for drug crimes, based not only on the weight of the drug proper but its carrier medium (in this case, blotter paper). Neal argued that if later, revised recommendations were applied—which fixed the weight of an LSD dose at .4 milligrams, regardless of carrier—his sentence would be substantially reduced. The Supreme Court ruled unanimously against Neal: his sentence was upheld as proper under the law in force at the time of his arrest. In a 2007 decision related to cocaine, however, the Court ruled that federal sentencing guidelines should be regarded as "advisory" rather than mandatory (*United States v. Booker*).

The Supreme Court has never taken on a case involving LSD as a sacramental drug essential to the practice of a religious group. A few such groups have been founded, including Timothy Leary's League for Spiritual Discovery, which lost a 1967 appeal in a lower court (see *League for Spiritual Discovery; Religion; Laws*). The most relevant recent case to come before the Supreme Court was *Gonzalez v. O Centro Espirita Beneficente Uniao do Vegetal* (2006). Uniao do Vegetal is a small religious group that prepares a sacramental tea made from an organic hallucinogen. The court ruled in favor of Uniao do Vegetal. Chief Justice John Roberts wrote the opinion, which cited the longstanding regulatory exemption granted to the Native American Church for the sacramental use of peyote. The court made

it clear, however, that any group seeking exemption must have a well established religious tradition, and must show that it does not engage in recreational use of the drug or promote its illegal distribution.

Talking Heads. This influential New Wave band released the latter-day psychedelic song "And She Was" in 1985. See *"And She Was."*

Tattoos. An urban legend about LSD-laced tattoos for children pops up from time to time in American cities. See *Blue Star.*

Temptations. The Motown group famous for soul vocals went through a psychedelic period in the late 1960s under producer Norman Whitfield. Influenced by psychedelic rock in general and by Sly and the Family Stone in particular (see *Psychedelic Rock; Sly and the Family Stone*), the Temptations produced songs with several psychedelic features. Vocally, they recorded multiple lead vocals that shifted from side to side on the stereo; instrumentally, they added harder rock beats and more guitar effects such as wah-wah and reverberation. Among the best known songs from their psychedelic period are "Ball of Confusion" and "Papa Was a Rolling Stone." Another hit single, "Psychedelic Shack," described a house full of happy trippers surrounded by incense, strobe lights, and poetry. Some Black activists criticized them for buying into a vision of psychedelic peace and love that made sense only for affluent majority youth, and after a time the group began introducing more elements of political protest.

Thelin Brothers. Ron and Jay Thelin founded The Psychedelic Shop in Haight-Ashbury, which became a gathering place for the growing hippie community. See *Psychedelic Shop.*

Thompson, Hunter S. New Journalist Thompson first wrote about LSD in *Hell's Angels* (1967), where he described the Angels' use of the drug. Thompson had introduced the bikers to Ken Kesey and the Pranksters, who shared their acid liberally (see *Kesey, Ken; Merry Pranksters*). Thompson wrote that acid made the bikers "oddly peaceful." But their psychedelic period ended soon enough. As Thompson summarized it, "After three or four months of chronic overindulgence on acid, most of the Angels began tapering off. A few suffered terrifying hallucinations and swore off the drug entirely. Some said they were afraid it would drive them crazy or cause them to wreck their bikes." This passage suggests Thompson's ambivalence about LSD. He appreciated the thrills but did not romanticize the experience to the degree that many of his contemporaries did.

Thompson dismissed the Leary camp as "well-educated truth seekers looking for wisdom in a capsule." He was more sympathetic with the Pranksters, although he found them a little cold; they weren't as sterile as the Learyites, but they lacked something in vitality and gregariousness. Kesey's La Honda gathering place "was public only in the sense that anyone who felt like it could walk through the gate on the bridge. But once inside, a man who didn't speak the language was made to feel very self-conscious. Acid freaks are not given to voluble hospitality; they stare fixedly at strangers, or look right through them." Thompson preferred the company of Hell's Angels for a good acid trip: "Dropping acid with the Angels was an adventure; they were too ignorant to know what to expect, and too wild to care. They just swallowed the stuff and hung on ... which is probably just as dangerous as the experts say, but a far, far nuttier trip than sitting in some sterile chamber with a condescending guide and a handful of nervous, would-be hipsters."

In *Fear and Loathing in Las Vegas*, written a few years after *Hell's Angels*, LSD has lost its nutty charm for Thompson. It's either the cause of terrible, useless madness, or (perhaps worse) not even interesting anymore. Early in *Fear and Loathing*, Thompson finds himself in the midst of a disturbing hallucination of lizard people and blood-soaked carpets; he tells himself to "ignore this terrible drug" and relax with a few cocktails in the hotel bar. Later his friend has an acid trip full of "hellishly intense introspection nightmares." For the most part in *Fear and Loathing*, though, Thompson shows more jadedness than alarm regarding LSD. Lurid hallucinations have lost their impact: "After a while you learn to cope with things like seeing your dead grandmother crawling up your leg with a knife in her teeth." He nonchalantly chews blotter acid "like baseball gum" and comments cynically about Leary and hippie culture:

This was the fatal flaw in Tim Leary's trip. He crashed around America selling 'consciousness expansion' without ever giving a thought to the grim meat-hook realities that were lying in wait for all the people who took him too seriously. After West Point and the Priesthood, LSD must have seemed entirely logical to him ... but there is not much satisfaction in knowing that he blew it very badly for himself because he took too many others down with him. Not that they didn't deserve it: No doubt they all Got What Was Coming To Them. All those pathetically eager acid freaks who thought they could buy Peace and Understanding for three bucks a hit.

In one passage, however, Thompson indulges in memories of his earlier and more upbeat LSD persona. Admitting that he "has never been able to accept the notion that you can get a lot higher without drugs than with them," he recalls a spectacular acid trip at a Fillmore concert, when he felt himself pushing up from the earth "like some kind of mutant mushroom." Remembering that night leads Thompson to an uncharacteristic moment of sentimental idealism:

Strange memories on this nervous night in Las Vegas. Five years later? Six? It seems like a lifetime, or at least a Main Era—the kind of peak that never comes again. San Francisco in the middle sixties was a very special time and place to be a part of. Maybe it *meant something*. Maybe not, in the long run ... but no explanation, no mix of words or music or memories can touch that sense of knowing that you were there and alive in that corner of time and the world.

To some extent, *Fear and Loathing* is an attempt to revive the old Prankster spirit. He and his attorney have their own version of the bus—a garish red convertible—and they take pleasure in provoking the public with scenes of hallucinogenic weirdness.

Thompson was the model for the character "Uncle Duke" in Garry Trudeau's *Doonesbury* comic strip. Uncle Duke—whose name comes from "Raoul Duke," Thompson's pseudonym in *Fear and Loathing in Las Vegas*—indulges frequently in psychedelic drugs, but like Thompson, his political and cultural instincts show no resemblance to hippie ideals.

Three Stigmata of Palmer Eldritch. This 1964 novel by Philip K. Dick was the work he most associated with LSD (see *Dick, Philip K.*). In an interview, Dick said that *Eldritch* "is my major novel of a hallucinogenic kind," which "deals with a tremendous bad acid trip, so to speak"—although he admitted that at the time he had only read about LSD. The novel features two fictional hallucinogens: "Can-D," which allows bored space colonists to merge with a figure resembling a Barbie doll, and "Chew-Z," which transports users to a version of transcendent afterlife. "Chew-Z" was discovered by the mysterious character of Palmer Eldritch, who markets it with a psychedelic slogan: "God promises eternal life. We can deliver it."

Tibetan Book of the Dead. Timothy Leary and his collaborators based their 1964 tripping manual on this Buddhist book, which collected instructions and meditations to prepare someone for the experience of dying. See *Psychedelic Experience; Zen Buddhism.*

Tie-Dye. An ancient craft for coloring clothes was adopted by hippies to create their signature look. Tie-dye designs appealed to LSD users as an attempt to mimic certain effects of psychedelic perception: vivid colors and swirling patterns brightened ordinary t-shirts in the way that LSD brightened objects of the routine sensory world.

To some degree, tie-dye designs resembled the effects created by liquid light shows at acid rock concerts of the period (see *Light Shows*). At the Diggers' Free Store in Haight Ashbury, tie-dyers used their craft to freshen old clothes they were giving away. The tie-dye process was useful for hippies not only because it was psychedelic, but because it was cheap and easy: all someone needed was a plain shirt, some rubber bands (to secure bunchings of the shirt that created distinctive patterns), and a few bottles of dye in bright colors.

In the few years following the Summer of Love, tie-dyed clothing moved from narrow association with hippie culture to a broader popularity in the world of fashion (see *Fashion, Psychedelic*). The Rit Dye company significantly increased their profits during these years by marketing their dyes along with instructions for tie-dying. In contemporary culture, tie-dying remains a common craft, and its associations with psychedelia have not interfered with its use at summer camps, school art classes, and similar mainstream institutions. Nevertheless, tie-dye will always be associated with the hippies, who embraced it to advertise their new appreciation for color.

TiHKAL. This 1997 book by Alexander and Ann Shulgin offers essays and chemical details about the tryptamine family of psychedelic drugs, which includes LSD. The title anagram's eccentric capitalization stands for *Tryptamines i Have Known And Loved.* *TiHKAL* was a sequel to *PiHKAL,* a similar book about phenethylamine psychedelics that prompted a search of Shulgin's lab by drug enforcement agents. See *Shulgin, Alexander; Shulgin, Ann.*

Tingler. This 1959 B-movie offered the first cinematic depiction of an LSD trip. The movie has survived in midnight festivals of campy classics; John Wilson, father of the Golden Raspberry Awards, listed it among his "100 Most Amusingly Bad Movies Ever Made." Vincent Price plays a doctor who has been researching a mysterious force inside the body that is triggered by intense fear. This force, which he names "The Tingler," attacks the spinal cord and will kill a person unless he or she screams wildly as an antidote. Director William Castle rigged some of the theater seats with a Tingler-like vibrating device, so that a few patrons could participate in the cathartic screaming.

Robb White, screenwriter for *The Tingler,* knew about LSD from clinical research being done at UCLA. In the movie, the doctor's assistant gives him a sample of LSD and warns him not to try it when he's alone. But the doctor has read a pamphlet entitled "Fright Effects Induced by Injection of Lysergic Acid LSD-25." If LSD is as frightening as advertised, he will be able to germinate his own Tingler and thereby advance his research. He injects himself with a double dose, which does the trick; the Tingler develops nicely, although ultimately he cannot suppress a Tingler-quelling scream. Vincent Price acted out Hollywood's first acid trip with gusto. He panicked over walls closing in on him and a claustrophobic loss of breath, all of which was aggravated by the presence of a lab skeleton. After his scream he passed out and put an end to cinema's first bummer.

"Tomorrow Never Knows." This John Lennon song from *Revolver* made the first obvious references to the psychedelic experience. See *Beatles.*

Trip. The *Trip* (1967) is the best known of B-movies about LSD. It was written by Jack Nicholson and featured Peter Fonda and Dennis Hopper in the cast; these three were also principals in *Easy Rider* two years later, another movie with psychedelic elements (see *Easy Rider*). Nicholson, Fonda, and Hopper had considerable experience with LSD. Director Roger Corman did not have their experience, but he took his first acid trip as he prepared to make the movie.

Fonda plays Paul Groves, a director of television commercials who is going through

a divorce. His personal problems take center stage during his LSD trip. When someone asks why he wants to try acid, he says, "Insight—I really think I'll find out something about myself." His trip has been organized in proper Timothy Leary format. He has a guide (Bruce Dern) and a house full of psychedelic props. Paul has prepared music and poems for inspiration. Just to be safe, he carries a capsule of Thorazine. During the early stages of the trip, his guide soothes him with phrases plucked verbatim from Leary's manual, *The Psychedelic Experience:* "Turn off your mind.... Relax, float downstream.... Trust me.... Those things are only in your mind; there's no reason to be afraid."

Paul's trip starts well (he rhapsodizes over an orange: "That's the sun in my hands!"), but soon he finds himself consumed by worries about sex and relationships. At different moments Paul imagines himself being accused and punished in inquisitorial settings. He sees a vision of his own bloodied face, followed by a shot of swirling crucifixes, and then his body covered for burial or burning. When he jumps back to reality in a panic, the guide offers the standard Leary comfort: "Relax, it's all in your mind." Paul calms down a little, but the guide can't prevent the nightmares from returning. Eventually Paul imagines a violent death for his guide and flees from the house. In the last part of his trip, Paul meets a woman and goes to her place for sex. *The Trip* ends with this bit of morning-after dialogue:

> WOMAN: "Did you find what you were looking for?"
> PAUL: "Yeah—I think I ... like, I love you."
> WOMAN: "And everybody else."
> PAUL: "Yeah—and everybody else."
> WOMAN: "It's easy now; wait till tomorrow."
> PAUL: "Yeah, well, I'll think about that tomorrow."

Studio executives, concerned that *The Trip* might make LSD seem too attractive, made two additions to Corman's work. One was a scrolling prologue that warned of the dangers of LSD. The other came in the film's last shot: they added a "cracked mirror" effect to the freeze frame of Paul, as if to undercut his version of hippie epiphany.

Tripper. David Arquette directed and starred in this LSD-themed slasher movie from 2006. *The Tripper* begins with a flashback to the Summer of Love, when a tree-hugging hippie annoys a logger and ends up on the wrong side of a chainsaw. In the main plot (set in the present), hippie revelers take LSD in the same forest; their chief antagonist wears a Ronald Reagan mask and uses an axe to dismember anyone wearing tie-dye. As the violence unfolds in kaleidoscopic color, Arquette portrays these hippies as unpleasant hedonists for whom the audience feels little sympathy.

Trips Festival. As the era of the Merry Pranksters and their Acid Tests neared its close (see *Merry Pranksters; Acid Test*), a couple of Pranksters envisioned something on a larger scale: a sort of supersized Acid Test. Mike Hagen mentioned the idea to Stewart Brand, and Brand took charge of organizing the event that came to be known as "The Trips Festival" (see *Brand, Stewart*). The Trips Festival was held for three consecutive nights in January, 1966 at the Longshoremen's Hall in San Francisco. Brand called on several of the principals from the Acid Tests, including the Grateful Dead, light show operators, and performance artists; he also enlisted the help of Bill Graham, soon to establish himself as Fillmore promoter, and Wes Wilson, who designed psychedelic op-art handbills (see *Grateful Dead; Graham, Bill; Wilson, Wes*). Several thousand people showed up for the festival, which received a lot of media attention—thanks in part to the drug arrest of Ken Kesey a week beforehand. The Trips Festival marked the first time that so many young people interested in psychedelic counterculture gathered in one place, and the first time that the emerging hippie community received national attention. As in the Acid Tests, the emphasis was on live psychedelic music, light shows, dancing, and of course LSD, the signature hippie drug (then still legal). LSD was made available in many forms, including a bag of tablets brought in by Owsley and passed around the crowd. The distinction between performers and audience was blurred, as festival technology enabled random acts of self-expression by the tripping participants.

The Trips Festival is often cited as the opening event of the hippie era, which would reach its apex (and begin its decline) in the Summer of Love the following year (see *Summer of Love*). During the festival, experimental filmmaker Ben Van Meter brought his camera to record what he called "the viewpoint of a goldfish in the Kool-Aid bowl." Eric Christensen's documentary *The Trips Festival Movie* came out in 2008 on a DVD that included Van Meter's film from 1966.

"Turn On, Tune In, Drop Out." In a speech from September of 1966—when the government was on the verge of making LSD illegal—Timothy Leary first uttered the words that became the most famous slogan of the psychedelic counterculture. He framed the slogan with surprisingly traditional religious terminology: "Like every great religion of the past, we seek to find the divinity within and to express this revelation in a life of glorification and the worship of God. These ancient goals we define in the metaphor of the present—turn on, tune in, drop out." Despite his efforts to link LSD with mainstream religion, the media focused solely on the six-word nugget that seemed to encourage young people to take LSD and resist socialization. In his memoir *Flashbacks,* Leary denied that he simply meant "get stoned and abandon all constructive activity"; but when he used the phrase again to keynote the Human Be-In (see *Human Be-In*), it stuck as an advertising slogan for LSD and hippie subversion of mainstream values.

Tusko. Tusko was the name of the elephant accidentally killed during an experiment with LSD in 1962. See *Elephant; West, Louis Jolyon.*

"25 or 6 to 4." The enigmatic title of this 1970 song by the rock band Chicago has led many listeners to speculate that its subject is LSD. If "25" stands for LSD-25, a popular theory proposes, that would help explain lyrics about flashing lights, a spinning feeling, and uncertainty about whether to try some more. Robert Lamm, the Chicago keyboard player who wrote the song, has deflated this theory with a much simpler explanation. He says that the title refers to a time in the middle of the night, when he was awake and trying to write a song: it was either 25 or 26 minutes before 4 A.M.

2001: A Space Odyssey. Stanley Kubrick's 1968 film has important associations with psychedelic culture, despite the fact that nothing in the film refers directly to drugs (see *Kubrick, Stanley*). Evidence for a psychedelic connection can be found both inside and outside the film. External evidence mainly has to do with audience reception and marketing in the late 1960s. MGM noticed that the audience for *2001* consisted disproportionately of countercultural youth, who were responding to it with something like religious enthusiasm. To take advantage, MGM began advertising *2001* as "The Ultimate Trip." As Vincent LoBrutto recalls, "The under-thirty crowds patiently and reverently waited in lines around the Capital Theater as if it were a church.... *2001* had a spiritual and religious power to the children of McLuhan, who stared at the screen and remained staring as the curtain closed after witnessing Bowman's spectacular rebirth. At one screening a young man ran down the aisle screaming, 'I see God!'"

The plot of *2001* certainly lends itself to psychedelic interpretation. This is a story of spiritual quest on the grandest scale, with the hero succeeding on behalf of all humanity. Astronaut Dave Bowman wins a power struggle against a resentful computer and earns rebirth into a higher form of being.

His transition begins with a famously trippy sequence called "Jupiter and Beyond the Infinite." Kubrick later said that it "was never meant to represent an acid trip," but he admitted that the association makes sense. Up to this point in the film, the dominant color has been white, but when Dave takes his trip through the Star Gate, colors start flowing like a psychedelic light show. Like most attempts at sublimity, the Star Gate sequence is easy to parody—in an episode of *The Simpsons*, for example, the Star Gate opens as Homer dials "10" on a massage chair—but there is philosophical substance to Kubrick's light show. Dave's colorful eye keeps coming back in full frame, as if to indicate that altered perception is the engine of evolution. What he will discover is not an improved tool or technology, but a new way to see. Kubrick represents the transfigured Dave as a cosmic baby, floating above the earth. Again, it's easy to parody (and *The Simpsons* have done that one, too), but the ending suggests neoteny on a grand scale: the new Dave has a baby's outsized eyes and capacity for wonder. Acidheads plausibly interpreted *2001* as an allegory of their own psychedelic ambitions.

Stanley Kubrick partly joined forces with his psychedelic fans—but only partly. In an interview he both welcomed and declined the allegory. "I have to say that it [the Star Gate] was never meant to represent an acid trip. On the other hand a connection does exist. An acid trip is probably similar to the kind of mind-boggling experience that might occur at the moment of encountering extraterrestrial intelligence." As the interview continues, he elaborates on his feelings about LSD:

> I've been put off experimenting with LSD because I don't like what seems to happen to people who try it. They seem to develop what I can only describe as an illusion of understanding and oneness with the universe. They seem very happy, very content and very pleased with the state of mind, but at the same time they seem to be totally unaware of the fact that it deprives them of any kind of

self-criticism which is, of course, absolutely essential for an artist to have. It's very dangerous to be zonked out by everything that you see and think of, and to believe all of your ideas are of cosmic proportions. I should think that if one had no interest in being an artist, this illusion of understanding would be delightful but for myself I think it is a pleasure which I'll forgo for as long as I'm interested in making films [quoted in LoBrutto].

Despite Kubrick's fears that LSD might lead to "zonked out," counterfeit versions of cosmic truth, his film gave acidheads the epic they were looking for: *2001* merged outer space with inner space and gratified their cravings for psychedelic revelation.

UFO Club. This famous but short-lived night club galvanized the London psychedelic scene that had its beginnings in "Spontaneous Underground" (see *Spontaneous Underground*). John Hopkins and Joe Boyd founded the UFO Club near the end of 1966 in a dancehall on Tottenham Court Road; it lasted less than a year. The club featured not only live bands but an array of features suggestive of acid tests (see *Acid Test*), including light shows, films, and the spontaneous freakish behavior of patrons who were tripping. Pink Floyd was the first band to play at the UFO. They were received so enthusiastically that they became a much bigger act, and soon a small venue like the UFO Club could not afford them (see *Pink Floyd*). Hopkins and Boyd were able to book other bands of note, including Procol Harum and The Incredible String Band, but in October they had to close the club. Their problems were not only financial but legal: London police had been putting pressure on UFO for drug activities, and Hopkins himself went to jail on drug charges.

Ultimate Spinach. This was the flagship of the psychedelic bands that were collectively promoted as the "Boston Sound" or the "Bosstown Sound" in late 1967 through 1968 (see *Bosstown Sound*). "Bosstown Sound" amounted to a publicity campaign devised by producer Alan Lorber of the MGM record label. Lorber managed three bands that formed the core of his promotion: Ultimate Spinach, Orpheus, and Beacon Street Union. The idea was to nurture an East Coast counterpart to the San Francisco acid rock scene that was becoming increasingly popular as media attention focused on hippie culture during the Summer of Love. Unfortunately for Lorber and his proteges, rock critics from the counterculture deplored the marketing strategy and criticized the bands as fauxpsychedelic epigones. The first Ultimate Spinach album sold reasonably well, but poor reviews in *Rolling Stone* and elsewhere led to diminished interest in subsequent recordings and tours.

The leader of Ultimate Spinach was Ian Bruce-Douglas, who wrote and sang most of their songs. Although the band has a few defenders who find merit in their work, for the most part critics have affirmed the original negative response. Rock historian Richie Unterberger summarizes their first album (*Ultimate Spinach*, 1968) as "a seriously intended psychedelic stew, with inadvertent comically awkward results. Bruce-Douglas' songs tended to be either dippily, humorlessly cosmic, or colored by equally too serious finger-pointing at mainstream society. The music aped the songwriting forms and guitar/keyboard textures of West Coast psychedelic stars, but sounded like ham-handed pastiches." Ultimate Spinach wilted after its second album in 1968, when Bruce-Douglas and most of his colleagues decided to leave the band.

USCO. An experimental group known as "The Company of Us" created psychedelic, multimedia works of art during the 1960s. Founded by Beat poet Gerd Stern and a young audio technician named Michael Callahan, USCO acknowledged two primary influences: LSD, and the theories of Marshall McLuhan. Members of USCO worked collectively and anonymously to produce psychedelic installations and performances. Stern recalled an early public performance in a San Francisco auditorium: "I was on acid during the performance. At one point, some guy—there was a piano on stage which had just been left there from something else—some guy jumped up on stage and started playing terrible chords. It was very disruptive. Michael McClure and I started roaring 'Ahrg, Grahrr!' at each other. It was really a very exciting piece of work." Other works by USCO contained more traditionally artistic elements—painting, sculpture, video sequences—but all of them showed a Prankster-like interest in psychedelic improvisation (see *Merry Pranksters*). When USCO visited Millbrook on Timothy Leary's invitation (see *Millbrook; Leary, Timothy*), friction developed over their contrasting styles. As Stern recalled, "Timothy started lecturing ... and we were appalled; it was the middle of this really turned-on show, and here was this professor standing up in the front going on and on. We happened to have a tape of Artaud screaming on a radio program while he was incarcerated in an asylum; in the middle of Timothy's lecture, we played Artaud screaming. It stopped everything."

Use of LSD. Estimates of how many people have used LSD vary considerably, and few attempts have been made to calculate a reliable figure. A study by the British Home Office estimated that by 1991 some 900,000 people aged 16–59 had tried the drug in the U.K. The most careful study was begun in the U.S. in 1975. Researchers at the University of Michigan undertook a long-term study to measure drug use among American students in twelfth grade (later expanded to include eighth and tenth graders). "Monitoring the Future: National Results on Adolescent Drug Use" was supported by the National Institute on Drug Abuse and has been updated each year since. When the study began in the mid 1970s, LSD was the most commonly used hallucinogenic drug, but its popularity among young Americans had already started to decline. Results over the

years indicate that LSD use dropped steadily through the 1980s, before rising somewhat in the first half of the 1990s; after 1996, numbers returned to lower levels, and in 2003 they reached historic lows.

The Michigan researchers measure four trends for each drug: use, perceived risk, disapproval, and perceived availability. In the case of LSD, each student would answer the following questions. "On how many occasions (if any) have you used LSD? How much do you think people risk harming themselves (physically or in other ways) if they try LSD once or twice? Do YOU disapprove of people trying LSD once or twice? How difficult do you think it would be for you to get LSD if you wanted some? Answers to the first question, at least through 2008, show LSD use near historic lows: only about 4 percent of twelfth graders, 3 percent of tenth graders, and 2 percent of eighth graders report having used the drug. However, those numbers do not correlate as one might expect with the second measure, "perceived risk." As the researchers summarize, "Since about 2000, perceived risk has declined steadily and substantially among eighth graders, declined modestly among tenth graders, but held fairly steady among twelfth graders." They offer two possible explanations for the apparent contradiction between low perceived risk and low use. One theory is that another hallucinogenic drug has taken the place of LSD for these students; likely candidates include MDMA (Ecstasy) and psilocybin. The other explanation for low use is diminished availability, especially after DEA agents shut down a major LSD factory in 2000. "Perceived availability" tracks fairly closely with "Use"—generally dropping through the years, except for the spike in the early 1990s.

In the category of "Disapproval" ("Do YOU disapprove of people trying LSD once or twice?"), the numbers are less orderly:

Disapproval of LSD use was quite high among twelfth graders through most of the 1980s but began to decline after 1991 along with perceived risk. All three grades exhibited a decline in disapproval through 1996.... After 1996, there emerged a slight increase in disapproval among twelfth graders, accompanied by a leveling among tenth graders and some further decline among eighth graders. In recent years disapproval of LSD use has diverged among the three grades, declining considerably among eighth graders, declining only a little among tenth graders, and increasing among twelfth graders.

Looking at these results, the Michigan researchers expressed concern that American eighth graders might be undergoing "generational forgetting" about LSD. If younger teens are indeed "becoming less knowledgeable about this drug's effects than their predecessors," the nation faces "a growing vulnerability to a resurgence of use."Focusing strictly on college students, Gallup pollsters tracked the use of LSD during the peak psychedelic years. In 1967, their polls indicated that only about 1 percent of American college students reported that they had ever tried LSD. By 1969 this number had climbed to 4 percent, and by 1970 to 14 percent. Subsequent polls and studies have shown that college use of LSD began to decline in the 1970s, and that figure has remained fairly low during recent decades. The Michigan researchers reported in 2005 that 5.6 percent of college students said they had tried LSD.

Varieties of Psychedelic Experience. In this 1966 book, Robert Masters and Jean Houston analyzed reports of numerous trippers on LSD and other psychedelics (see *Masters, Robert; Houston, Jean*). Each chapter of *Varieties* focused on a distinct theme related to the trippers' experiences, including body image, social relations, aesthetic perception, and religious feeling.

Velvet Underground. This rock band was the central attraction in Andy Warhol's version of an Acid Test, the "Exploding Plastic Inevitable." See *Warhol, Andy*.

Vietnam. A study of flashbacks among American soldiers in Vietnam indicated that approximately 10 percent of them used LSD during their tour of duty (Stanton). Lee and Shlain quote an officer from the Army Security Agency about the acid scene in Vietnam: "*Apocalypse Now*—that's how it really was. After a while, Vietnam *was* an acid trip. Vietnam was psychedelic, even when you weren't tripping" (see *Apocalypse Now*). The most popular brand of LSD in Vietnam was Orange Sunshine (see *Orange Sunshine*).

Vinkenoog, Simon. Dutch poet Vinkenoog, appointed poet laureate for the Netherlands in 2004, was known for embracing LSD and surrounding countercultural causes. He participated in the Albert Hall poetry reading organized by Allen Ginsberg in 1965 that helped to spark the London underground scene (see *Ginsberg, Allen*). In 1968 he wrote an article about LSD for the magazine *Bres*, and shortly after that he translated into Dutch *The Psychedelic Experience* (see *Leary, Timothy; Psychedelic Experience*). Even after his recognition as poet laureate he continued to associate himself with psychedelia: Vinkenoog spoke at the 2006 Basel symposium marking the 100th birthday of Albert Hofmann (see *Hofmann, Albert*). He once described his first LSD trip as an unpleasant one, but only because of the hospital setting: "In 1959, LSD was inflicted on my by a team of unqualified doctors-to-be who messed up some of my most beautiful experiences ever by having me fill in silly forms, by hooking me up to an electroencephalograph going momo-momo, etc." (quoted by Krippner in Masters and Houston, *Psychedelic Art*).

Voznesensky, Andrei. Well known Russian poet who admired and was admired by American Beats, Voznesensky visited San Francisco during the psychedelic era. He joined Lawrence Ferlinghetti in reading poetry between Jefferson Airplane sets at the Fillmore (see *Ferlinghetti, Lawrence; Jefferson Airplane; Fillmore*). Allen Ginsberg wanted to introduce his Russian friend to LSD, but the poet had Soviet chaperones and Ginsberg never found an opportunity (see *Ginsberg, Allen*).

Ward, R.H. Ward wrote *A Drug-Taker's Notes* (1957), one of the first detailed accounts of tripping on LSD. He took the drug six times under the supervision of an English psychiatrist. Ward, who had read Huxley (see *Huxley, Aldous*), hoped to achieve a transcendent religious experience: to "touch the fringes of ecstasy" and reach "communion with God." Although he noted that LSD sparked a sense of wonder and produced intense emotions, he warned that the drug was as likely to lead to hell as heaven, and he compared hallucinogenic epiphanies unfavorably with mystical experiences not induced by drugs.

Warhol, Andy. In 1966, at the height of his popularity, Warhol produced a New York multimedia show called "Exploding Plastic Inevitable" that shared several features with the Acid Tests of California (see *Acid Test*). Like the Acid Tests, Warhol's show revolved around a rock concert that was enhanced by strobe lights and projected photos and films, with the audience drawn into the performance as dancers and living screens. Instead of the Grateful Dead, Warhol featured the Velvet Underground as house band. Lou Reed of Velvet Underground had used LSD among other drugs while in college at Syracuse, but his songs did not resemble typical San Francisco psychedelic music (see *San Francisco Sound; Psychedelic Rock*). One of his signature songs performed at "Exploding Plastic Inevitable" was "Heroin," with lyrics about the compelling attractions of that drug. If the style of "Exploding" imitated psychedelic aesthetics, the music swerved in a different direction. As critic Jim DeRogatis described it, "Where the West Coast bands produced cheerfully transcendent psychedelia, the Velvets specialized in bad-trip rock, reveling in the grit and grime of the New York streets—an approach and an attidude that was distinctly out of step during the Day-Glo Summer of Love."

Wasson, R. Gordon. A banker turned psychedelic researcher (with particular expertise in hallucinogenic mushrooms and their importance for world religious traditions), Wasson collaborated with Albert Hofmann and Carl Ruck on *The Road to Eleusis: Unveiling the Secrets of the Mysteries.* The three men theorized that an ergot alkaloid—the organic foundation for LSD—lay at the heart of the Eleusinian mysteries of ancient Greece (see *Eleusinian Mysteries; Hofmann, Albert; Ruck, Carl*). Wasson advocated the use of the term "entheogen" to describe LSD and similar drugs, which he preferred to "psychedelic"—the former indicating deep religious meaning, the latter hippie recreation (see *Entheogen; Psychedelic*).

Water Supply. As the CIA and the military conducted their tests of LSD as a possible weapon (see *MK-Ultra*), it occurred to them that an enemy—most likely the Soviets—might try to spike with LSD the water supply of a large American city. Because minute quantities of acid produce dramatic psychotropic effects, an agent could theoretically carry enough of the drug in his pocket to disable a city the size of Los Angeles. The CIA took the possibility seriously enough to hire an expert consultant, Dr. Nick Bercel, one of several Los Angeles psychiatrists who had been experimenting with psychedelic psychotherapy (see *Bercel, Nick*). Bercel put a tiny amount of LSD into a glass of water and analyzed the results. He told the CIA not to worry: the chlorine routinely added to city water had neutralized the LSD. Nevertheless, the CIA continued to speculate about a smaller-scale spiking of a sensitive target, such as a warship or an Air Force base. One purpose of their testing program was to gauge the effects of such an event and plan countermeasures.

During the Summer of Love in San Francisco, government officials worried more about hippies than communists. A few hippie leaders had suggested that spiking San Francisco's water might be a fine thing to try. City officials (including Supervisor Dianne Feinstein) turned to a local medical expert for advice. Dr. David Smith told them the reassuring news about chlorine (see *Smith, David*). He also mentioned that Siamese Fighting Fish can be deployed in the water supply to provide an early warning system for LSD contamination: tiny amounts of LSD would disorient the fish and make them swim upside down.

Although no foreign agent or prankster ever managed to get LSD into a municipal water supply, the threat has persisted in the popular imagination. In the 1968 movie *Wild in the Streets,* youngsters put LSD into Washington's water to swing a vote their way (see *Wild in the Streets*); an *X-Files* episode showed a malign agent pumping LSD into the water pipes of Mulder's apartment building; and in *The Simpsons,* the rival town of Shelbyville spiked Springfield's water and gave Marge her first ever psychedelic experience (see *Simpsons*).

Watts, Alan. An English expatriate who wrote and lectured about Eastern spirituality, Watts experimented with LSD in the early 1960s. In 1962 he published a short book that detailed his psychedelic experience: *The Joyous Cosmology: Adventures in the Chemistry of Consciousness.* Watts' book resembled Huxley's *The Doors of Perception* in its combination of minute sensory descriptions and philosophical reflections, but unlike Huxley, Watts did not undergo any moments of anxiety that hinted at psychological danger (see *Huxley, Aldous*). He wrote that LSD enabled him to see beyond the generalities of normal perception and recognize the richness of nature: "But here the depth of light and structure in a bursting bud go on forever. There is time to see them, time for the whole intricacy of veins and capillaries to develop in consciousness, time to see down and down into the shape of greenness, which is not green at all, but a whole spectrum generalizing itself as green—purple, gold, the sunlit turquoise of the ocean, the intense luminescence of the emerald." Sounds from an organ "blow forth in immense, gooey spludges" that "acquire texture: expanding circles of vibration finely and evenly toothed like combs." Attending a mass, he claimed to see through the priest's mere "performance": "I began to congratulate the priest on his gamesmanship, on the sheer courage of being able to put up such a performance of authority when he knows precisely nothing." Watts' psychedelic reflections emphasize the artifice of normal identity and the interdependence of contrary cosmic forces. For all his serious philosophizing, however, he also includes a moment when he becomes "helpless with hysterics" watching a friend load his car with trash: "The Divine Comedy. All things dissolve in laughter.... But our laughter is without malice, for in this state of consciousness everything is the doing of gods."

Wavy Gravy. Born Hugh Romney, Wavy Gravy renamed himself after joining the Merry Pranksters (see *Merry Pranksters*). When Ken Kesey went to jail on drug charges, Wavy Gravy joined Ken Babbs as unofficial leaders of the Pranksters (see *Kesey, Ken; Babbs, Ken*). Eventually he left them to found the Hog Farm, a group of hippies who lived communally and did various jobs associated with rock concerts, political protests, and philanthropic causes. The Hog Farm was recruited by promoters to provide security at Woodstock. Wavy Gravy referred to his Woodstock security team as the "Please Force," because they asked politely when they wanted someone to cooperate. Wavy Gravy was known not only for his non-confrontational style but his clown persona: he dressed in wild colors (including tie-dye false teeth) and enjoyed clown-like tricks and antics. He was considered "Official Clown" of the Grateful Dead. In later years he founded Camp Winnarainbow, where needy children could participate in various artistic activities. To help fund these campers, Ben and Jerry's created Wavy Gravy ice cream—vanilla based, with an emphasis on nuts (see *Ben and Jerry's*).

Weil, Andrew. Weil, a physician who became famous for advocating a more liberal approach to drugs, was an undergraduate at Harvard in the early 1960s, when Timothy Leary conducted experiments with LSD and other hallucinogens (see *Leary, Timothy; Harvard*). As Don Lattin explains in *The Harvard Psychedelic Club*, the young Weil actually helped to get Leary fired: Weil contributed to an expose in the *Harvard Crimson* that brought to light irregular activities by Leary and his colleagues. Whatever his feelings about Leary, Weil himself was fascinated by psychotropic drugs and their potential therapeutic uses. He wrote an undergraduate thesis on the mind-altering effects of nutmeg. Weil's first and most influential book was *The Natural Mind*, in which he argued that humans naturally seek out forms of altered consciousness, and that what we call "drugs" are not foreign invaders of a human mind; rather, drugs trigger chemical processes that are built into the brain's evolved structure.

West, Louis Jolyn. Psychiatrist West did research connected with the CIA's MK-Ultra program (see *MK-Ultra*). Having worked with American prisoners of war from Korea, West became an authority on brainwashing and dissociative states; one element of his research involved LSD and other hallucinogens. In a 1962 experiment, West accidentally killed an elephant that he injected with LSD. See *Elephant*.

White, George Hunter. White, a tough narcotics cop, was chosen by MK-Ultra to run an operation codenamed "Midnight Climax" (see *MK-Ultra*). The CIA wished to test LSD outside labs and clinics in "real life" situations. White chose as his subjects men who picked up prostitutes in San Francisco for the evening; such men would be unlikely to stir up legal trouble if the drugging scheme were exposed. He had arranged for the women to bring their johns back to his apartment for drinks spiked with LSD. From behind a two-way mirror, White observed the unsuspecting trippers, took notes,

and drank a pitcher full of martinis. He nicknamed LSD "Stormy," because it appeared to be causing symptoms of insanity. White shut down Midnight Climax in 1965, just as "Stormy" was starting to attract trippers without any help from the CIA.

"White Angel." A highly regarded short story with LSD at its core, "White Angel" by Michael Cunningham was chosen for *The Best American Short Stories 1989*, and was later featured in a widely-used textbook, *The Scribner Anthology of Contemporary Short Fiction* (1999). The story forms part of Cunningham's novel *The Home at the End of the World*, which was made into a film of the same name. "White Angel" tells the story of two brothers living in Cleveland at the end of the 1960s: sixteen year-old Carlton and nine year-old Bobby (who likes to be called "Frisco"). Bobby worships his older brother, who does his best to include Bobby in his dreams of countercultural utopia. Carlton gives his little brother a half dose of LSD one morning, and the two of them trip happily in the snow. As Bobby explains, "We have taken hits of acid with our breakfast juice.... This acid is called windowpane. It is for clarity of vision, as Vicks is for decongestion of the nose." Bobby's acid trip produces two such moments of clarity. As he sees doves taking off, "transforming themselves from steel to silver in the snow-blown light," he realizes that the drug is working: "Everything before me has become suddenly, radiantly itself." The second moment comes as Bobby and Carlton are sitting by a window. Carlton tells him, "You and I are going to fly, man," and Bobby confirms that they did just that: "We raise ourselves up off the cocoa-colored deep-pile wool-and-polyester carpet by a sliver of an inch. Sweet glory. The secret of flight is this—you have to do it immediately, before your body realizes it is defying the laws. I swear it to this day." The scene recalls *Peter Pan*, with LSD taking the place of fairy dust.

"White Angel" ends tragically, when

Carlton accidentally runs through a sliding glass door and bleeds to death in the family's living room. It is ironic that the story begins with windowpane and ends with shattered glass. But Cunningham does not imply that LSD was the problem for Bobby and Carlton: this is no anti-drug parable. Carlton was not on acid when he had his accident, and Carlton's use of the drug is generally portrayed in a positive light.

White Lightning. One of Owsley's best known brands of LSD came in small tablets known as "White Lightning," which he made in collaboration with Tim Scully and Melissa Cargill (see *Owsley; Scully, Tim; Cargill, Melissa*). These tablets contained doses of 270 micrograms and were famous for their purity. Owsley's lab turned out approximately 300,000 of them from 1966–67.

"White Rabbit." This 1967 hit single by the Jefferson Airplane used Alice in Wonderland imagery to advertise psychedelic tripping. See *Jefferson Airplane; Slick, Grace; Alice*.

Who. The Who's rock opera *Tommy* (1969) portrayed LSD more as threat than therapy for the damaged protagonist. See *Acid Queen*.

Wild in the Streets. In this 1968 political farce, the youthful counterculture gains control of the American government. LSD enters the movie in two main elements of its plot. When the youngsters need help to swing a vote their way, they spike the Washington water supply. While members of Congress are tripping, their young guides steer them to vote in favor of lowering the minimum age for national office. Once in power, the youngsters again turn to LSD to achieve their goal of clearing away unwanted older people. They send recalcitrant 30-plus citizens to concentration camps, where they are dosed with acid to keep them from rebelling against their exclusion from productive society. In deploying LSD as a chemical weapon, *Wild in the Streets* reimagined the Summer of Love as a conspiracy to brainwash America. The movie's far-fetched dystopian vision exploited fears of generational conflict, one of the most common themes of public discussion in the turbulent year of 1968.

Wilson, Bill. The founder of Alcoholics Anonymous met Aldous Huxley in the mid 1950s and became an LSD enthusiast. Wilson, who had heard about Osmond and Hoffer's success with psychedelic therapy for alcoholism (see *Osmond, Humphry; Hoffer, Abram; Alcoholism*), took his first acid trip in 1956 under the supervision of Gerald Heard and Sidney Cohen (see *Heard, Gerald; Cohen, Sidney*). He found the experience greatly inspiring, on a par with his first spiritual epiphany that had sparked his therapeutic work. Wilson later summarized his thoughts about the potential benefits of LSD: "It is a generally acknowledged fact in spiritual development that ego reduction makes the influx of God's grace possible. If, therefore, under LSD we can have a temporary reduction, so that we can better see what we are and where we are going—well, that might be of some help. So I consider LSD to be of some value to some people, and practically no damage to anyone" (Alcoholics Anonymous).

Wilson, Brian. The creative leader of the Beach Boys acknowledged that LSD had an important influence on his life and music. See *Beach Boys*.

Wilson, Wes. Wilson was one of the earliest and most prolific artists of the psychedelic poster (see *Psychedelic Posters*). While working for a San Francisco printer, Wilson designed a handbill for the Trips Festival (see *Trips Festival*); he took LSD at the festival and found it inspiring. Thereafter, his work reflected psychedelic perception: "I selected my colors from my visual experiences with LSD," Wilson has said. He created many of the earliest posters for concerts at the Avalon and the Fillmore, producing as many as six posters per month. Soon he agreed to become the house designer for Bill

Graham's Fillmore concerts. He worked for Graham until May of 1967, when he became frustrated with what he considered insufficient compensation for his efforts.

Wilson used space and drew letters in distinctive ways that would become staples of psychedelic postering. He liked to fill up the whole rectangular sheet of a poster, with images, letters, and blocks of color in any remaining spaces. This sometimes led to confusion between positive and negative spaces, especially for people who were unfamiliar with his style. His baroque lettering techniques also contributed to legibility problems for the uninitiated. Wilson's letters curved around adjacent images on the posters, and he drew letters so that they appeared to be undulating or melting. He sometimes drew figures of naked women at the center of his posters, and like other psychedelic artists, he made use of mythic images such as the mandala, the yin-yang, and the peace symbol. In Wilson's final poster for the Fillmore, all of these characteristic elements are present. The letters spelling "Grateful Dead" curve and melt so that they are barely legible, and underneath the lettering, a naked, pregnant woman hold a crystal ball inscribed with a yin-yang design. What makes this last poster particularly interesting, however, lies at the bottom: in the space between the words "Fillmore" and "Auditorium," Wilson drew a dark, blockish dollar sign on what looks like the top of a skull. Wilson was clearly expressing his unhappiness about what he viewed as Graham's exploitation of his talent.

Windowpane. A common brand of LSD was called "Windowpane" because it came in translucent gelatin sheets divided into four small squares. The gelatin coating helped to protect LSD from exposure to air. The name was also used metaphorically, as in this remark from Michael Cunningham's short story "White Angel" (see *"White Angel"*): "This acid is called Windowpane. It is for clarity of vision, as Vicks is for decongestion of the nose."

Wolfe, Tom. In 1968, New Journalist Wolfe published a bestselling book about Ken Kesey and the Merry Pranksters that attempted to give mainstream readers an insider's look at psychedelic culture. See *Electric Kool-Aid Acid Test.*

Woodstock. LSD was one of the two most prevalent drugs at the Woodstock Festival in August, 1969. Joel Makower's oral history suggests that virtually everyone was smoking marijuana, and that a good many of the half million attendees took acid at some point during the festival. A few arrests were made for possession of LSD, but for the most part, the widespread distribution and consumption of the drug went unchallenged by police. Apparently doubts were raised doubts about the purity of some of the acid, as indicated by this public announcement included in the *Woodstock* movie: "There's a rumor circulating that the brown acid going around is poison. Cool it. It's just badly manufactured."

Because festival organizers had anticipated heavy use of LSD, they set up several so-called "freak-out tents" for anyone who panicked due to a bad trip. According to statistics recorded on the website *woodstock69. com*, roughly 400 people visited the tents to seek help. The freak-out tents were staffed by two different teams: the doctors and the Hog Farmers. The doctors came ready to administer Thorazine, the antipsychotic drug that puts an end to an acid trip. The members of Hog Farm were LSD veterans from the early years, including Merry Pranksters like Wavy Gravy (see *Wavy Gravy*). Unlike the doctors, the Hog Farmers preferred to counsel the person experiencing a bummer. As James E. Perone explains, the veteran acidheads thought that the use of Thorazine would leave trippers with unfinished psychological business; talking them through their distress would help them understand the experience and regain control of their mental state. By one method or the other, doctors and acid counselors prevented any incidents of serious harm from bad trips.

The only major drug-related casualty at Woodstock was a death from heroin overdose.

In 1994, at a festival organized to mark the twenty-fifth anniversary of Woodstock, marijuana and LSD were again the drugs of choice. Joseph Treaster of *The New York Times* described "the sweet aroma of marijuana wafting across the fields of the Woodstock '94 festival last weekend, and tabs of LSD changing hands as easily as candy bars." Psychologist Bruce L. Wilson told Treaster that he worried about bad trips for the new generation of Woodstockers, less acid-savvy than their predecessors. Teenagers "got into trouble with LSD at the festival because they were trying the drug for the first time and underestimated its effect" (*NYT,* August 21, 1994). Ang Lee's 2009 film *Taking Woodstock* includes a depiction of one innocent character's first acid trip, which begins with some uneasiness but develops into a mellow, colorful experience.

World Psychedelic Centre. When Michael Hollingshead left Millbrook in October, 1965 (see *Hollingshead, Michael; Millbrook*), he returned home to London in hopes of spreading the psychedelic movement. He founded the World Psychedelic Centre in a large Chelsea apartment provided by an Etonian friend also fond of acid. Hollingshead had brought from Millbrook thousands of doses and hundreds of copies of *The Psychedelic Experience* (see *Psychedelic Experience*); he hosted numerous celebrities and artists at the Centre, including musicians Paul McCartney, Mick Jagger, Donovan, and Eric Clapton, writer William S. Burroughs, and film director Roman Polanski. After a few months the tabloids ran stories of acid-spiked drinks at the Centre's parties, and in March the police raided and closed down the Centre.

Yellow Submarine. The Beatles song from *Revolver* inspired an animated film with the same name. The film had a successful release in 1968 and has remained an icon of the psychedelic era. Director George Dunning supervised scores of animators as they created psychedelic imagery to accompany the songs that anchor the film. Noted artist Heinz Edelmann served as art director and helped to develop the connective plot, which offers a simple hippie allegory. Peaceful, music-loving "Pepperland" is attacked by "Blue Meanies," who drain all the fun (and color) from the place. The mayor of Pepperland dispatches a yellow submarine to get help from the Beatles, and after a series of lyrical adventures, they return to liberate Pepperland and redeem the Blue Meanies. At the end, everyone grooves together as one happy community.

By the time *Yellow Submarine* was released, the Beatles were well known users of LSD and champions of psychedelic culture (see *Beatles*). The film's marketers made no effort to disguise its psychedelic message. At the top of the promotional poster, in soft pink lettering, they quoted a line spoken by the George Harrison character: "IT'S ALL IN THE MIND, Y'KNOW!" Nowhere does the message come through more clearly than in the sequence based on "Lucy in the Sky with Diamonds." As the Beatles come upon an unfamiliar landscape, one of them speculates, "It looks like the foothills ... the foothills of the headlands." These turn out to be "headlands" in a literal sense. We soon see rows and rows of transparent heads, each of which contains a colorful word or image: flags (both British and American), bright geometric and organic shapes, Einstein's formula for energy and mass, the word "Freud," among many others. As "Lucy in the Sky with Diamonds" begins, the animators shift mainly to images of females—but they resist the temptation to illustrate the song in point-for-point correspondence. Instead of a girl with kaleidoscope eyes, for example, we see young women who look like Busby Berkeley showgirls from the 1930s, fluidly shifting through various shapes and colors. At the end of the song, the theatre of the transparent head closes up, leaving us bereft of showgirls.

Another scene in *Yellow Submarine* conducts a psychedelic reshaping of time rather than space. In the middle of "When I'm Sixty Four," this prosaic message appears: "Sixty four years is 33,661,440 minutes, and *one minute* is a long time. Let us demOnstrate." Starting with zero (the "O" from "demonstrate"), the animators count to 60. Successive numbers take their turn in the frame, each one decorated with novel imagery. The bland zero gives way to more colorful single digits, which mutate into more complex double-figured shapes. "12," for example, has a "1" with an animal smile and a "2" that loops around a Victorian gentleman's ear. By the time the 40's roll through as full-screen op art posters, the audience may well forget the point of the countdown. Even with a nemesis as impersonal and relentless as time, *Yellow Submarine* wants us to realize that "it's all in the mind, y'know!"

Zachariah. This 1971 film was publicized as "the first electric Western." Psychedelic band Country Joe and the Fish played a gang of musical bank robbers (see *Country Joe and the Fish*). Written in part by members of the Firesign Theater (see *Firesign Theater*), *Zachariah* parodied elements of Hesse's *Siddhartha*, and its loose plot allowed several rock stars to perform; Elvin Jones, for example, in the role of a gunfighter, played a memorable drum solo. Producers had asked John Lennon to provide a song for the movie, but he declined. *Zachariah* can be classified as an "acid Western," a subgenre that combines countercultural values with elements of the traditional Western (see *Acid Western*).

Zap Comix. This underground but popular series of comic books began in the late 1960s as the brainchild of Robert Crumb (see *Crumb, Robert*). Crumb has said that LSD sparked a creative burst that significantly altered his artistic style and led to the creation of *Zap Comix*. *Zap* cartoonists used a variety of aesthetic and narrative gestures, but all of them reflected the influence of psychedelic perception, and all of them implied a critique of mainstream American culture with its underlying repressions and neuroses. Among other regular contributors to *Zap* were Rick Griffin and Victor Moscoso, two prominent designers of psychedelic posters during the peak years of the San Francisco acid scene (see *Psychedelic Posters; Griffin, Rick; Moscoso, Victor*). Although *Zap Comix* saw its greatest popularity during the late 1960s and early 1970s, Crumb and his colleagues continued to produce new issues into the twenty-first century.

Zappa, Frank. Zappa produced a few albums that are classified as "psychedelic," but Zappa himself never took LSD or any other hallucinogen, and he often subjected hippie culture to sharp satire. Zappa's satirical muse led him to ridicule with equal energy the mainstream American suburban culture and the psychedelic counterculture that grew up in its midst. Because Zappa's work was filled with iconoclastic messages and experimental musical forms, many people assumed that he partook of the same mind-altering drugs favored by The Beatles, The Grateful Dead, Jimi Hendrix, and other musical celebrities of the psychedelic era. In fact, Zappa avoided all those sorts of drugs; he smoked marijuana once, didn't like it, and never bothered with anything else. Nevertheless, his first album, *Freak Out!* (1966), appears on the list of "Best Psychedelic Albums of All Time" (*Q Magazine*). The title lyric does nothing to discourage such a classification: in the song "It Can't Happen Here," Zappa sings about mainstream America's denial of the subversive culture already in its midst. Record producer Tom Wilson, who sponsored *Freak-Out*, was tripping on acid as he tried to supervise the strange sounds coming through his studio speakers. But the sounds all came from the brain of a man who disdained chemical shortcuts to creativity.

In the wake of The Beatles' *Sergeant Pepper's Lonely Hearts Club Band* (see *Beatles*), Zappa decided to produce a satirical rejoinder. The album cover parodied the famous

Sergeant Pepper collage, with the name of Zappa's band along the bottom ("MOTH-ERS," spelled out in vegetables instead of flowers), and the title of the album neatly lettered on a bass drum: *We're Only in It for the Money.* Some of the songs clearly satirize psychedelic and hippie pretensions. "Flower Punk," for example, mimics Jimi Hendrix' "Hey Joe," but substitutes lyrics that make fun of the Haight-Asbury scene. For all its satirical edge, *We're Only in It for the Money* also contains songs that sound like genuine psychedelic calls for expanded consciousness. "Absolutely Free" begins with Zappa defining "discorporate"—the first word in the song, it means to leave your body—and continues in a frankly psychedelic mode, both musically and lyrically. He calls for mental liberation from the dismal routines of ordinary American life. Frank Zappa thus holds a unique position in psychedelic music: he called for altered consciousness but took no drugs, and joined a psychedelic canon even as he was making fun of its pretentious cant.

Zen Buddhism. LSD enthusiasts of the 1960s forged connections between the psychedelic experience and the meditative practices of Zen Buddhism (see *Religion*). For many people, an LSD trip challenges a common sense belief in the stable "reality" of the external world, and in this sense the psychedelic experience would seem a good match with Buddhist ideas of emptiness and detachment. The most influential work linking LSD and Zen Buddhism came from psychedelic evangelists Timothy Leary, Richard Alpert, and Ralph Metzner. The three men collaborated on *The Psychedelic Experience,* a manual that adapted The Tibetan Book of the Dead for the purpose of counseling people taking LSD trips. The book sold well and was translated into several languages (see *Psychedelic Experience*). As Rick Fields explains, Buddhist scholars in America offered divergent opinions about the LSD-Zen relationship. Some, like D.T. Suzuki, were skeptical that any drug experience could

nurture, let alone replicate, true meditative work. Many serious Zen practitioners doubted that acidheads were capable of the necessary discipline and focus. Others, including Alan Watts, considered LSD a potentially valuable aid to those seeking wisdom (see *Watts, Alan*). Watts was reluctant to generalize about the psychedelic experience (because of so many variables in set and setting), but in his own case the drug had led him to a state of mind "both like and unlike what I understood as the flavor of Zen." LSD had helped him reach an understanding of certain paradoxes underlying Zen wisdom. Despite the mixed reviews of LSD from Zen teachers, young acidheads of the late 1960s began to frequent Buddhist zendos as the next step in their quest for enlightenment.

When trained Zen Buddhists took LSD themselves, the results varied considerably. The first (and worst) such trip was recorded by Sidney Cohen in his survey of psychedelic psychiatry ("Side Effects"). One psychiatrist reported having given LSD to two Zen Buddhist teachers, "in order to compare the drug state with the transcendent state achieved through meditation. Both Zen teachers became so uncomfortable that termination with chlorpromazine became necessary." Timothy Leary recalled a better acid trip by a Buddhist holy man. Ralph Metzner gave the drug to Lama Anagarika Govinda, at his request, and "after thirty years of meditation, the Lama had experienced the *bardo Thodol* in its living sweating reality" (*Flashbacks*).

Another acid trip by a Buddhist holy man was very different from these other two, but this guru's reaction helps to explain both the discomfort of the two teachers and Govinda's meditative revelation. The account comes from a book by Ram Dass (see *Alpert, Richard*), *Miracle of Love: Stories about Neem Karoli Baba.* When Alpert met his guru in 1967, he gave him a huge dose of LSD (900 micrograms), "eager to see what would happen. He allowed me to stay for an hour, and nothing happened. Nothing whatsoever. He just laughed at me." On a second try, when the guru took even more (1200 micrograms), he asked Alpert, "'Have you got anything stronger?' I said I didn't. Then he said, 'These medicines were used in Kulu Valley long ago. But yogis have lost that knowledge. They were used with fasting. Nobody knows how to take them now. To take them with no effect, your mind must be firmly fixed on God. Others would be afraid to take. Many saints would not take this.' And he left it at that."

Bibliography

Abel, Ernest L. *Psychoactive Drugs and Sex.* New York: Plenum Press, 1985.

Abel, Ernest L. *Psychoactive Drugs and Sex.* New York: Plenum Press, 1985. Print.Abramson, Harold A. *The Use of LSD in Psychotherapy and Alcoholism.* Indianapolis: Bobbs-Merrill, 1967.

Alcoholics Anonymous. *"Pass It On": The Story of Bill Wilson and How the A. A. Message Reached the World.* New York: Alcoholics Anonymous World Services, 1984.

Alexander, Marsha. *The Sexual Paradise of LSD.* North Hollywood: Brandon House, 1967.

American Psychiatric Association. *Diagnostic and Statistical Manual of Mental Disorders-IV.* Washington, D.C.: American Psychiatric Association, 1994.

Anonymous [Beatrice Sparks]. *Go Ask Alice.* New York: Avon, 1971.

Asher, Harry. "They Split My Personality." *Saturday Review* 1 June 1963.

Austin, Joe. "Rome Is Burning (Psychedelic): Traces of the Social and Historical Contexts of Psychedelia." *Summer of Love: Art of the Psychedelic Era.* Ed. Christopher Grunenberg. London: Tate, 2006.

Badiner, Allan Hunt, and Alex Grey, eds. *Zig Zag Zen: Buddhism and Psychedelics.* San Francisco: Chronicle Books, 2002.

Bergquist, Laura. "Curious Story Behind the New Cary Grant." *Look* 1 Sept. 1959.

Black, David. *Acid: The Secret History of LSD.* London: Vision, 1998.

Blackman, Cally. "Clothing the Cosmic Counterculture." *Summer of Love: Psychedelic Art, Social Crisis, and Counterculture in the 1960s.* Ed. by Christopher Grunenberg and Jonathan Harris. Liverpool: Liverpool University Press, 2005.

Blaszczyk, Connie. "Randall Grahm on Wine, Words, and Subversive Thinking." *Zinezone.com.* 9 June 2010.

Blewett, Duncan. *The Frontiers of Being.* New York: Award, 1969.

Boon, Marcus. *The Road of Excess: A History of Writers on Drugs.* Cambridge: Harvard University Press, 2002.

Boucher, Geoff. "California Girls: The Beach Boys." *Los Angeles Times.* 12 Aug. 2007. *Losangelestimes.com.* 18 March 2009.

Brother, Eric. "Dock Ellis and the Electric Baseball Game." *High Times* Aug. 1987.

Brown, David Jay. "Psychiatric Alchemy with Oscar Janiger." May 1990. *Mavericksofthemind.com.* 22 Nov. 2008.

Bryan, John. *Whatever Happened to Timothy Leary?* San Francisco: Renaissance Press, 1980.

Burleigh, Nina. *A Very Private Woman: The Life and Unsolved Murder of Presidential Mistress Mary Meyer.* New York: Bantam, 1998.

Busch, A. K., and W. C. Johnson. "Lysergic Acid Diethylamide as an Aid in Psychotherapy." *Diseases of the Nervous System* 11 (1950): 204.

Buskin, Richard. *Sheryl Crow: No Fool to This Game.* New York: Billboard Books, 2002.

Caporael, Linda. "Ergotism: The Satan Loose in Salem." *Science* 192 (April 1976): 21.

Carmichael, Michael. "Wonderland Revisited." *London Miscellany* 28.1 (1996): 19–28.

Castaneda, Carlos. *The Teachings of Don Juan: A Yaqui Way of Knowledge.* Berkeley: University of California Press, 1968.

Cateforis, Theo. *The Rock History Reader.* London: Routledge, 2007.

Chandler, Arthur L., and Mortimer A. Hartman. "LSD-25 as a Facilitating Agent in Psychotherapy." *Archives of General Psychiatry* 3 (1960): 286–99.

Chapman, Rob. "The Legend of *Smile*." *Mojo* Feb. 2002.

Chayefsky, Paddy. *Altered States: A Novel.* New York: Harper & Row, 1978.

Clark, Walter Houston. *Chemical Ecstasy: Psychedelic Drugs and Religion.* New York: Sheed and Ward, 1969.

Cohen, M. M., and M. J. Marmillo. "Chromosomal Damage in Human Leukocytes Induced by Lysergic Acid Diethylamide." *Science* 155 (March 1967): 1417–19.

Cohen, Sidney. "Lysergic Acid Diethylamide: Side Effects and Complications." *Journal of Nervous and Mental Disease* 130.1 (Jan. 1960): 30–40.

_____, and Keith S. Dilman. "Complications Associated with Lysergic Acid Diethylamide." *Journal of the American Medical Association* 181.2 (1962): 161–62.

Cover, Arthur. "Philip K. Dick." *Vertex* 1.6 (Feb. 1974).

Cunningham, Michael. "White Angel." *Scribner Anthology of Contemporary Short Fiction.* Ed. by Lex Williford and Michael Martone. New York: Simon & Schuster, 1999.

Dass, Ram. *Miracle of Love: Stories about Neem Karoli Baba.* New York: E. P. Dutton, 1979.

Davidson, Bill. "The Hidden Evils of LSD." *Saturday Evening Post* 12 Aug. 1967.

DeCurtis, Anthony. "George Harrison Gets Back." *Rolling Stone* 22 Oct. 1987.

DeRios, Marlene Dobkin, and Oscar Janiger. *LSD, Spirituality, and the Creative Process.* Rochester: Park Street Press, 2003.

DeRogatis, Jim. "The Great Albums: The Velvet Underground and Nico." *Chicago Sun–Times.* 24 March 2002. *Suntimes.com.* 10 Jan. 2010.

Dick, Philip K. "Faith of Our Fathers." *Dangerous Visions.* Ed. Harlan Ellison. New York: Doubleday, 1967.

_____. *Martian Time-Slip.* New York: Ballantine, 1964.

_____. *The Three Stigmata of Palmer Eldritch.* New York: Doubleday, 1965.

DiPrima, Diane. "Holidays at Millbrook." *The Portable Sixties Reader.* Ed. Ann Charters. New York: Penguin, 2002.

Dishotsky, Norman I. "LSD and Genetic Damage." *Science* 172 (April 1971): 431–40.

Dittman, Michael J. *Jack Kerouac: A Biography.* Westport, CT: Greenwood Press, 2004.

Dittman, Michael J. *Jack Kerouac: A Biography.* Westport: Greenwood Press, 2004. Print.Dunlap, Jane [Adelle Davis]. *Exploring Inner Space: Personal Experiences under LSD-25.* New York: Harcourt, Brace, and World, 1961.

Dyck, Erika. *Psychedelic Psychiatry: LSD from Clinic to Campus.* Baltimore: Johns Hopkins UP, 2008.

Ebert, John David. *Twilight of the Clockwork God: Conversations on Science and Spirituality at the End of an Age.* Tulsa: Council Oak Books, 1999.

Eisner, Bruce. "Timothy Leary: The Man Behind Both the Internet and the LSD Revolutions." *Bruceeisner.com.* Bruce Eisner's Vision Thing: Creating a Sensible Culture. 15 Feb. 2006. 11 June 2010.

Ferlinghetti, Lawrence. *The Secret Meaning of Things.* New York: New Directions, 1968.

Fields, Rick. "A High History of Buddhism." *Tricycle Magazine: The Buddhist Review.* 6:1 (Fall 1996). *Tricycle.com.* 28 Nov. 2008.

Fisher, Gary. "Treatment of Childhood Schizophrenia Utilizing LSD and Psilocybin." *MAPS Newsletter* 3 (Summer 1997): 18–25.

Freedman, A. M., et al. "Autistic Schizophrenic Children: An Experiment in the Use of LSD-25." *Archives of General Psychiatry* 6.1 (1962): 203–13.

Gehman, Richard. "Ageless Cary Grant." *Good Housekeeping* Sept. 1960.

Gehr, Richard. "Omega Man: A Profile of Terence McKenna." *Levity.com.* 5 April 1992. 15 Oct. 2009.

Ginsberg, Allen. *Deliberate Prose: Selected Essays, 1952–1995.* Ed. Bill Morgan. New York: HarperCollins, 2000.

Gips, Elizabeth. *Scrapbook of a Haight-Ashbury Pilgrim: Spirit, Sacraments, and Sex in 1967/68.* Santa Cruz: Changes Press, 1991.

Gleick, James. *Genius: The Life and Science of Richard Feynman.* New York: Pantheon Books, 1992.

Graves, Robert, and Frank L. Kersnowski. *Conversations with Robert Graves.* Jackson: University Press of Mississippi, 1989.

Greenfield, Robert. *Timothy Leary: A Biography.* New York: Harcourt, 2006.

Grigoriadis, Vanessa. "Daniel Pinchbeck and the New Psychedelic Elite." *Rolling Stone* 7 Sept. 2006.

Grof, Stanislav. *LSD Psychotherapy: Exploring the Frontiers of the Hidden Mind.* Alameda: Hanter House, 1994.

Gunn, Thom. *Moly.* London: Faber and Faber, 1971.

_____, and Clive Wilmer. *The Occasions of Poetry.* London: Faber and Faber, 1982.

Gurley, George. "Coultergeist." *New York Observer.* 25 Aug. 2002. *Observer.com.* 11 June 2010.

Hall, Donald, and Dock Ellis. *Dock Ellis in the Country of Baseball.* New York: Coward, McGann and Geoghegan, 1976.

Harvey, Robert C. *The Art of the Comic Book: An Aesthetic History.* Jackson: Unioversity Press of Mississippi, 1996.

Henke, James, Parke Puterbaugh, Charles Perry, and Barry Miles. *I Want to Take You Higher: The Psychedelic Era, 1965–69.* San Francisco: Chronicle Books, 1997.

Hertsgaard, Mark. *A Day in the Life: The Music*

and Artistry of the Beatles. New York: Delacorte Press, 1995.

Herzstein, Robert Edwin. Henry R. Luce, Time, and the American Crusade in Asia. Cambridge: Cambridge University Press, 2005.

Heylin, Clinton. Bob Dylan: Behind the Shades: A Biography. New York: Summitt Books, 1991.

Hofmann, Albert. LSD, My Problem Child: Reflections on Sacred Drugs, Mysticism, and Science. Santa Cruz: MAPS, 2009.

Hollingshead, Michael. The Man Who Turned On the World. New York: Abelard-Schuman, 1973.

Hooper, Judith. "John Lilly: Altered States." Omni Jan. 1983.

Horgan, John. Rational Mysticism: Dispatches from the Border between Science and Spirituality. Boston: Houghton Mifflin, 2003.

Hunter, Robert. A Box of Rain. New York: Viking, 1990.

Huxley, Aldous. Brave New World. New York: Harper Perennial, 1998 (1932).

_____. The Doors of Perception. London: Chatto and Windus, 1954.

_____. Island. New York: Harper Perennial, 2002 (1962).

Huxley, Laura Archera. This Timeless Moment: A Personal View of Aldous Huxley. New York: Farrar, Straus and Giroux, 1968.

Izumi, Kiyo. "Perceptual Factors in the Design of Environments for the Mentally Ill." Psychiatric Services 27 (Nov. 1976): 802–06.

Jackson, Phil, and Charles Rosen. Maverick: More Than a Game. New York: Playboy Press, 1975.

Katz, Sidney. "My Twelve Hours As a Madman." Macleans 1 Oct. 1953: 32–52.

Kleps, Arthur. The Boo-Hoo Bible: The Neo-American Church Catechism. San Cristobal: Toad Books, 1971.

Knickerbocker, Conrad. "William S. Burroughs." Paris Review Fall 1965.

Koenig, David. Mouse under Glass: Secrets of Disney Animation and Theme Parks. Irvine: Bonaventure Press, 1997.

Krassner, Paul. Paul Krassner's Psychedelic Trips for the Mind. New York: Trans-High, 2001.

Kripal, Jeffrey John. Esalen: America and the Religion of No Religion. Chicago: University of Chicago Press, 2007.

Lattin, Don. The Harvard Psychedelic Club: How Timothy Leary, Ram Dass, Huston Smith, and Andrew Weil Killed the Fifties and Ushered in a New Age for America. New York: HarperOne, 2010.

Leary, Timothy. Flashbacks: An Autobiography. Los Angeles: J. P. Tarcher, 1983.

_____. The Politics of Ecstasy. New York: Putnam, 1968.

_____, Richard Alpert, and Ralph Metzner. The Psychedelic Experience: A Manual Based on the Tibetan Book of the Dead. New York: University Books, 1964.

Lee, Martin A., and Bruce Shlain. Acid Dreams: the CIA, LSD, and the Sixties Rebellion. New York: Grove Press, 1985.

Lee, Marty, and Eric Noble. "Interview of Peter Berg and Judy Goldhaft." The Digger Archives. 29 April 1982. Diggers.org. 3 May 2009.

Lester, Paul. "Brian Wilson: Royal Festival Hall, London." Uncut April 2002.

LoBrutto, Vincent. Stanley Kubrick: A Biography. New York: D. I. Fine Books, 1997.

Luck, Georg. "Review of The Road to Eleusis." American Journal of Philology 122.1 (Spring 2001): 135–38.

MacDonald, John D. One Fearful Yellow Eye. Philadelphia: Lippincott, 1966.

Macey, David. Michel Foucault. London: Reaktion, 2004.

Makower, Joel. Woodstock: The Oral History. New York: Doubleday, 1989.

Markoff, John. What the Dormouse Said: How the Sixties Counterculture Shaped the Personal Computer Industry. New York: Viking, 2005.

Masters, Robert, and Jean Houston. Psychedelic Art. New York: Grove Press, 1968.

_____. The Varieties of Psychedelic Experience. New York: Holt, Rinehart, and Winston, 1966.

McNally, Dennis. A Long Strange Trip: The Inside History of the Grateful Dead. New York: Broadway Books, 2002.

Mezz, Dave. "On the Haight with Charles Perry." Vox. 26 July 2007. Voxmagazine.com. 22 March 2009.

Mikkelson, Barbara. "The Scarlet Linkletter." Snopes.com 15 Aug. 2005. Web. 28 Oct. 2008.

Miles, Barry. Hippie. London: Cassell Illustrated, 2003.

Mockingbird Foundation. The Phish Companion: A Guide to the Band and Their Music. San Francisco: Backbeat Books, 2004.

Moore, Alan. V for Vendetta. New York: DC Comics, 1989.

Moore, Gerald. "LSD: The Exploding Threat of the Mind Drug that Got out of Control." Life 25 March 1966.

Morris, Sylvia Jukes. Rage for Fame: The Ascent of Clare Boothe Luce. New York: Random House, 1997.

Mullis, Kary B. Dancing Naked in the Mind Field. New York: Pantheon, 1998.

Newland, Constance [Thelma Moss]. Myself and I. New York: Coward-McCann, 1962.

Nin, Anaïs. The Diary of Anaïs Nin, 1947–1955. Ed. Gunther Stuhlmann. New York: Harcourt Brace Jovanovich, 1974.

Oates, Joyce Carol. "Dylan at 60." Studio A: The

Bob Dylan Reader. Ed. by Benjamin Hedin. New York: Norton, 2004.

O'Brien, Michael. *John F. Kennedy: A Biography*. New York: St. Martin's, 2005.

Olson, Eric. "Family Statement on the Murder of Frank Olson." *Frankolsonproject.com*. 8 Aug. 2002. 28 July 2008.

Pahnke, Walter. "LSD and Religious Experience." *LSD, Man, and Society*. Ed. by Frank Barron, Richard C. DeBold and Russell C. Leaf. Middletown CT: Wesleyan University Press, 1967.

Peet, Preston. *Under the Influence: The Disinformation Guide to Drugs*. New York: Disinformation Co., 2004.

Perone, James E. *Woodstock: An Encyclopedia of the Music and Art Fair*. Westport, CT: Greenwood Press, 2005.

Perry, Charles. *The Haight-Ashbury: A History*. New York: Random House, 1984.

Pinchbeck, Daniel. *Breaking Open the Head: A Psychedelic Journey into the Heart of Contemporary Shamanism*. New York: Broadway Books, 2002.

Platt, John A. *London's Rock Routes*. London: Fourth Estate, 1985.

Poirier, Richard. *The Performing Self: Compositions and Decompositions in the Languages of Contemporary Life*. New York: Oxford University Press, 1971.

Powell, William. *The Anarchist Cookbook*. New York: L. Stuart, 1971.

Pynchon, Thomas. *The Crying of Lot 49*. Philadelphia: Lippincott, 1966.

Rees, Alun. "Nobel Prize Genius Crick Was High on LSD When He Discovered the Secret of Life." *Daily Mail*. 8 Aug. 2004. *Dailymail.co.uk*. 17 Oct. 2008.

Regis, Edward. *The Biology of Doom: The History of America's Secret Germ Warfare Project*. New York: Henry Holt, 1999.

Rensin, David. "The Bill Gates Interview." *Playboy* 8 Dec. 1994.

Richards, Chris, and David Malitz. "Stanley Mouse Talks Grateful Dead, Zig-Zags, Hot Rods, Hippies, and What Journey Took from Jimi." *Post Rock*. *Washington Post*. 10 April 2009. Web. 17 Jan. 2010.

Roberts, Andy. *Albion Dreaming: A Popular History of LSD in Britain*. London: Marshall Cavendish, 2008.

Rosenbaum, Jonathan. "Acid Western: *Dead Man*." *Chicago Reader*. 27 June 1996. *Chicagoreader.com*. 12 Nov. 2008.

Sandford, Christopher. *Clapton, Edge of Darkness*. London: V. Gollancz, 1994.

Savage, Charles. "LSD-25: A Clinical-Psychological Study." *American Journal of Psychiatry* 108 (June 1952): 896–900.

Sewell, R. Andrew, John H. Halpern, and Harrison G. Pope. "Response of Cluster Headache to Psilocybin and LSD." *Neurology* 66 (2006): 1920–22.

Shulgin, Alexander T., and Ann Shulgin. *PiHKAL: A Chemical Love Story*. Berkeley: Transform Press, 1992.

_____. *TiHKAL: The Continuation*. Berkeley: Transform Press, 1997.

Siff, Stephen. "Henry Luce's Strange Trip: Coverage of LSD in *Time* and *Life*, 1954–68." *Journalism History* 34 (Fall 2008).

Sigafoos, J., et al. "Flashback to the 1960s: LSD in the Treatment of Autism." *Developmental Neurorehabilitation* 10.1 (2007): 75–81.

Slick, Grace, and Andrea Cagan. *Somebody to Love? A Rock-and-Roll Memoir*. New York: Warner Books, 1998.

Smith, Huston. *Cleansing the Doors of Perception: The Religious Significance of Entheogenic Plants and Chemicals*. New York: Jeremy P. Tarcher/Putnam, 2000.

Spitz, Bob. *Dylan: A Biography*. New York: McGraw-Hill, 1989.

Stafford, Peter G. *Psychedelics Encyclopedia*. Berkeley: Ronin, 1992.

_____, and Bonnie H. Golightly. *LSD, the Problem-Solving Psychedelic*. New York: Award Books, 1967.

Stanton, M. Duncan. "Drug Flashbacks: Reported Frequency in a Military Population." *American Journal of Psychiatry* 129 (6 Dec. 1972): 751–55.

Steadman, Ralph. *The Joke's Over: Bruised Memories: Gonzo, Hunter S. Thompson, and Me*. New York: Harcourt, 2006.

Stevens, Jay. *Storming Heaven: LSD and the American Dream*. New York: Atlantic Monthly Press, 1987.

Szulc, Tad. "The CIA's Electric Kool-Aid Acid Test." *Psychology Today* 11 (Nov. 1977).

Tendler, Stewart, and David May. *The Brotherhood of Eternal Love*. London: Panther, 1984.

Thompson, Hunter S. *Fear and Loathing in Las Vegas*. New York: Vintage, 1971.

_____. *Hell's Angels: A Strange and Terrible Saga*. New York: Random House, 1967.

Thompson, Peter. *Jack Nicholson: The Life and Times of an Actor on the Edge*. Secaucus: Carol, 1997.

Time.com. "Peter Fonda: Did We Blow It?" 21 April 2000. 14 Dec. 2008.

Turner, Fred. *From Counterculture to Cyberculture: Stewart Brand, the Whole Earth Network, and the Rise of Digital Utopianism*. Chicago: University of Chicago Press, 2006.

Turner, Fred. *From Counterculture to Cyberculture: Stewart Brand, the Whole Earth Network, and the Rise of Digital Utopianism*. Chicago: University of Chicago Press, 2006. Turner, Steve. *The*

Gospel According to the Beatles. Louisville: Westminster John Knox, 2006.

Unterberger, Richie, et al. *All Music Guide to Rock: The Experts' Guide to the Best Recordings in Rock, Pop, Soul, R & B, and Rap.* San Francisco: Miller Freeman Books, 1997.

Verbeten, Sharon. "Ready, Set, Action." *Dolls Magazine.* 1 Nov. 2008. *Dollsmagazine.com.* 11 Feb. 2009.

Ward, R. H. *A Drug Taker's Notes.* London: Gollancz, 1957.

Wasson, R. Gordon, Albert Hofmann, and Carl A. P. Ruck. *The Road to Eleusis: Unveiling the Secret of the Mysteries.* New York: Harcourt Brace Jovanovich, 1977.

Watson, James D. *The Double Helix: A Personal Account of the Discovery of the Structure of DNA.* New York: Atheneum, 1968.

Watts, Alan. *The Joyous Cosmology: Adventures in the Chemistry of Consciousness.* New York: Pantheon, 1962.

Weil, Andrew. *The Natural Mind: A New Way of Looking at Drugs and the Higher Consciousness.* Boston: Houghton Mifflin, 1972.

Wenner, Jann. "Lennon Remembers." *Rolling Stone* 21 Jan. and 4 Feb. 1971.

_____, and Charles Reich. "The *Rolling Stone* Interview: Jerry Garcia." *Rolling Stone* 20 Jan. and 3 Feb. 1972.

West, L. J., C. M. Pierce, and W. D. Thomas. "Lysergic Acid Diethylamide: Its Effects on a Male Asiatic Elephant." *Science* 138 (Dec. 1962): 1100–03.

Witt, Peter N., and Charles F. Reed. "Spider-Web Building." *Science* 149 (10 Sep. 1965): 1190–97.

Wolfe, Tom. *The Electric Kool-Aid Acid Test.* New York: Farrar, Strauss and Giroux, 1968.

Zinberg, Norman Earl. *Drug, Set, and Setting: The Basis for Controlled Intoxicant Use.* New Haven: Yale University Press, 1984.

Index